Language in Geographic Context

Multilingual Matters

Please contact us for the latest book information:
Multilingual Matters, Bank House, 8a Hill Road,
Clevedon, Avon BS21 7HH, England.

MULTILINGUAL MATTERS 38
Series Editor: Derrick Sharp

Language in Geographic Context

Edited by

Colin H. Williams

What is language but many words?
Words, only words, but oh what power is contained therein!

MULTILINGUAL MATTERS LTD
Clevedon · Philadelphia

TO WILBUR ZELINSKY

**who professes an infectious joy and wonderment
at the rich diversity of human culture**

Library of Congress Cataloging-in-Publication Data

Language in geographic context.

  (Multilingual matters ; 38)
  1. Areal linguistics.   2. Language policy.
3. Language planning. I. Williams, Colin H.
II. Series.
P130.L36 1988   409   88–5122

British Library Cataloguing in Publication Data

Williams, Colin H.
  Language in geographic context.——
  (Multilingual matters; 38).
  1. Geographical linguistics
  I. Title
  410

  ISBN 1–85359–002–9
  ISBN 1–85359–001–0 Pbk

Multilingual Matters Ltd
Bank House, 8a Hill Road, &   242 Cherry Street
Clevedon, Avon BS21 7HH   Philadelphia, PA 19106–1906
England   U.S.A.

Copyright © 1988 C.H. Williams, W.F. Mackey,
T. Lundén, W.W. Bostock, J.E. Ambrose, C.W.J. Withers,
W.T.R. Pryce and D. Cartwright.

Index compiled by Meg Davies, Society of Indexers.

Typeset by Photo·graphics, Honiton, Devon
Printed and bound in Great Britain by
Short Run Press Ltd., Exeter EX2 7LW

Contents

APPLICATIONS

Foreword

HAROLD CARTER

Emeritus Professor of Geography
University College of Wales, Aberystwyth

It is a great pleasure to write a foreword to this volume of essays dealing with language in a geographical context. The book is indicative not only of a growing awareness of the significance of the spatial characteristics of language, but also of the realization by geographers of the supreme importance of language both as a symbol and an integral part of culture or way of life. There are, therefore, two aspects to this book, its contribution to geolinguistics itself and its contribution to issues of much wider significance.

In regard to the first of these aspects it must be admitted that there is as yet little established in the nature of geolinguistic theory; little in the way of a set of core concepts which can be adopted as a basis for future research. This book, consisting as it does of chapters by different authors, does not seek in any systematic way to set up such an infrastructure, but nevertheless it makes a significant contribution towards it, and represents a major step in the formulation of an identifiable theory-based study which can be called geolinguistics. In particular, the sections dealing with the development and principles of geolinguistics and the methodologies within its practice push forward our understanding of the spatial study of languages. Hopefully it will convince socio-linguists that a spatial approach has much to offer in the comprehension of the relations between languages, of language change and especially of language loss and language maintenance.

The second aspect which I have mentioned is of a broader nature. The book is limited to examples and case studies taken from the Western world but the inclusion of discussions on the macro scale and issues related to language planning are pointers to much wider horizons. Cultural conflict has been one of the continuous themes of history; one becoming more prevalent as increased mobility and a more complex pattern of migration engendered clashes of peoples. In many ways the dominance of a Marxist interpretation of the class-based nature of conflict, and the contemporary pre-occupation with somatic differences expressed in the concept of racism, have pushed aside the much more widespread and universal generation of conflict through cultural differences. Of those differences the two major symbols are language and religion, very often themselves closely associated. It is perfectly clear that the most explosive situations are created when all the sources of antagonisms occur together; when an economically disadvantaged population, physically distinct, usually by skin colour, and with a separate cultural inheritance finds itself over and against a different and dominant group. These issues are discussed in the book but the fact remains that cultural and hence linguistic differences transgress the boundaries of economic status and physical appearance.

It follows that the matters which are dealt with in the book are not abstract and what are misguidedly called academic problems. Here is an area where clashes across the world are most evident, form Northern Ireland to the Punjab, from Brittany to Sri Lanka, from the Basque country to Zimbabwe, from the inner cities of Britain to those of Australia. Any work which gives insight into the past nature and present character of culture conflict is of the greatest importance. And it needs to be stressed that disaccord arises out of spatial contiguity and overlap. Territory is at the very centre of contention and space or territory are fundamental geographic principles.

There are, therefore, a series of different approaches for the reader of this book. It can be taken as a distinctive and original contribution to the development of geolinguistics exploring especially its development and methodological basis. It can be read as a series of specific studies of well researched Western areas, on a variety of scales, where changing language patterns have been consistently important. Finally it can be considered as a book throwing light on culture conflict and providing insight into its nature. I commend all these. As we lift our eyes from the minutiae of local economic regeneration, which seems to dominate funded research, to the major problems which beset the world, then geolinguistics must figure larger and larger in schemes of geographical, and I hope linguistic, teaching and research. It is right and proper that they should.

Preface

This volume has grown from a conviction that geographers have paid too little attention to the analysis of language groups within contemporary advanced industrial societies. It offers an introduction to the scope and principles of geolinguistics and illustrates its application at international, state and local scales of analysis.

As a student in the late 1960s and early 1970s I was taught the value of an inter-disciplinary approach to socio-economic questions by inspiring teachers of Geography and Politics at the University of Wales. Underlying this approach was a conviction that the contemporary concerns with social planning, modernization and development were best served by recognizing their complexity and by the adoption of cross-cultural and inter-disciplinary perspectives. However, when attention was focussed on the minority groups of advanced industrial societies, such questions as language defence and religious affiliation were treated in a rather off-hand manner and consigned to a residual cultural explanation, which on closer inspection turned out not to be an explanation at all, but rather a denial of their significance. Now this attitude intrigued me, for it taught me much about the way in which academic priorities are shaped by the conventional wisdom of prevailing political ideologies. The neglect of language in particular concerned me and in the subsequent 15 years I have sought to collaborate with others to promote the formal study of language within geography. An early outlet for this research in the geography of language was the Discussion Papers in Geolinguistics series started in the late 1970s, and with which all the contributors to this current volume have been associated. The interest shown in these research papers convinced me that there was a far wider interest among fellow travellers than was reflected in the pages of the established geography journals alone, hence the origins of this volume.

Preparations and thinking on the contents of this volume were greatly assisted by a British Academy Award in 1980–82 and by an invitation to be a Fulbright Scholar in Residence at that most stimulating centre of geographic thought in Happy Valley, The Pennsylvania State University, 1982–83. I am grateful to both organizations for their support.

I am, naturally, delighted that when approached the contributors so readily agreed to provide the chapters, and I hope the finished product will be sufficient reward for their labours.

A number of people have commented on individual chapters and I wish to acknowledge the constructive comments received from Professor Richard Wood, Professor P. O'Farrell, Dr. M. Keane, Mr. D. Fennell, Professor John Edwards. At an earlier stage Mr. J.M. Pickering of The Pennsylvania State University Press offered advice and editorial assistance which proved valuable.

Closer to home the many discussions with John Ambrose of North Staffordshire Polytechnic are very much appreciated, as is the support of Professor George Kay and my colleagues in the Department of Geography and Recreation Studies, North Staffordshire Polytechnic. Many of the maps were skilfully prepared by our departmental cartographer, Mrs Jane Williams, and my secretary, Ms Karen Wootton, deserves a special acknowledgement for her patient assistance in the typing of portions of the manuscript.

I would like to thank Professor Harold Carter, the doyen of Welsh geographers, for agreeing so readily to write a foreword, and for his general encouragement of our efforts. I would also like to thank Derrick Sharp for his faith in this project and for his editorial assistance, and Mike and Marjukka Grover of Multilingual Matters for their enthusiasm and practical interest in the work of spreading our concerns beyond the world of geographers. Finally, my greatest debt is to my family, who have so often supported my interest and fascination with the inventiveness of human language and my concern that minority languages be better represented in the affairs of modern life.

May Day, 1987   Colin H. Williams
Stone, Staffordshire

Acknowledgements

We are grateful to the following for their permission to reproduce copyright material:
Dr. H.L.I. Humphreys for our Figures 5.3 and 5.12 (after Humphreys, 1979); Dr S.Williams and the Editor of Cambria for Figure 5.6 (after Williams, 1981); Franco Angeli Editore for our Figure 5.2 (after Aarebrot, 1982); Croom Helm Publishers for our Figure 5.3 (after C.H.Williams, 1985); T. Lundén and Edizioni LINT for our Figures 5.4, 5.5, 5.6, 5.7a,b,c (after Lundén, 1973); H. Carter and the Director of the University of Wales Press for our Figures 7.7, 7.8, 7.9 (after Aitchison & Carter, 1985), Figures 7.10 and 7.11 (after Pryce, 1978); the Editor and Publishers of Etudes Celtiques, CNRS for our Figures 7.13, 7.14 and Table 7.6 (after Williams, 1981 and 1982); P. White and the Editor of Area for our Figure 7.5 (after Emery & White, 1975); the Editor of Canadian Public Policy for permission to use portions of our revised chapter eight, which appeared in its original form as "An Official Languages Policy for Ontario", vol.XI, No 3, 1985 pp. 561–77; the Editor of Europa Ethnica for our Table 9.1 and 9.2 (after Coakley, 1980); Dr G. Fitzgerald and the Officers of the Royal Irish Academy for our Figures 9.1 and 9.2 (after Fitzgerald, 1984).

1 An Introduction to Geolinguistics

COLIN H. WILLIAMS
Department of Geography and Recreation Studies,
North Staffordshire Polytechnic, Stoke-on-Trent, U.K.

The geolinguist's task

Imagine, if you would, the surface of the earth devoid of its people, inhabited only by non-human animal life roaming its disparate and diverse topographic regions. Next imagine an omnipotent hand dipping into a jarful of people, who between them speak over 6,000 languages, and then his distributing these people in a random fashion all over the world. Now imagine the long wanderings of these people searching for their brothers and sisters in this seemingly chaotic linguistic jumble. Finally, imagine the omniscient being charging some Herculian-like figure to provide an ordered explanation for the resultant distribution pattern and for the relationship between land and language and you have in allegorical form the essence of the geolinguist's task.

Fortunately for us, the task we have set ourselves in this volume is a far more modest, and we hope, realizable one. It is to reflect some current thinking and illustrate some of the potential of geolinguistic analysis.

For many years Geography was essentially the science of distributed phenomenon in space and over time, but language *per se* hardly ever figured as a prominent element in geographic studies. There were, of course, pioneering studies, as we detail below both in this and in successive chapters, but there was little systematic work which deserved the title of geolinguistics. Even today, one is hesitant about using the term geolinguistics, as if it referred to a widely shared and understood body

1

of theory and practice at the interface of geography and the language sciences.

I have detailed elsewhere some of the sources of geolinguistic analysis.[1] In this introductory chapter I want to highlight some of these contributory sources and suggest how the contents of this present volume both extend these early concerns and also develop new themes and points of departure for future studies.

In essence geolinguistics is a developing branch of human geography which reflects the increasing concern of its parent discipline with social problems, and with devising more appropriate methodologies for the analysis of time-honoured questions of social investigation. Its concern is with the relationship between languages and their physical and human contexts, hence the title of this book. It may seek among other things to illumine the socio-spatial context of language use and language choice; to measure language distribution and variety; to identify the demographic characteristics of language groups; to "assess the relative practical importance, usefulness and availability" of different languages from the economic, psychological, political and cultural standpoints of specific speech milieux; to understand variations in their basic grammatical/ phonological and lexical structures, and to measure and map "their genetic, historical and geographical affiliations and relations".[2] Until we achieve a greater integration of the work of linguists and social scientists, the geographer's major contribution will continue to be that of the synthesiser emphasizing the application of general social processes to specific places.

There is little explicit agreement as to what constitutes the core of geolinguistic analysis, but it may prove helpful to outline some of the sources which have contributed to its growth. The earliest identifiable interest lay in the work of European cultural geographers such as Vidal de la Blache, H.J. Fleure, Jules Gillieron, Edmond Edmont and their successors, for example, Estyn Evans and E.G. Bowen.[3] They were concerned to portray the essence of the cultural perspective, treating human aspirations and artefacts as a contingent but nevertheless integral part of the environment. Lukerman (1965: 128–37) suggests that

> "the *genre de vie* or the culture of a population or place is explicitly an historical accumulation of habit. Human inventiveness and freedom are, above all, a social fact, not an individual exploit ...
>
> "The essence of French writing on *genre de vie* is an express emphasis on the historical background of social

behaviour and on the force of social habit as the mechanisms of relationship with the physical environment."

These ideas, as W.T.R. Pryce (1982: 131–49) has shown, represented a fundamental shift away from a human geography dominated by physical influences. Thus, for example, students of the Celtic languages such as E.G. Bowen, Estyn Evans and later Emrys Jones, among others, were beginning to adopt normative concepts in order to explain spatial culture systems, and increasingly they focussed on language as a culture surrogate for group identity on the Celtic fringe. Their pioneering work, based on a combination of census analysis and fieldwork interpretation, has laid the foundation for the more comprehensive, sophisticated multi-variate analyses of today discussed by Pryce & Williams in Chapter 7.

A second source of inspiration for geolinguistic analysis came from the interesting work of dialectologists and the compilers of linguistic atlases. Despite initial methodological problems relating to the training of fieldworkers, the construction of reliable questionnaires, the selection of informants and the consequent verification of the accuracy of dialect mapping, considerable progress has been made in this field. The present volume does not concern itself with dialectology, although it acknowledges that this is an important aspect of the fruitful inter-relationship between linguists and geographers in the past. The reason for this omission is that I take dialectology to be concerned with language issues *per se*, rather than with language in its contextual, geographical sense, which is our primary concern here. Indeed, in a recent collection of essays Peter Trudgill (1983: 6) makes a strong case for distinguishing between different ends of a continuum of language in society: conceiving "sociolinguistics and geolinguistics more as methodologies for doing linguistics through the study of language variation", and locating dialectology more "toward the linguistic end of the 'language in society' spectrum". Nevertheless, we should acknowledge the tremendous advances made in harnessing the power of social scientific and spatial explanation by dialect analysis and dialectological methods. Chambers & Trudgill (1981) have argued persuasively for the existence of dialectology as a unified sub-discipline comprising dialect geography, urban dialectology and human geography. Its unity is provided by the theoretical underpinning of variation theory, the set of premises and hypotheses which arises as a consequence of accepting the variable as a structural unit in the grammatical model. In consequence much of our knowledge of the processes of linguistic change and the diffusion of new forms derives from the very detailed work of linguists such as Trudgill, Haugen, and Mackey (see, for example, Trudgill, 1983; Haugen, 1966; Mackey, 1980a), and of the compilers of linguistic atlases such as Kurath (1939–43), Wagner (1964), Mather & Speitel, (1975), among others.[4]

The only institutional outlet for geolinguistic research was founded in 1965 as the American Society for Geolinguistics. Its aims and range of activities reflect Mario Pei's concern to "channel sociolinguistic information to the informed layman". Its annual journal *Geolinguistics* is a catholic expression of its concern with "disseminating up-to-date knowledge concerning the present day languages of the world" (*Geolinguistics*, 1984, Vol. X, p. ii). However, little of its published work is informed by geographical perspectives. The society's view of the "geographic input" is confined to the occasional selection of material from cases outside the United States, interpreting the *geo* of geolinguistics in a very passive way.

A far more spatially aware interpretation of geolinguistics was pioneered by Professor Bill Mackey and his associates at the International Center for Research on Bilingualism at Laval University, Quebec. His life-long researches have been devoted to a systematic analysis of languages in contact. Early work of his sought to devise methods of standardizing and weighting the various degrees of "power" each language may wield, their attraction at global, regional and local scales and their status potential for prospective speakers, who, for a variety of reasons, are undergoing a process of language shift. More recent work has involved the study of language death, the polyglossic spectrum, and, as we shall see in Chapter 2, the elaboration of geolinguistic principles (see, for example, Mackey, 1973, 1980b, 1985, 1986).

A related source of cross-cultural comparative analysis was the modernization school of social change in the 1950s and 1960s, as represented by the work of Deutsch (1966) and Lerner (1964). In their attempt to develop a communication approach to socio-political change, great emphasis was placed upon language, both as a symbol of independence, and as a carrier of new ideas, particularly of nationalism's potency as a mobilizing ideology. As a result of this early lead we now have a plethora of well conceived and executed case studies of languages in conflict for many sovereign states (for example, Weinstein, 1983; Rokkan & Urwin, 1982). Several political scientists in particular have made a special attempt to integrate various perspectives from politics, sociology and geography in their discussions of applied language policy. Jonathan Pool (1969, 1976, 1978) has devoted considerable attention to the questions of selecting a national language in newly independent, ex-colonial states, and to concerns over language planning, particularly in the USSR. Ken McRae (1964, 1974, 1975, 1983, 1986) has systematically explored the cultural co-existence of national languages in Canada, Switzerland, Finland and Belgium and has provided an outline of the various principles by which language rights might be accorded within multilingual states; principles which have become accepted tenets of the literature on language planning.

The most consistent and innovative concern to emphasize the territoriality of language behaviour by a political scientist is that expressed by Jean Laponce (1975, 1984a,b, 1985, 1987). His researches have developed from the pragmatic concern of relating language shift to political conflict through the particular problems of accommodating francophone grievances in the Canadian political system, to his most recent exploration of neuropsychological explanations for the spatial behaviour of minority linguistic groups — a fascinating area of future research in the life sciences.

While most political scientists and sociologists analysed the political implications of language-related behaviour at the international or state-provincial scale, sociolinguists and anthropologists were often more concerned with identifying the influence of the local environment on linguistic change and on speech strategies in small face-to-face situations. Place was to become an important determinant of behaviour in establishing the rules of code switching, the identification of diglossic situations and the development of vernacular and dialect speech forms.[5] The net effect of these case studies is that we now have an impressive array of data, interpretations and survey text books to inform such crucial policy questions as the development of bilingual education programmes, the granting of language rights to minority groups desirous of being served by government officials in their own tongue, and in the process of language nativisation or indigenisation.[6]

However, it is rare for non-geographers to accord to space a significant role in language-studies. Apart from the spatially informed work of Trudgill, Mackey and Laponce, few of the scholars cited thus far conceived of space as anything but a container, a passive context for more detailed linguistic analysis. This relative neglect of a spatial perspective is understandable when one considers that most scholars conceive of geography in two-dimensional and rather simplistic terms. If they adopt geographical assumptions at all in their research, it is in the hope of demonstrating the direct influence of distance, topography or the built environment upon their analysis of social structure in general, and of language in particular. This conception of space in nineteenth century social physics terms is limiting in the extreme. Whilst one would not wish to argue that geolinguistic analysis has yet reached the theoretical realism found in other parts of Human Geography, notably the analysis of "social relations and spatial structures",[7] it does nevertheless offer a more positive, practical appreciation of the role of space, territory and scale as useful additional elements to be emphasized in a more holistic socio-linguistic practice. It is in this spirit of consolidating the spatial perspective that the chapters in this volume are offered. We make no claims that we are establishing a new field, or have a unique insight which others ignore to their cost. Rather, this collective work is offered as a gentle reminder that the spatial perspective, and its attendant methodologies, is able to enrich the, by now, voluminous literature of linguistic studies. If in passing it also encourages fellow geographers to treat language as a more significant variable in their researches we shall have been doubly satisfied.

These various developments have prompted a more systematic study of the geography of language, and in this book we consider four aspects of this revival of interest: the elaboration of geolinguistic origins and principles; the macro-social context of language in social space; the various methodological issues of data collection, interpretation and reconstruction of historical language territories; and the application of geolinguistic principles in state language planning.

In Chapter 2, Bill Mackey sets forth the scope and principles of contemporary geolinguistics, dividing his critique into the four stages deemed essential to any standardized investigation of language and space. The four stages are observation, description, interpretation and prediction. In his far-ranging and authoritative discussion he is at pains to emphasize the contingent nature of much of our primary data on language. Caution and careful scrutiny of sources are the watchwords of his assessment of the descriptive role of geolinguistics, for all too often our cartographic and numerical analyses can be misleading, and at times downright false. Eleven basic questions of interpretation inform his discussion of the problems of language distribution, attraction, power, status, expansion, extinction and replacement. General and specific hypotheses are formu-lated, some of which are examined in other chapters in this volume.

The most dynamic process he illustrates is that of language replacement and extinction. We may readily relate the myriad examples throughout history which come to mind, and in the context of this volume several of the more notable cases from the Celtic realm and Scandinavia will be fully documented, for the territorial extension and diffusion of language has dominated geolinguistic analysis at the nation state scale.

However, whilst acknowledging the significance of previous work in this tradition it is perhaps worth signalling here the challenge which faces us in detailing the ecology of language shift at the urban scale and heed Mackey's call to examine the implications of changing language patterns in the major metropolitan regions of the world.

It is also time to re-examine our assumptions regarding language and territory, for two simultaneous processes are operating to challenge our predilection for the neat categorization and reification of socio-linguistic behaviour. The first may be summarized in the general challenge to centralism, known as "the ethnic revival".[8] A leading sector of this revival in the ethnic intelligentsia, whose stress on the authenticity of language and the inviolability of an ethnic homeland gives a literal interpretation to the search for roots in the soil, community and landscape of one's *own* people. The second process is the internationalization of language, what Mackey describes as the "definitive liberation of language from its traditional bounds of time and space . . . (when) language is no longer inevitably attached to spacial boundaries as it was in the past, when its speakers had to be limited to one or a few areas of the globe" (p. xx). What is the relationship between these two apparently contradictory processes at either end of the scale continuum? Is the former a primordial reactive strategy to cope with the new threats and demands of the latter? What is the relationship between the mass media and the reproduction of language and its broader cultural items at the local scale? Does the conquest of the "tyranny of distance" inevitably mean that our geographical framework now has to be totally re-thought? Or if, as Ambrose & Williams claim (1981: 53–71), scale does make a significant difference to the identification of linguistic practices, is it more a matter of integrating the newer perspectives with the older in a far more sensitive manner? Clearly much remains to be researched; our hope is that the principles suggested in Mackey's chapter will clarify and structure the lines of future investigations in geolinguistics.

In order to illustrate the macro-social context of geolinguistics Thomas Lundén and William Bostock have prepared complementary chapters. Professor Lundén's emphasis is on the historical evolution of linguistic territories within one broad region, namely Norden, whilst in contrast Professor Bostock's emphasis is on the global penetration of one language, namely French. Taken together, both chapters illustrate well the inherent relationship between socio-political and technological processes. Norden is characterized by a diversity of languages in their respective environments from the Frisian and Germanic presence in lowland Schleswig, to Finnish and Sami in the Arctic circle some 960 miles to the north. Lundén assesses the impact of mass processes such as state-formation and national integration, modernization and technological change on the various language communities in Norden. He suggests that each change in the ecological bases of socio-economic development produces an additional stress on languages in contact. Norden is a useful context for such analyses because most of the principles discussed by Mackey apply here. Within one large region one may examine the whole continuum of language in society from the Sami's concern to protect a threatened ecosystem to the adoption of Norwegian, and more lately, English as a medium of trans-national interaction. The effects of the adoption of English as a lingua franca are not fully documented in this chapter, but one may cite evidence from Finland to suggest that Swedish at least is under threat as the obvious second-language choice of some young Finns, despite the attempts by government to consolidate its position.[9]

In Chapter 4 we reverse the perspective. Rather than ask how several languages interact in one region, we ask how a single language, French, can unite people in very disparate regions worldwide. Trans-national languages have been significant elements of imperial rule since Persian, Greek and Roman times and greatly influenced the spread of capitalism and the development of the modern world system.[10] Professor Bostock examines the authenticity of *la Francophonie* as an international movement. After tracing the fluctuations of French as a language of international trade and diplomacy he details those trans-national agencies who use French and thereby reinforce its power-base as a medium for the spread of specific values and ideologies. Mackey has drawn attention to the need to specify and measure the relative status of languages and the power of their speakers, a need well illustrated in Bostock's discussion of those agencies which promote the use of French in as varied a context as Quebec or Niger. Whilst we may be familiar with the role of agencies such as *l'Académie Française* or the *Alliance Française* in reinforcing language standardization or in providing the material artefacts to construct the "identity shield" of modern French for the Lebanon or Louisiana,[11] it is likely that we are less familiar with the operation of the leading francophone Agency for Cultural and Technical Co-operation established in 1969 at Niamey in Niger. Its 30 full-member states represent a powerful multicultural pressure group. Fears of French state dominance and of neo-colonial practices are considered to be ill-founded by Bostock, who cites the fact that the Agency's founders were non-French francophones and that many of its leading lights, according to Gordon, subscribed to the initial Malagasy view that the organization could be used as "a vehicle of protest against colonialism and as a medium in which to express black identity".[12] In one of those remarkable transformations where the colonial medium is used to preach anti-colonial messages, French became a language for liberation just as English did in India. It is even more remarkable, given the pillage of Black Africa, that so many of *la francophonie*'s most ardent advocates are to be found in the former colonial possessions of French West and Equatorial Africa. The paradox is well illustrated in David Gordon's magisterial survey of the French language, particularly in the search of the élites in new nations for authenticity and national congruence.

"In the case of Black Africa where borders have been among the cruellest cases of the 'rape of geography by history' (Jacques Ancel's phrase), nations, in the legal sense, have been created where no common language other than that, on an élite level, of the colonizer existed to help form a nationality — the vernacular language, rather than being a component of national identity, serves in most of these linguistically heterogeneous countries as a force for disruption and loss of national identity ... In fact, in the cases of many new nations seeking to develop a sense of national identity among their people, leaders are confronted with a challenge which the older nations of the West did not have to face, the challenge of adopting, standardizing and universalizing a language which will both serve development and modernization and at the same time have legitimacy, 'authenticity', in the eyes of the masses." (Gordon, 1978: 17).[13]

Élite-mass relations also figure in the meaning of *la francophonie*, for critics have derided its authenticity as a mass movement, claiming that it is élite-dominated and of little relevance to the populations of French-speaking polities. Bostock is not convinced by such criticisms but does raise a more profound, and disturbing, question concerning French as an international symbol of shared values in multicultural societies. This question relates to the parallel development of one form of *francité*, that is the attempt to reserve "*francophonie* for whites only". Such racist tendencies have not been fully realized and, as yet, do not threaten the more integrative values attached to the current interpretation of *francophonie* as a global movement.

In the next three chapters we focus on the methodological issues which structure geolinguistic investigations. John Ambrose and I survey the problems encountered when attempting to measure language border areas. We demonstrate, with reference to the work of Scandinavian scholars, how issues of scale, geo-political location and national communication systems all influence the initial definition and subsequent legal recognition of boundaries. However, we argue that legal requirements do not necessarily accord with the functional realities of personal interaction and group behaviour in border areas and report on the several advantages obtained by adopting a behavioural approach to measuring language boundaries. In the absence of reliable census evidence we argue that detailed socio-cultural investigation is the only feasible method of establishing linguistic boundaries. Such investigations are demonstrated with reference to the Breton language boundary and suggestions are made as to how one may map and record changes in the border area over time. Of particular importance is the identification of a "zone of collapse", defined as an area where the language potential of the indigenous population is not realized in a wide range of social domains. Once individuals in such zones begin to abandon one language in favour of another, for whatever reason, we enter a phase of language shift. Language shift is very well documented in the socio-linguistic literature, but reference is rarely made to the precise geographical referents of such shift patterns. We argue that there is a crucial geographic distribution pattern in this process, and such patterns need to be investigated so as not to misinterpret local variations. Too often, it seems, gross generalizations are made about language situations, when aggregate linguistic and social data are collected in a small number of locations. The subsequent extrapolation of this data to cover a whole territory results in misinformation which can be critical, especially when one incorporates such results into the public decision-making realm of formal language planning. This point is well illustrated in a parallel study of the Welsh borderland where we urge sensitivity to local conditions and to the recognition of the scale factor in geolinguistic studies.

> "The scale problem has particular implications for language planners in their consideration, for example, of the zone of collapse ... this may seem to form a linguistic buffer zone protecting the more strongly Welsh core areas to the west. Examination at increasingly large scales has shown, however, that the zone is not equipped to perform the function effectively; it is an area in flux, where morale is low and where no two localities share exactly the same problems; quite the last place where the 'grand design' for language planning should be attempted — and yet at the same time the place in need of the most urgent and comprehensive measures for the protection of the individual Welsh speaker." (Ambrose & Williams, 1981: 70).

Locating the boundary of a language under threat is a necessary precursor to the wider task of identifying the mechanism of language shift wherever it might occur throughout the territory. Given the complex socio-economic and psychological factors which influence language choice, it is imperative that the origins of shift processes be correctly investigated. This demands a thorough knowledge of the various social correlates of language in space and over time. Charles Withers provides such a study of the decline of Gaelic in Scotland from the seventeenth century to the present time. Special attention is paid to the shrinkage of the *Gaidhealtachd* and to the retreat of Gaelic from a large number of speech domains. He identifies two distinct processes which influence the geography of Gaelic's decline. The first are those agencies which sought to anglicise the Highlander as a result of a conscious drive toward linguistic uniformity in the kingdom. These include military, religious and educational bodies, the operation of whose policies is a subject of much debate within Scottish history and social science (see also Withers 1984; Durkacz, 1983; Mackie, 1978; Webb, 1978; Mitchison, 1980). The second process is the related but necessarily more wide-ranging incorporation of the Gaelic territory into the space-economy of Britain and the burgeoning world system. Withers argues that there are many strands to this incorporation, each of which deserves careful scrutiny, for they have a collective and incremental impact on language shift. They would include, for example, the role of temporary migration to the Lowlands as an agent of language shift, the immigration of English speakers and the emigration of Gaels, changes in the traditional social organization and agrarian economy of the Highlands; in short, the transformation of a Highland society to suit the dictates of an expanding state-wide political economy.[14] Given the structural integration of the Gaelic territory into the British state there seems little chance of the language fulfilling an autonomous role. Indeed, compared with the Welsh and Irish situations, there is even less to be optimistic about in terms of the reproduction of a distinct Gaelic culture. Withers cautions that "there is still much to be done to provide a contemporary relevance and sound future for Gaelic" (p. 162). Despite the mini-revival of the past generation in the Celtic lands, Gaelic still lacks a co-ordinated strategy for community survival. Rural decline on the one hand and the failure to institutionalize the language in the affairs of the local state on the other, leave the language in a very tenuous position indeed.[15]

In the third of our methodological chapters Reece Pryce and I survey the quality of language data from mid-eighteenth century Wales to the present. That historical geolinguistics can be undertaken for such a continuous period is itself quite remarkable in comparison with many other language-contact situations world-wide. However, as the chapter demonstrates, these data sources are not without their problems, in particular those of partiality in the questions asked regarding language affiliation and competence, those regarding the integrity of official data and those problems associated with the interpretation of such data. The major data source is, of course, the decennial census, which has asked a question on language since 1891. The chapter scrutinizes the census evidence, detailing those improvements in successive surveys which relate to the categorization of data, the selection of appropriate areal units for data collection and analysis, and the selection of additional census questions which relate to the reading and writing ability of the population. Clearly there remain difficulties in interpreting what precisely the aggregate data so collected actually reveal about language in society, for the census is a mass self-administered questionnaire. There is little direct verification of the degree of language fluency as reported in the aggregate census results, but one may supplement this nevertheless valuable source by detailed socio-cultural surveys and in-depth interviewing at representative sites.

Further refinements to the analysis of intercensal changes concern the adoption of specific geo-statistical methodologies, such as plotting long-term changes on cartesian co-ordinate graphs, or constructing the location quotient to record changes in the distribution of Welsh speakers. The location quotient is able to demonstrate the linguistic status of a particular locality in relation to that prevailing within the wider regional context, offering a series of relative comparisons which we argue complements the more orthodox intercensal comparisons based on absolute change only.[16] These descriptive measurements have been supplemented in the past two decades by the adoption of multi-variate statistical techniques such as factor analysis, and the chapter reports on an attempt to construct more sophisticated socio-cultural environments using the principal components analysis technique. The resultant regions, so obtained, are not only of interest in their own right but are also capable of being used as a preliminary framework for the implementation of a range of government services. The adoption of this technique is a major advance on previous univariate language analysis, because it incorporates some 48 variables for the 168 Local Authority units in Wales prior to 1974, placing the co-variation of language in a wider structural context (see Williams, 1979, 1982a,b, especially Chapter 6).

Although the census has been the dominant source for most geolinguistic analysis in Wales it is by no means the only fruitful avenue for the reconstruction of historical patterns of language distribution. Place name evidence, field names in estate records, tithe surveys and parish registers have also been used to good effect in many local studies. However, it is to ecclesiastical sources that one must turn for the most comprehensive national pre-census source, and in this chapter we summarize and assess the significance of both Anglican and non-Established religious sources. Previous studies had assumed that various church records were unrepresentative of local conditions. We accept this criticism as valid for the nineteenth century, but argue that prior to the growth of mass nonconformist congregations, there are good grounds for accepting that the church returns are valid as indicators of local language of worship conditions. The vast body of church data has been examined by Reece Pryce in a series of published papers and we report on the significance of this source for constructing national maps showing language zones and overall trends in language change for the period 1750 to 1900 (see Pryce, 1972, 1978, 1986).

A final source for the identification of language zones is the image which the general public might hold of where within Wales specific languages, namely Welsh and English, predominate or are threatened. There are admittedly procedural problems of how to measure perceived "mental maps" of culture regions, and, indeed, there remains a lively debate as to whether such mental constructs have any validity whatsoever, outside of the derived "realities" constructed by the researcher. Nevertheless, as the perceived environment is often claimed to influence behaviour and attitudes, it is important to recognize the relevance of phenomenological and other subjective "explanations" in interpreting reactions to language decline and territorial shrinkage. If, as is often argued, a crisis mentality exists within Wales, then it is surely interesting at the very least to attempt to locate in geographic space *where* this crisis is assumed to be most acutely felt!

In the final section of the book we concentrate on the application of geolinguistic research in the field of state language planning and regional development. Professor Don Cartwright examines the possibility of establishing a formal language zone in Ontario to encourage the reproduction of francophone culture and language maintenance in the east and north of the province. He argues that the existing system of gradually introducing provincial services into the two official language communities is unlikely to halt the erosion of French within this zone of transition, and this for very good reasons. In recent decades, Canada has experienced the profound effects of linguistic territorialization whereby francophones are becoming more concentrated in Quebec and anglophones in the rest of Canada. By concentrating its resources on providing parallel institutions to serve both French and English language communities the state is in effect practising an inappropriate form of language planning. What is needed, argues Professor Cartwright, is less conventional status planning and more functional and formal organization of territory. The designation of an Official-Languages Zone in eastern and northern Ontario would require very careful measurement of the mother-tongue populations, their distribution patterns, their use of either or both official languages in specific domains, and the calculation of how feasible such a designation might be, given the current political climate and recent failure of the government's related scheme to establish bilingual districts within Canada. Each of these considerations is fully discussed and their implications for Canadian unity and francophone aspirations realized. Given Professor Cartwright's previous researches and positions of responsibility as research co-ordinator of the Federal government's Bilingual Districts Advisory Boards, we should not be surprised at the sophisticated and authoritative arguments he deploys in favour of the establishment of an official-languages policy for Ontario, as a matter of extreme urgency, lest the territorialization processes engulf Ontario's francophone population.

Throughout this volume great stress has been laid on the contextual element of language and territory. Most of the languages discussed have been threatened minority languages, languages often devoid of an institutional framework which serves to protect and nurture them at whatever scale in the political hierarchy. We have acknowledged that who speaks what language to whom, when and under which conditions is an important research question for socio- and geo-linguistics. However, we have also seen that *where* a language group is physically located in macro, environmental terms is also germane to the range of possibilities given to such groups. The final case study chapter examines the plight of the Irish language within its homeland, the *Gaeltacht*. This territory is characterized as a dependent, marginal periphery on the edge of Europe, exposed to all the problems which other beleaguered languages in Western Europe have faced for centuries. However, unlike the Welsh, Breton, Corsican, Frisian and Scots–Gaelic situations, the Irish-speaking communities have been subjected to a succession of government attempts to bolster and stabilize their numbers, thereby seeking to preserve a distinct Irish milieu. Whilst acknowledging the traumatic effect on Irish of the pre-independence colonial rule exercised by the British crown, my chapter is also critical of the methods by which autonomous Irish governments have sought to "save" their national tongue. By concentrating on the relationship between economic marginality, regional development and the intervention of state bureaucracies, the tensions and structural limitations of the Irish situation may be seen to good effect. The lessons gleaned from the Irish experience related to language planning, the nature of state-directed modernization and economic development and of bilingual education are salutary and timely reminders that even with political independence there is no guarantee that indigenous languages will flourish. It is quite another matter, and one of considerable social concern to all involved, as to what constitutes appropriate remedial action by independent governments anxious to save threatened languages.

Notes to Chapter 1

1. For elaboration of the first part of this chapter see Williams, 1984.
2. See the aims of the American Society of Geolinguistics, founded in 1965, which are in turn derived from Mario Pei's section on geolinguistics in his *Invitation to Linguistics* (1971).
3. For an account of the work of E.G. Bowen, see Carter & Davies (1976); and for an appreciation of his influence in the writings of others see Davies (1986).
4. For a review of the cartographic development of language mapping see Zelinsky & Williams (1988).
5. See among others in the vast field of sociolinguistics the representative work of Labov (1972), Milroy (1980), Fishman (1971, 1972, 1981).
6. Recent survey texts which reflect current thinking are Edwards (1985) and Trudgill (1984).
7. This is the title of a recent "state of the art" book which attempts to fuse human geographic and sociological theory and apply the resultant synthesis to empirical analysis; see Gregory & Urry (1985), and for a critical review of its achievement see Gregson (1987: 93–107). It should be clear that while I applaud this attempt at synthesis, I do not mean to imply that the essays in the current volume offer a specific "Giddensian" treatment of language in geographic context, though undoubtedly this would be an important addition to our stock of knowledge and an intriguing research task to boot.
8. Two good investigations of this complex phenomenon are Smith (1981) and Fishman *et al.* (1985).
9. See Reuter (1981: 130–43), Allardt (1977, 1979), Alapuro (1980).
10. On ancient imperial systems see Smith (1986); on language and colonialism see Anderson (1983) and Gordon (1978); on the growth of the world system see Wallerstein (1980), and a geographic interpretation in Taylor (1985).
11. The phrase is taken from Gordon (1978: 115–46, chapter 4).
12. Bostock is here paraphrasing Gordon (1978: 89).
13. Gordon (1978: 17) on national congruence, that is the attempt to make state and national co-extensive entities, see Williams (1986: 196–230); see also Williams & Smith (1983: 502–18).
14. For a very stimulating analysis of the relationship of state-formation and the reproduction of culture see Corrigan & Sayer (1985); see also Harvie (1981)

for a discussion of state-wide trends which have shaped Scottish history in the present century.
15. For an intriguing Third World perspective on rural decline see Baviskar *et al.* (1980) and Baviskar *et al.* (1983).
16. For exemplification of the location quotient technique see Emery & White (1975: 26–30).

References

ALAPURO, R., 1980, *Finland: An Interface Periphery*. Helsinki: R.G.C.S. No. 25.

ALLARDT, E., 1977, *Finland's Swedish Speaking Minority*. Helsinki: R.G.C.S. No. 17.

—— 1979, *Implications of the Ethnic Revival in Modern Industrialized Society*. Helsinki: Societas Scientiarum Fennica, 12.

AMBROSE, J.E. & WILLIAMS, C.H., 1981, On the spatial definition of 'minority'. In E. HAUGEN *et al.*, *Minority Languages Today*. Edinburgh: Edinburgh University Press. 53–71.

ANDERSON, B., 1983, *Imagined Communities*. London: Verso.

BAVISKAR, B.S. *et al.*, 1980, *Rural Decline in the U.K.: A Third World View*. Langholm: The Arkleton Trust.

BAVISKAR, B.S. *et al.*, 1983, *Development Institutions and Approaches in Three Rural Areas of the U.K.* Langholm: The Arkleton Trust.

CARTER, H. & DAVIES, W.K.D. (eds) 1976, *Geography, Culture and Habitat*. Llandysul: Gomer Press.

CHAMBERS, J.K., 1981, Geolinguistics of a variable rule, *Discussion Papers in Geolinguistics*, 5.

CHAMBERS, J.K. & TRUDGILL, P., 1980, *Dialectology*. Cambridge: Cambridge University Press.

CORRIGAN, P. & SAYER, D., 1985, *The Great Arch: English State Formation as Cultural Revolution*. Oxford: Blackwell.

DAVIES, W.K.D. (ed.) 1986, *Human Geography from Wales: Proceedings of the E.G. Bowen Memorial Conference, Cambria*, Vols 12 & 13.

DEUTSCH, K.W., 1966, *Nationalism and Social Communication*. Cambridge, Ma.: MIT Press.

DURKACZ, V.E. 1983, *The Decline of the Celtic Languages*. Edinburgh: John Donald.

EDWARDS, J., 1985, *Language, Society and Identity*. Oxford: Blackwell.

EMERY, F. & WHITE, P., 1975, Welsh speaking in Wales according to the 1971 census, *Area*, 7. 26–30.

FISHMAN, J.A. (ed.) 1971, 1972, *Advances in the Sociology of Language*. 2 Vols. The Hague: Mouton.

—— 1981, *Never Say Die*. The Hague: Mouton.

FISHMAN, J.A. *et al.*, 1985, *The Rise and Fall of the Ethnic Revival*. Berlin: de Gruyter.

GORDON, D.G., 1978, *The French Language and National Identity*. The Hague: Mouton.

GREGORY, D. & URRY, J. (eds) 1985, *Social Relations and Spatial Structures*. London: Macmillan.

GREGSON, N., 1987, Human geography and sociology: Common ground or common object? *Political Geography Quarterly*, 6,1. 93–101.

HARVIE, C., 1981, *No Gods and Precious Few Heroes*. London: E. Arnold.

HAUGEN, E., 1966, *Language Conflict and Language Planning: The Case of Modern Norwegian*. Cambridge, Ma.: Harvard University Press.

KURATH, H. (ed.) 1939–43, *Linguistic Atlas of New England*, 3 vols. Providence, R.I.: Brown University.

LABOV, W., 1972, *Language in the Inner City: Studies in Black English Vernacular*. Philadelphia: University of Pennsylvania Press.

LAPONCE, J.A., 1975, Relating linguistic to political conflicts: The problem of language shift in multilingual societies. In J.G. SAVARD & R. VIGNEAULT (eds), *Multilingual Political Systems: Problems and Solutions*. Quebec: Laval University Press.

—— 1984a, *Langue et Territoire*. Quebec: Les Presses de l'Université Laval.

—— 1984b, The French language in Canada: Tensions between geography and politics, *Political Geography Quarterly*, 3. 91–104.

—— 1985, The multilingual mind and multilingual societies: In search of neuropsychological explanations of the spatial behaviour of ethno-linguistic groups, *Politics and Life Sciences*, 4,1. 3–9.

—— 1987, Assessing the neighbour effect on the vote of francophone minorities in Canada, *Political Geography Quarterly*, 6,1. 77–87.

LERNER, D., 1964, *The Passing of Traditional Society*. New York: The Free Press.

LUCKERMAN, F., 1965, The '*calcul des probabilités*' and the *Ecole Française de Géographie*, *The Canadian Geographer*, 9, 128–37.

MACKEY, W.F., 1973, *Three Concepts for Geolinguistics*. Quebec City: C.I.R.B.

—— 1980a, The ecology of language shift, *Zeitschrift für Dialektologie und Linguistik. Beihefre*, 32. 35–41.

—— 1980b, The ecology of language shift. In P.H. NELDE (ed.), *Sprachkontakt und Sprachkonflikt*. Wiesbaden: Franz Steiner. 35–41.

—— 1985, La mortalité des langues et le bilinguisme des peuples. In PIEPER & STICKEL (eds), *Studia Linguistica Diachronica et Synchronica*. Berlin: Mouton de Gruyter, 537–61.

—— 1986, The polyglossic spectrum. In J.A. FISHMAN *et al.* (eds), *The*

Fergusonian Impact. Vol. 2. Berlin: Mouton de Gruyter. 237–43.

MACKIE, J.D., 1978, *A History of Scotland.* Harmondsworth: Penguin.

MATHER, J.Y. & SPEITEL, H.H., 1975, *The Linguistic Atlas of Scotland.* London: Archon.

MCRAE, K.D., 1964, *Switzerland: Example of Cultural Co-existence.* Toronto: Canadian Institute of International Affairs.

—— (ed.) 1974, *Consociational Democracy: Political Accommodation in Segmented Societies.* Toronto: McClelland and Stewart.

—— 1975, The principle of territoriality and the principle of personality in multilingual states, *International Journal of the Sociology of Language*, 4. 33–54.

—— 1983, *Conflict and Compromise in Multilingual Societies, Switzerland.* Waterloo: Wilfred Laurier University Press.

—— 1986, *Conflict and Compromise in Multilingual Societies, Belgium.* Waterloo: Wilfred Laurier University Press.

MILROY, L., 1980, *Language and Social Networks.* Oxford: Blackwell.

MITCHISON, R. (ed.) 1980, *The Roots of Nationalism.* Edinburgh: John Donald.

PEI, M., 1971, *Invitiation to Linguistics.* Southbend, Indiana: Gateway Editions.

POOL, J., 1969, National development and linguistic diversity. *La Monda Lingvo-Problemo*, 1. 140–56.

—— 1976, *The Politics of Language Planning.* Paper presented to the I.P.S.A. World Congress, Edinburgh

—— 1978, Soviet Language Planning: Goals, Results, Options. In J.R. AZRAEL (ed.), *Soviet Nationality Policies and Practices.* New York: Praeger, 223–49.

PRYCE, W.T.R., 1972, Approaches to the linguistic geography of Northeast Wales, 1750–1846, *National Library of Wales Journal*, 17. 343–63.

—— 1978, Welsh and English in Wales, 1750–1971: A spatial analysis based on the linguistic affiliation of parochial communities, *Bulletin, Board of Celtic Studies*, 28. 1–36.

——1982, The idea of culture in human geography. In E. GRANT & P. NEWBY (eds), *Landscape and Industry.* Middlesex Polytechnic: Faculty of Social Science Publications.

—— 1986, Wales as a culture region: Patterns of change, 1750–1971. In I. HUME & W.T.R. PRYCE (eds), *The Welsh and their Country.* Llandysul: Gomer Press. 26–63.

REUTER, M., 1981, The status of Swedish in Finland in theory and practice. In E. HAUGEN *et al.* (eds), *Minority Languages Today.* Edinburgh: Edinburgh University Press. 130–43.

ROKKAN, S. & URWIN, D.W. (eds), 1982, *The Politics of Territorial Identity*. London: Sage.
SMITH, A.D., 1981, *The Ethnic Revival*. Cambridge: Cambridge University Press.
—— 1986, *The Ethnic Origin of Nations*. Oxford: Blackwell.
TAYLOR, P., 1985, *Political Geography*. London: Longman.
TRUDGILL, P., 1983, *On Dialect: Social and Geographical Perspectives*. Oxford: Blackwell.
—— (ed.) 1984, *Applied Sociolinguistics*. London: Academic Press.
WAGNER, H. (ed.) 1964, *Linguistic Atlas and Survey of Irish Dialects*. Dublin: D.I.A.S.
WALLERSTEIN, I., 1980, *The Modern World – System II*. New York: Academic Press.
WEBB, K., 1978, *The Growth of Nationalism in Scotland*. Harmondsworth: Penguin.
WEINSTEIN, B., 1983, *The Civic Tongue: Political Consequences of Language Choices*. New York: Longman.
WILLIAMS, C.H., 1979, An ecological and behavioural analysis of ethnolinguistic change in Wales. In H. GILES & B. SAINT-JACQUES (eds), *Language and Ethnic Relations*. Oxford: Pergamon Press.
—— 1982a, The spatial analysis of Welsh culture, *Etudes Celtiques*, XIX. 283–322.
—— (ed.) 1982b, *National Separatism*. Cardiff: University of Wales Press.
—— 1984, On measurement and application in geolinguistics. *Discussion Papers in Geolinguistics*, 8.
—— 1986, The question of national congruence. In R.J. JOHNSON & P.J. TAYLOR (eds), *A World in Crisis?* Oxford: Blackwell. 196–230.
WILLIAMS, C.H. & SMITH, A.D., 1983, The National Construction of Social Space, *Progress in Human Geography* 7. 502–18.
WITHERS, C.W.J., 1984, *Gaelic in Scotland*. Edinburgh: John Donald.
ZELINSKY, W. & WILLIAMS, C.H., 1988, The mapping of language in North America and the British Isles. *Progress in Human Geography*, 12.

2 Geolinguistics: Its Scope and Principles

WILLIAM F. MACKEY
*International Centre for Research on Bilingualism,
Laval University, Quebec, Canada*

The relation between land and language has been of concern ever since rulers have had to govern areas where languages other than their own were spoken. The expansion of multilingual empires such as those of the Habsburgs and the Ottoman Turks, as well as the creation of nation-states, made necessary the identification of areas where the official or national language was not that of the inhabitants.

In this context, it is significant that one of the first official acts of the Constituent Assembly established by the French Revolution was the creation in 1793 of a commission with the mandate of eliminating regional languages and dialects spoken in the territory covered by the new republic — *une et indivisible* launching one of the earliest geolinguistic surveys (Grégoire in De Certeau *et al.*, 1975).

Within the new nation-states, however, the boundaries which separated the languages and dialects housed within their territory have often remained unclear. It was not until the end of the nineteenth century and the early twentieth that standard and more exact methods of investigation were applied to the study of the relation between language and territory. As such studies have multiplied, the need for some basic principles and more standard methods has become evident. All such studies suppose a choice of perspective from which observation of language on areas of the globe takes place within defined limits. This also supposes the possibility of identifying and grouping the language phenomena observed at a given place and at a given time. This is followed by an interpretation of what has been identified and analysed, which may lead to some prediction based on projections of observed trends. Let us take each of these in turn: observation, identification, interpretation and prediction.

Observation

Anyone planning to undertake a geolinguistic study must first decide what to observe — where.and when, at what level and how closely. At one extreme, there is the observation of the usage of linguistic forms (words, sounds and expressions) as each varies from one locality to another. At the other extreme there are the wide-ranging area surveys of language use (home languages, working languages and special purpose languages) covering large areas of the globe (the Americas, the South Pacific, Europe and the Indian Sub-Continent). In between there are case studies and language use profiles varying in range and intensity. The most detailed of these was an off-shoot from the rigorous methods developed for the study of comparative philology, which had by then included standard criteria of proof of the origin of word forms, the relation between them and the order of their modification within and between languages of common ancestry. It was noted that the form of words varied both in time and space; the form of a word depended on when and on where it was used.

The geography of linguistic forms

Those who applied to language the theory of the evolution of biological species, observed that the evolution of word forms away from the original — or proto-language — depended on their geographic location. In the regional differentiation of Vulgar Latin, for example, in the course of its development into Italian, Spanish, French, Rumanian and other Romance Languages, the differentiation of the forms was studied as a function of the geographic distance between where they were observed and where they originated. Such names as "areal linguistics" or "spatial linguistics" were applied to this study (Bartoli, 1945).

During the same period, philologists became aware of the great variety of word forms as they were then used in the spoken dialects of Europe, presumably fathered by one proto-language, so much so, that one was expected to discover the origin and distribution of each of its forms before generalizing on the history and geography of a language or dialect. *Chaque mot a son histoire* became the dictum of the new study, which was then called "linguistic geography", the object of which was to identify variations in word forms from one locality to the next and to map out the areas where the same forms were used. This required the development of field techniques, on-the-spot recording of usage and pronunciation, and the plotting of word forms on language maps. A set of such maps constituted a "linguistic atlas" of the area covered. Before such an atlas could be completed, a number of problems had to be solved: sampling validity, field methods, recording accuracy, team work and financing. Yet, within a few decades, every nation which could afford it was supporting the development of an atlas of its own national language (Gilliéron & Edmont, 1912; Haust, 1953; Wrede *et al.*, 1953; Kurath, 1939).

Since the main outcome, from the point of view of the nation-state, was the identifying of regional dialects, it is not surprising that specialists in this area of language research become known as "dialect geographers" or simply "dialectologists". Since the publication of the first linguistic atlases, a great deal of time and effort has been expended on the improvement of methods and techniques of recording and quantification.

The geography of language functions

At the other end of the scale of observation (the macro sciences) are the methods adopted in the study of the geographical distribution of languages inside political frontiers. The study of such questions has come within the province of political science, particularly that of political geography, which has included the analysis of language territoriality in culturally segmented societies, ethnic cleavage along language lines and the development of the politics of accommodation in multinational states (McRae, 1974). Such bodies as the International Political Science Association have devoted more than one conference to such questions (Savard & Vigneault, 1975).

Case studies and profiles

Between these two extremes of micro and macro geolinguistic observation lies a range of case studies in the context of such disciplines as sociology, geography, linguistics, social psychology and anthropology. There have, for example, been studies of how one of the last surviving dialects of a moribund language has vanished from a given locality

(Dorian, 1981). Profiles have been established outlining the structure, domains and degrees of use of languages in a single region, such as those made as part of the sociolinguistic component of the Anthropological Survey of India (Bhattacharya, 1979). We have studies on certain forms of territorial accommodation (Cartwright, 1981). There are some spatial definitions of language groups (Ambrose & Williams, 1981), studies of the distribution of a single language in a number of different countries (Valdman, 1979), and models of territorial separatism (Williams, 1982). All these studies suppose a relationship between land and language; but the nature of the relationship is not always the same. From this growing multidisciplinary literature, therefore, it is becoming more and more difficult to extract any general truths based on commonly held geolinguistic distinctions.

After the choice of perspective (1), the problem in establishing geolinguistic distinctions is of three orders: descriptive (2), interpretative (3) and predictive (4). Let us now consider each of these.

Description

The main problems of geolinguistic description are the identification of the unit of observation (a language or language variety), the location of the units, their territorial segmentation, their functions and evolution.

Identification

When we say that Language X is the language of a certain area, what do we mean? Is it the language exclusively used in that area? Is it the language of the home? Or do we refer to the area's official or regional language, or to some combination of the above? For answers to these queries, we may have to turn to the questions on which the data were gathered — in most cases the national census. It then becomes necessary to study the meaning or meanings of each of the census questions and the degree of reliability of the responses. For example, the Canadian census refers to "mother tongue" as "the first language learned and still understood", which does not mean that the language is still spoken, or that it is necessarily the language of the home.

The value of language data from census sources depends on the questions, the responses and the records. The usefulness of the language question depends on what is meant (its semantic coverage) and what is understood (like the degree of specificity and possible ambiguity of the responses). The semantic area covered in language-related census questions varies considerably from one country to the next. They may include mother tongue (the language of the mother), the first language learned, the home language, the language best known, the language of the ethnic group, and the like. Most of the questions, however, may be grouped into two types: questions on language use and questions on language ability. The accuracy of the responses will depend on the form of the question and on the area in which it is interpreted. Analysis of the 1961 censuses in India, in South Africa and in Canada have shown that errors due to a misinterpretation of the language questions are quite frequent. A knowledge of a second language may be claimed by people inhabiting a unilingual area whereas, in a bilingual area, the same degree of competence would not be worth mentioning.

Language maps based on such data are often misleading. When one examines a map of the Irish *Gaeltacht*, for example, "Irish-speaking" is not used in the same sense as "French-speaking" is used on a language map of Acadia. Nor does the latter have the same meaning as "French-speaking" on a language map of "Francophonie" where most of the areas shown refer to the use of French as an auxiliary, national, regional, official or school language (see Bostock, this volume, Chapter 3).

Secondly, when identifying the languages it is not always clear what Language X does or does not include. Some geolinguistic studies, for example make no distinction between language varieties, treating all continental Germanic dialects as a single entity (Cornish, 1936). Other studies will distinguish between such varieties as Bavarian, Lower Saxon and the different Allemanic dialects of peripheral areas. Unfortunately, these distinctions are not always consistent. The same study which distinguishes Low Saxon as a dialect of German — incomprehensible to other German speakers — will class Galician, not as a dialect of Portuguese, but as a separate language, because it is used in a different country.

Location

In trying to locate the areas in which different languages are spoken one finds similar discrepancies, which make accurate geolinguistic descriptions difficult to obtain. One finds, for example, widely used school maps of the world's chief languages where each country is coloured according to its official language — red for English, blue for French, and so on. The impression left by such maps is that the more territory under a country's jurisdiction, the more important its national language. Uninhabited stretches of Canada's Northland, vast enough to engulf half of Europe, are colour-coded as English and French speaking areas of the globe. If, in real life, one were to encounter someone along these solitary reaches of the Arctic seas, it would probably be a speaker of an Amerindian language, possibly Inuktitut. Since only people speak languages, the basis for their geographic distribution has to be, not political or physical, but demographic. Where are the people located and what languages do they use?

One way of assuring that only inhabited areas are included in language maps is to have computers generate the maps on the basis of language usage data (Mackey & Cartwright, 1977, 1979). Although this does limit the mapping to inhabited areas, it still has the disadvantage of imperfectly representing the density of the population speaking any one language. A sparsely populated city like Oslo could cover the same area as a densely populated city like London or New York. To avoid this problem, techniques for generating three-dimensional languge maps have been used — albeit on a small scale (Taylor, 1977, 1980). Here densely populated areas appear as hills or mountains on a surface representing the territory in which one or more languages are spoken.

Segmentation

In the geographic representation of language distribution it has often been difficult to draw the line between where one language begins and the other ends. What, in sum, is to be considered as a language border? One can use both subjective and objective data as a basis for determining a language border. One can ask people on the spot to point it out, and one can note the spots in which one language rather than the other is used. In either case the results are not always clear-cut (Williams, 1977, 1981).

Techniques for the use of direct field observations and records of language use in determining language borders fall within the tried and true traditions of linguistic geography whereby each language variable is plotted on a map of the area; identical plots (same form) are then linked together by a continuous line (an isogloss). Where many isoglosses appear together in bundles, as they often do along physical or political frontiers, there is a language or dialect boundary. In many cases, however, the isoglosses are widely spaced and wander irregularly on either side of the political frontier. Here we have as a boundary a transition zone which may in itself constitute a language or dialect area. Although such techniques have succeeded in separating one language from another, they give no idea of interlingual distance or the mutual intelligibility of languages and dialects (Mackey, 1971). Castilians next to speakers of Galician will have less trouble than if they were to be faced with the problem of understanding Basque. A language boundary is not always a language barrier.

What is of more than academic importance, however, is the relationship between boundaries — that is, the geopolitical segmentation of the language map. Wars have been fought to settle such relationships. With 5,445 languages (Grimes, 1984) and few sovereign states (159 United Nation members in 1985) — all with "sacred" frontiers, there are certainly bound to be language boundaries within and between these states. But these boundaries are not all of the same type; nor are their relations to the relevant political frontiers. The type of geopolitical segmentation of a language area may be a decisive factor in determining the potential for ethnic accommodation on the one hand or language conflict on the other.

We can identify five types of geopolitical segmentation between two language areas (that of Language X and that of Language O), *viz.*: split, spread, implant, overlap and overflow (See Figure 2.1). There is a difference, for example, between the overflow of a language area into the territory of another sovereign state, as in the case of Austrian German in the North of Italy, and that of a stateless language like Basque, split by the political frontier between two sovereign states — France and Spain. Both are different from the meeting and overlap of language areas of two sovereign states on the territory of a third, as is the case of the dialects of French and Dutch in the middle of Belgium. Contrariwise, there are certain languages which are spread between two or more sovereign states. Like the Gipsy enclaves in Europe and the Soviet Union they are often multinational in character. Finally, there are the hundreds of intranational frontiers implanted within the political boundaries of sovereign states. In certain multinational federations like India and the Soviet Union, some of these frontiers are accorded official status (Haarmann, 1982). All the above types may be found within a single multinational federation, like, for example, Yugoslavia (Mackey & Verdoodt, 1975).

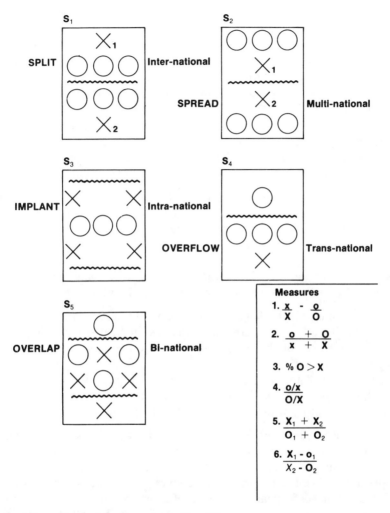

FIGURE 2.1. *Geopolitical segmentation (S)*

Functions

So far, we have limited our problem of description to a single dimension — as if the distribution of languages were made on the basis of one person–one language. In reality, however, large areas of the world are populated by persons who must be at least bilingual, if not trilingual, and sometimes quadrilingual. In much of Africa below the Sahara, for example, in countries like Cameroon, Senegal and Zaire, the vernacular or home language is insufficient. One must be able to use the language spoken outside the home, the language of the area. If one travels outside the region, a vehicular language will be needed. And if one goes beyond primary school, another language of wider cultural communication is required. A young Zaïrian student who has seen military service may have mastered Togbo as a home language, Kikongo as the regional language, Lingala for military service, and French as a school language (Mackey, 1986). In other words, as a unit of language demography he may have to be counted four times. But not on the same map. He would not appear on a map of mother-tongue speakers of French, for example; but rather on a map of those who use French as a school language.

What we are mapping here is not really a language but a language function. Each language function deserves its own map: schooling, government administration, trade, religion, science and technology. Some languages of schooling, like French and English, are found in all quarters of the globe. Those who use these languages as auxiliary tongues sometimes outnumber those who speak them as home languages. Such was the status of Latin in Europe for more than a millenium.

Mapping all the languages of the world according to their special functions is not such a formidable task as might first meet the eye. For it becomes evident that the more specialized the function — measured by the number of years required to master it — the fewer the language options. Of all the languages in the world, a physicist, no matter what his home language, may find use for less than half a dozen; he may even be able to get by with a single scientific language.

Some of the world's languages constitute universal components in a sort of extraterritorial diglossia, practised by all adherents to a certain faith or function. For some languages are indispensable for certain specialities, like Islamic practices (Arabic) or computer sciences (English). Some languages appear as being useful or even necessary in a number of different functions. They possess what might be called a multiglossic distribution. They can therefore be mapped and weighted, not only according to the number of areas in which they occupy a certain function (like education, for example), but also on the number of functions they fill (education, administration, liturgy). These functions, however, are by no means stable. A generation ago, the language of schooling in the Sudan was English; today it is Arabic. This leads us to our second set of problems, those having to do with the dynamics of language change in different parts of the world.

Evolution

Both the function of a language and its territorial extension can evolve in time. So we must study the territorial changes separately from the functional ones.

Territorial change

The data on which language maps are based are not stable. Over a period of time, a language or family of languages which may have covered a continent can completely disappear. If we were to compare a language map of pre-Roman Europe with one of the Europe of Charlemagne and another of contemporary Europe, we would be faced with three different pictures.

Covering most of Europe in the first picture (circa. 250 BC) would be the Celtic dialects, extending from Scotland in the north all the way down to, and including, the Anatolian plain (modern Turkey), and from the Portuguese coast in the west to the Carpathian Mountains in the east. Excluded from this vast Celtic-speaking area would be the basins of the Adriatic and Mediterranean seas, including much of Spain and most of Italy (with the exception of Cisalpine Gaul). Dominating the Mediterranean Basin would be Etruscan, extending from the Valley of the Po to the Bay of Naples, the rest of Italy occupied by the Italic dialects, some of which, like Latin, covered tiny areas within the Etruscan domain. A few centuries later the picture has completely changed. The Celtic dialects have receded to the British Isles; and Latin has expanded from its tiny hillside enclave to cover all of Western Europe from the English Channel to the Coast of Africa. Eventually, we have a language map which approximates that of contemporary Europe, showing that the descendants of the spoken Latin of the Roman Legionnaires have evolved into separate species, as it were, known as the dialects of French, Italian, Spanish, Portuguese, Rumanian and other Romance Languages.

Here we have two distinct geolinguistic phenomena of language change. The first has to do with changes in the population; the second with changes in the languages. In the first case, vast areas have become inhabited by people speaking languages different from those of the previous occupants. In the second case, the language, spoken by several generations of peoples with different ethnic tongues, has become so fragmented from one part of this vast empire to the other as to constitute such mutually incomprehensible languages as French, Spanish, Italian and Rumanian. To explain the nature of this differentiation, comparative philologists have used the geological analogy of the substratum. But this provided only a partial explanation. Just as important was the superimposition of other languages (superstrata) like those of the Allemanic invaders on the territory occupied by the Latinized Celts (Gallo-Romans) (Mackey, 1983a).

The identification of the areas covered by the substratum, the superstratum and the adstratum of a language required the use of such geographic techniques as typonomy. The plotting of place names of foreign origin permitted the mapping of areas occupied by peoples speaking a language which had long disappeared. Archaeological techniques provided further evidence, especially when they supplied decipherable inscriptions.

Functional change

Language maps of the past, as indeed those of the present, can be interpreted only in the knowledge that in any area a number of different languages are likely to co-exist, sometimes with different and distinct functions — administrative, religious and cultural. And the functions attached to each language change in importance and evolve in time. Latin, for example, the cultural and ecclesiastical language of Europe in past centuries, no longer enjoys these functions. The rate of decline of one language and the rise of another in any given area can be measured for each of its functions. Take, for example, the fate of the languages of science and learning from Antiquity to the Modern Period. In Europe, the main language of science has changed from Greek to Latin to Italian to French to German to English. It is only in this century, however, that it has been possible to quantify this function with any degree of precision. Exact records of scientific publications dating back to the end of the nineteenth century now permit one to measure their relative use over time (Mackey, 1984) (See Figure 2.2).

Accurate descriptions of the past and present distribution of languages and their functions are prerequisite to any sort of generalization on the causes and consequences of language change. These descriptions are basic to the interpretation of data and to the generation of geolinguistic hypotheses.

Interpretation

With enough descriptive information at our disposal we could begin to seek answers to some of the basic geolinguistic questions.

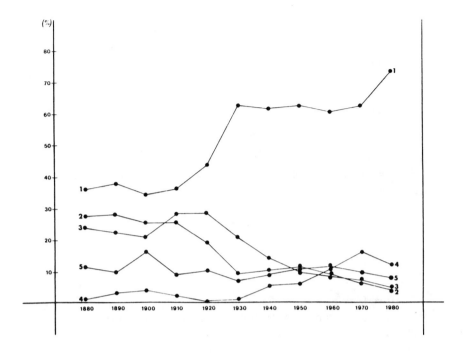

FIGURE 2.2   *The languages of science* (1880 to 1980)

Articles in scientific journals during the past century (1880 to 1980) according to language of publication: English (1), French (2), German (3), Russian (4) and other languages (5), the latter accounting for percentages ranging from 11.9 in 1880 to 7.3 a century later. These other languages, along with the percentage of their most productive year recorded in the sample, include: Italian (10.5), Spanish (4.4), Japanese (2.18), Polish (1.17), Rumanian (0.82), Portuguese (0.75), Hungarian (0.62), Dutch (0.52), Chinese (0.5), Czech (0.47), Serbo-Croatian (0.43), Norwegian (0.32), Ukranian (0.27), Danish (0.23), Azerbajani, Bulgarian, Finnish, and Turkish (0.18 each), Slovak (0.08), Korean (0.07), Hebrew and Slovenian (0.05 each), Armenian and Greek (0.03 each), Esperanto, Georgian, Indonesian, Latin, and Lithuanian (0.02 each). For some widespread languages like Arabic, Bengali, and Hindi, with speakers numbering about a hundred million each, no titles were found in the years sampled. For the last year sampled (1980) the leading "other" languages were: Japanese (2.18), Italian (0.98), Polish (0.85), Spanish (0.75), and Chinese (0.5), the remaining 2% being shared by the above 22 languages. Journals in the physical sciences, medicine, mathematics, biology, chemistry, and the earth sciences were sampled by decade (horizontal axis) from the most complete inventories. Figures for each language (vertical axis) contain maximum probable errors for percentages ranging between 0 and 1% (± 0.06%), between 1 and 10 (± 2%), between 10 and 20 (± 2.5%) and between 20 and 80 (± 3%). This study was done in Quebec at the International Centre for Research on Bilingualism by Minoru Tsunoda between 1980 and 1983 under the direction of W.F. Mackey. A more complete report of the research was published in Tokyo by Sophia University Linguistic Institute for International Communication under the title "Les langues internationales dans les publications scientifiques et techniques" in *Sophia Linguistica* 1983, pp. 140–55.

What determines the distribution of languages on the face of the globe? Why do certain language areas expand and others contract? Why do languages disappear from vast areas they once covered? What is required for the estimation of the life expectancy of a language? Does the rise of one language suppose a proportionate fall in the use of other languages? What attracts people to the use of one language rather than another? Why are some languages more stable than others? Are the status and power of attraction of a language simply reflections of the status and power of the nations for whom it is the national language? Or is language status independent of national status? How does language status develop? What are its components? What are the causes of language extinction? Here are some basic questions which we should attempt to answer. They have to do with the problems of language distribution, language attraction, language power and status, expansion, extinction and replacement.

Language distribution

If we look at what we know about language distribution on the face of the globe, we can allow ourselves a few general observations, as a line of departure. Is the number of languages, in the aggregate, universally proportional to the density of the population? To begin with we can note that the density of population diminishes as we approach the poles and increases as we near the equator; so does the diversity of languages. Secondly, we note that in the inhabitable regions, the languages are not equally distributed. Thirdly, the number of speakers per language varies in the extreme, ranging from a few hundred to a few hundred million. Fourthly, distribution is not proportionate to number. Some languages, like English claiming speakers which number in the hundreds of millions, are used in many different parts of the world; but so are certain languages like Gipsy Romany which counts less than a million speakers.

Language attraction

The higher the status of a language, the more users it attracts. The number of people who read and understand high-status auxiliary languages, like English and French, may actually exceed the number of native speakers of those languages. For French, it has been estimated to be more than triple the number of native speakers of which there are approximately 80 million, as against some 250 million people who use the language as an auxiliary tongue (Dalby, 1982). This dominance as an auxiliary medium cannot be said of languages that have little or nothing to offer. Learning an auxiliary language represents an investment on which some return is normally expected.

Language power and language status

Although all languages have been shaped by the people who have used them, their relative status is independent of the power of their speakers. Some languages have maintained their dominance and status long after their native speakers have ceased to exercise any form of political or economic influence. Ancient Greek, the language of people under Roman subjugation, was the prestige language of Imperial Rome. And long after the Roman Empire had ceased to exist, its language remained the vehicle of the highest functions of church and state.

It is not only a question of cultural capital. Aramaic, for example, the native speech of a small desert tribe, devoid of political or military importance, became the most widespread international language in the empires of Babylon, Assyria and Persia — even replacing Hebrew as a vehicular language in the Palestine of the seventh century BC. Thanks to alphabetized cursive script capable of being written rapidly on papyrus, it soon took over the functions of official languages whose writing required stone inscription or cumbersome clay impressions in cuneiform characters. Through this one dominant function, Aramaic eventually covered all trade routes of Antiquity throughout the Middle East and much of Asia, India and Africa.

Of course, the competition at the time was admittedly minimal. For the first few millenia after the invention of writing, the number of standardized written languages was probably less than a dozen. Even after the invention of the alphabet the number of written languages did not increase rapidly. Written languages were mostly associated with official, administrative, religious and ecclesiastical documents, or court literature. By the year one thousand of our era, the Western world could count only ten official standardized languages. Before that number was to double, it took an additional eight centuries, in spite of the intervening invention and development of printing. With the rise of the nation-state, however, the rate of increase began to accelerate — 20 additional standard languages appearing at the dawn of the nineteenth century; that number doubled some 40 years later. In the twentieth century, the number of languages reduced to writing can now be counted in the hundreds. It is admittedly true, however, that some are more standardized than others (Kloss & McConnell, 1978).

Standardization is undoubtedly a factor in language status. It is inherent in the language. But there are other components of language status, external ones, which depend on the characteristics of the populations of users of a language — demographic, economic, cultural and geographic, accounting for the expansion of certain languages at the expense of others.

Language expansion

Not only the number of native speakers of a language but also the number of people who use it as a regular auxiliary language contribute to its expansion. This total must be weighted by factors which permit users of a language to spread the language through their cultural productivity, their geographic mobility and their economic influence. In weighting the demographics, such indicators as books in print, gross national product and tourism have been used (Mackey, 1973).

These are some of the factors which have made certain languages attractive to others and, along with political, military and commercial expansion, have contributed to the power of these languages. What we do not know, however, is the extent to which language power is the sum of its correlates (Laponce, 1984).

Language extinction

Let us now look at the other side of the coin. What factors contribute to the demise of a language? We shall see that these are not simply the lack of prestige. The cause of the death of a language may be both multiple and complex.

The simplest is genocide. We do not have to go back to ancient times to demonstrate its effects. The twentieth century provides it share of examples: Armenians, Ukranians, European Jews, Kalmuks, Ingouches, Ibos, Bengalis, Tutsis and the Volga Germans — to name only these (Conquest, 1970). The effect of genocide on the survival of a language depends on the concentration and number of survivors — if any. Next is famine, such as that which reduced by a third the Celtic speaking population of Western Ireland in the middle of the nineteenth century.

And this, it seems, occurred at a time when the Irish speaking populations, having been already decimated by the expropriation of their lands and the interdiction of their language were showing signs of revival (De Fréine, 1976).

Thirdly, there is fragmentation. The deportation of the Acadians in the eighteenth century and the diaspora of Sephardic Jews in the fifteenth are examples. Emigration and the settlement of language groups in isolated or mountainous regions also contribute to linguistic fragmentation.

Finally, there are the effects of formal interdiction as a matter of national policy. Official barring of the use of Irish in the sixteenth and seventeenth centuries as well as the interdiction of minority languages and patois in France after the French Revolution — of Basque, Breton, Catalan and Provençal — contributed to the decline of these languages, if only because their use was forbidden in school.

Language replacement

Having assessed the factors which contribute to language expansion on the one hand and language extinction on the other, can we now classify documented cases of language replacement? It seems that we can identify two main types. First, there is the extension of the territory where a language is used. Second, there is expansion through an increase in the number and density of speakers of a language.

Territorial expansion

How has the territorial coverage of languages expanded? One well-documented means is territorial conquest by the speakers of the expanding language. By what process does this take place? We can identify three types: displacement, integration and interdiction.

Displacement This has little to do with cultural, social or administrative influence; it is the linguistic effect of territorial encroachment. The conquerors come to stay, bringing with them their families and friends. The natives, if they are not killed or impressed into slavery, are driven to the barren lands or to the periphery. Their language becomes eventually associated with deprivation, servitude and menial labour, so that the generations which succeed find little profit in maintaining their ancestral culture. Such was the fate of the Celtic languages in Britain under Anglo-

Saxon and Norman rule, as well as that of hundreds of native languages of the New World under their Spanish, English or French rulers.

Integration   The more powerful institutions of the conqueror are here systematically imposed on the occupied nations. This type is characterized by the progressive annexation of territory, the creation of satellites or provinces, each under a governor and controlled by a permanent garrison, protecting colonization from the mother land by merchants and settlers who create their own institutions. The colonization of the Roman Empire is a case in point. It extended the use of Latin throughout Europe to the extent that the successors of the imperial tongue became the national languages of the modern European states.

Interdiction   Contrariwise, the conqueror maintains the existing institutions of the occupied land, imposing on them the use of his language. Typical of this type of language replacement are the many changes in domination along the borderlands of Europe during the past five centuries. During the nineteenth century, for example, Polish institutions in the East were forced to operate in Russian, while in the West of the country they were obliged to function in German. The outcome of wars between the great powers often decided which school language at any given period would be used in Alsace, Lorraine, Trieste, Alto Adige and the Banat. Quite often the school language changed from one generation to the next.

Demographic increment

Within the same territorial confines, the importance of a language may increase with the rise in the number of speakers. Two means of demographic increment in the number of speakers are the assimilation of outsiders and the increase in the birth rate (procreation of the linguistic species, as it were).

Assimilation   Historically, the assimilation of foreigners has been of two types: the acculturation of invaders and the integration of immigrants.

Acculturation of invaders   There are records of peoples who have gained a country but lost their language in the process; the invaders dominate the conquered people but are acculturated by them. This was the case of the Norse-speaking Normans in France, who abandoned their language in favour of Old French (Gallo-Roman). It was also the case of the Germanic-speaking Franks, who adopted the language and civilization of the Gallo-Romans whom they had conquered. In all such cases, what eventually prevails is the weight of the dominant culture, with its more stable institutions, its written traditions, its established and functioning bureaucracy and its accumulated store of useful knowledge. If these cultural forces are weighted in favour of the invaders, however, it is the language of the conquered which tends to disappear.

The integration of immigrants   With the phenomenal increase in the mobility potential during the past century, emigration and immigration have taken on an important dimension in the shaping of national policies — economic, cultural and linguistic. The bilingual children of millions of guest workers in Western Europe, especially since the end of the Second World War, have been instrumental in increasing the number of speakers of the languages of the host countries.

The most successful examples of the long-term linguistic effects of immigrant integration, however, can be found in the New World, where the addition of millions of speakers to languages like English and Spanish can be attributed to immigration from countries where these languages were unknown. The ethnic origin of more than a third of the population of the United States and Canada, according to the most recent surveys, is not English, French or Spanish. The birth rate of these descendants of immigrants has also contributed to the increase in the number of speakers of English in North America.

Natality   Increase in the birth rate of peoples speaking the same language can, with certain limitations, increase the number of speakers of that language. The rate of increase depends also on the survival rate as well as on life expectancy. In highly industrialized nations where the birth rate may be low, the increased life expectancy of the population may compensate, at least during their life time.

The second limitation has to do with the incidence of exogamy. When people speaking a majority language intermarry with minority language speakers the next generation become bilingual speakers of the majority language, whereas the third generation tend to become unilingual speakers of that language.

In practice however this tendency is attenuated by the forces of ethnic and cultural nucleation. Some ethnic groups maintain a strict interdiction against exogamy. Linguistic nucleation of ethnic minorities, promoting endogamy, assures the survival of their language at least as an additional tongue or home language (Mackey, 1985). Concentrations of Italians in New York, Montreal, Buenos Aires and São Paulo have contributed to the survival of the Italian language in the New World.

Each of these types of language replacement is applicable not so much to the language as to the territory it covers. The same language, throughout its history, may alternate between roles. It can be, at turns, the victim and the beneficiary of different types of replacement according to the nature of the languages and peoples with whom it comes in contact. Take the case of Persian, for example. Under the Achaemenid Dynasty (668 to 330 BC) the Persian Empire had no equal. Yet its language was of little interest, since the languages of rich cultures it had conquered were purveyors of ancient and prestigious civilizations. Contrariwise, a dozen centuries later during the Samanid Dynasty of the tenth century of our era, after having been conquered by both Muslim and Mongol, Persia witnessed the adoption of its language by its conquerors and its extension throughout the Ottoman Empire and into parts of India where it flourished until the nineteenth century, when it was progressively supplanted by English.

Prediction

In the social sciences, prediction is not prophecy. Although we do now know which events — many haphazard — will shape the fate of languages in the future, we are able on the basis of the past evolution of a language and its present status to hazard certain projections — very much as the human ecologists have done for the environment. The value of these projections lies in the possibility of doing something about them — of reversing unwanted trends if and when possible. Projections also help us estimate the life expectancy of certain languages.

The ecology of language shift

If we look at the peoples of the globe, therefore, and the languages they speak, we are faced with a panorama which reveals a great diversity. The picture is also a rapidly changing one, as the growing mobility of populations and the phenomenal expansion in the availablity and use of communications media make each country ethnically and linguistically more complex. More and more people from different and widespread areas speaking different tongues are moving into the same limited areas, as the rate of world urbanization increases (Mackey, 1980).

It is true that some parts of the world are still largely rural. There are, for example, countries like Tanzania, 80% of whose 19 million people live on small farms. But this country, like many others, is running out of arable land. Moreover, as such countries develop, they begin to resemble industrialized societies where fewer and fewer people produce more and more of the food. In countries like Canada, the United States and Australia, for example, only 3 or 4% of the population produce food for the remaining millions, and there is even some of it left over for export. The demographic result is that more and more people are living in bigger and bigger cities. The trend seems to be world-wide.

All the evidence seems to point to the probability that the demographic locus of the future will be in the multilingual megapolis. Already some of the world's largest cities have become multilingual — some of them situated in countries like France and England, which for centuries were associated with one and a single language. Such nations are now faced with a rapidly increasing cosmopolitan school population. In London, more than a hundred languages are now spoken by the schoolchildren; the same is true for New York and Paris — and for Los Angeles, where one pupil in five has a mother tongue which is not English. Here, English no longer holds an absolute majority. Spanish seems to be on the rise, since one third of the population speak the language and two thirds of the kindergarten population have Spanish as their mother tongue. With 104 home languages (in 1982), everyone in Los Angeles is now a member of a language minority.

In cities like these, minority languages may some day become majority languages, dominating beyond their territorial borders. Already, the first Puerto Rican city in the world is no longer in Puerto Rico; it is in New York. Miami is a leading Cuban city where Spanish is an official language. To find the second Mexican city in the world, one must look beyond the borders of Mexico to Los Angeles county in the USA. Changing language patterns such as these were created during the past few decades following the increasing mobility of the world's population. This increasing ease with which large numbers of people can now relocate at long distances from their countries of origin has created a growing pressure for multilingual education. Stable unilingual countries are no longer immune to these pressures, especially if they harbour one or more of the stateless nations of what has been called the Fourth World. Here the advent of linguistic irredentism, the revolt of language minorities and the rise of regionalism have engendered the practice of the politics of accommodation whereby more local languages have had to be recognized, taught and used in the schools (Mackey, 1974, 1975).

According to a recent study by the United Nations Fund for Population Activities, which used as a base the year 1950 when less than half the world's population lived in cities, the proportion by the end of the century will exceed three quarters — the greatest increase being in the developing nations, where the rate of urbanization will have more than doubled. It is these same countries, most of them multilingual, which will have accounted for 90% of the boost in the world's population to beyond the six-billion mark by the end of the century. If the trend toward the democratization of societies also continues the increasingly multilingual cities will witness demand for more languages as media of schooling while, as in the past, the traditionally dominant language groups will not easily accept solutions which might lessen their linguistic hegemony. Some of these groups — often more affluent — have begun building their own peripheral towns, leaving the inner city with no dominant language. Paradoxically, as some high density areas of the globe move toward a state of geolinguistic entropy, the world as a whole has become linguistically more interdependent. For this century has witnessed the definitive liberation of language from its traditional bounds of time and space. Both the written and the spoken word can now endure in permanent records. At the same time, language is no longer inevitably attached to spatial boundaries as it was in the past when its speakers had to be limited to one or a few areas of the globe. In this century, following the revolution in mass communications media, some languages are understood by some people in all parts of the globe. And since 1967 it has become technically possible for all of them to intercommunicate. That was the year when the communications satellite Intelsat III was launched into orbit over the Indian Ocean, closing a network permitting world-wide communication. At that moment, for the first time in the history of mankind, no part of the globe was completely out of touch with the rest of the world. Since then, hundreds of satellites have made this technical possibility more feasible for a few of the world's languages. Such languages are no longer the exclusive property of a single state; for them, the identity of land and language no longer holds.

For all these reasons, language problems, in many parts of the globe, have come to dominate public policy. It is true that language-related problems — population mobility, ethnic diversity and language inequality — have existed in the past. But then, there were fewer people on earth, inhabiting fewer places and changing homes less often and more slowly. Few could read or write, and if they tried to learn, the choice of languages in which there was anything to read was extremely limited. The many millenia from the beginning of recorded history to the beginning of the modern period, around the year 1000 of our era, yield records of only a few dozen written languages.

The life expectancy of languages

Both the number of speakers and their distribution seem to be factors which favour the life expectancy of a language. These seem to depend, however, on the existence of other factors such as status, function and standardization.

Any language which has survived for more than a millenium despite multiple unfavourable circumstances is characterized by the presence of at least one factor which favours longevity. A study of the external history of such languages might permit us to put forward certain hypotheses.

The distribution hypothesis

The duration of a language over time is a function of its distribution in space. To refer back to the distribution of languages in Europe during the third century BC, we can note that, although the dominant Etruscan civilization, more refined and powerful than that of the Celts, was conveyed in a written language of high status, it covered an area many times smaller. While Etruscan has long been a dead language, the Celtic languages live on — albeit in peripheral areas.

The status hypothesis

The life expectancy of a language is a function of its status, and the status of a language is measured by the number and importance of the functions it fulfils. The more functions a language drops, the more status it loses. Latin, at one time filled all the functions of language — tribal, vernacular, national, colonial, immigrant, international, diplomatic, scientific and liturgical. One by one, these functions were assumed by other languages until in the end it ceased to be used as the exclusive liturgical language of the Roman Catholic Church.

Not only the number of functions determines the status of a language, but also its relative importance. The relative importance is determined by the culture in which the language operates. in cultures where sacred texts are valued most highly, the language of the texts — whether it be Koranic Arabic or Vedic Sanskrit — will have the highest status. Contrariwise, in cultures with a high regard for science and technology it is the language of scientific discourse which will be seen as having the most important function.

Predominance in one function does not presume dominance in all. French, for example, suffered a general decline in international prestige after the battle of Waterloo and the dismantling of the Napoleonic Empire; but for more than a century after the Congress of Vienna, it continued to be used as the leading and sometimes as the exclusive language of diplomacy.

The demographic hypothesis

Majority languages have tended to expand, since they often rank as the most important simply on account of their numerical superiority. Should all speakers of one language have equal choice of intermarrying with speakers of another language, the statistical projections of language dominance seem to favour survival of the majority language, often at the expense of minority languages in the same area. On this basis language demographers have made statistical projections showing the eventual demise of many minority languages. (See Table 2.1). Whatever the determinants of the life and death of languages, we can know them only on the basis of well-defined descriptions where the language varieties are identified and located with precision along with the forces that affect their use.

Conclusion

From the foregoing it seems evident that the scope of geolinguistics extends beyond the boundaries of traditional disciplines which, although convenient at the outset, like most man-made boundaries, are essentially arbitrary.

The data required to understand the relation between land and languages as they are used by people of differing cultures are not the property of any one science. Yet we are still dependent upon certain disciplines for data that have traditionally made up their staked-out fields of observation — especially those of anthropology, history, geography, sociology and linguistics. These data, however, are not always usable outside the discipline that has generated them in units of observation which are peculiar to it. Each considers language, land and people according to the principles, requirements and current orientation of its field as defined by generations of practitioners past and present.

TABLE 2.1   *Exogamic Projection of Canadian Language Demography**

	First	Second	Generations Third	Fourth	Fifth
English	14,446,235	19,140,188	21,160,947	21,396,816	21,399,475
French	5,546,025	2,166,749	238,128	2,659	
Italian	425,235	47,476	305		
German	213,350	17,453	59		
Ukranian	144,760	9,420	20		
Greek	86,830	4,710	7		
Chinese	77,890	3,626	4		
Portuguese	74,765	2,947	2		
Polish	70,960	2,314	1		
Hungarian	50,670	1,364			
Dutch	36,170	827			
Serbo-Croat	29,285	580			
Yiddish	26,330	453			
Hindi-Urdu	23,110	344			
Finnish	18,280	237			
Spanish	17,710	200			
Arabic	15,260	149			
Czech	15,090	126			
Russian	12,590	89			
Japanese	10,500	62			
Estonian	10,110	50			
Lithuanian	9,985	40			
Slovak	9,465	30			
Lettish	9,250	21			
Danish	4,690	8			
Rumanian	4,455	5			
Flemmish	3,190	3			
Swedish	2,210	1			
Norwegian	2,160	1			
Welsh	1,175				
Icelandic	995				
Slovenian	375				

Note: According to the double hypothesis of random choice of partner and the most popular language as home language
Source: Laponce, 1984: 85.

The resulting incongruity becomes evident in the scientific status of multidisciplinary specializations like psycholinguistics and sociolinguistics, the principles of which seem to vary from one study to the next, depending on whether it was penned by a psychologist, a linguist or a sociologist (Mackey, 1983b & c).

In order to benefit from the enormous potential of these disciplines — in data, method and technique — it is necessary that some basic principles of observation and interpretation be applied uniformly to each of them, at least as their output concerns the language varieties, the language users and the language areas of the world.

References

AMBROSE, JOHN & WILLIAMS, COLIN H., 1981, Scale as an influence on the Geolinguistic Analysis of a Minority Language. *Discussion Papers in Geolinguistics*, 4.

BARTOLI, M.G., 1945, *Saggi di linguistica spaziale*. Torino: Bona.

BHATTACHARYA, S.S., 1979, Sociolinguistic profile of Tripura, *Journal of the Indian Anthropological Society*, 14. 189–98.

CARTWRIGHT, DONALD G., 1981, Language policy and the political organization of territory: A canadian dilemma. *The Canadian Geographer* 25, 205–24.

CONQUEST, ROBERT, 1970, *The Nation Killers*. London: Macmillan.

CORNISH, VAUGHAN, 1936, *Borderlands of Language in Europe and their Relations to the Historic Frontiers of Christendom*. London: Sifton.

DALBY, DAVID, 1982, Languages of the world. *Atlas of Mankind*. London: Mitchell Beazley.

DE CERTEAU, MICHEL, JULIA, D. & REVEL, J., 1975, *Une politique de la langue: La Révolution française et les patois*. Paris: Gallimard.

DE FRÉINE, SEAN, 1976, *The Great Silence*. Dublin: Mercier.

DORIAN, NANCY C., 1981, *Language Death: The Life Cycle of a Scottish Dialect*. Philadelphia: University of Pennsylvania Press.

GILLIÉRON, J. & EDMONT, E., 1902–1912, *Atlas linguistique de la France*. Paris: Champion.

GRIMES, BARBARA (ed.) 1984, *Languages of the World* (10 ed.). *Ethnologue* vol. 10. Dallas: Wycliffe Bible Translators.

HAARMANN, HARALD, 1982, *Elemente einer Soziologie der kleinen Sprachen Europas*. Bd. I: *Materialien zur Sprachökologie*. Hamburg: Buske.

HAUST, J., 1953, *Atlas linguistique de la Wallonie*. Liège: Vaillant-Carmanne.

KLOSS, HEINZ & MCCONNELL, GRANT D., 1978, et seq. *The Written Languages of the World: A Survey of the Degree and Modes of Use* (vol. 1). (ICRB Publication E-10). Quebec: Presses de l'Université Laval (vols 2–7 in preparation).

KURATH, HANS (ed.) 1939, *Linguistic Atlas of New England*. Providence, R.I.: Brown University Press.

LAPONCE, JEAN A., 1984, *Langue et territoire*. (ICRB Publication A-19) Québec: Presses de l'Université Laval.

MACKEY, WILLIAM F., 1971, 1972, 1976, *La distance interlinguistique* (ICRB Publication B-32) Quebec: International Centre for Research on Bilingualism. Reprinted as chapters 9–11 of W.F. Mackey. *Bilinguisme et contact des langues*. Paris: Klincksieck 1976, pp. 221–307. Abstracted as "Interlingual Distance". *Information Sciences Abstracts* (72-1088) (1972):2.

—— 1973, *Three Concepts for Geolinguistics* (ICRB Publication B-42) Reprinted as *Methodik der Geolinguistik*, In *Sprachen un Staaten* (vol. 2) (Nationalitäten und Sprachenfragen in weltpolitischer Perspektive) Hamburg: Stiftung Europa-Kolleg 1976.

—— 1974, Géolinguistique et scolarisation bilingue *Etudes de linguistique appliquée* 15 (1974): 10–33.

—— 1975, Current trends in multinationalism. In W.F. MACKEY & A. VERDOODT (eds.), *The Multinational Society*, Rowley, Ma.: Newbury House. 329–54.

—— 1980, The ecology of language shift. *Zeitschrift für Dialektologie und Linguistik. Beihefte* 32 (1980): 35–41. Summary in: *Sprachkontakt und Sprachkonflikt I* edited by Peter H. Nelde. Brussels: Forschungstelle für Mehrsprachigkeit 1979, pp. 161–62.

—— 1983a, La mortalité des langues et le bilinguisme de peuples. *Anthropologie et Sociétés* 7 (1983) 3: 3–23.

—— 1983b, Sociolinguistics: The past decade. In SHIRÔ HATTORI & KAZUKO INOUE (eds), *Proceedings of the Thirteenth International Congress of Linguistics*. Tokyo: CIPL. 325–50.

—— 1983c, Sociolinguistics and the synchronic fallacy. *Academiae Analecta* (Medelelingen van Koninklijke Academie van België) 45 (1983) 4: 79–90.

—— 1984, Mother-tongue education: problems and prospects. *Prospects* 14 (1984) 1: 36–49.

—— 1985, The sociobiology of ethnolinguistic nucleation, *Politics and the Life Sciences* 4: 11–21.

—— 1986, The polyglossic spectrum. In *The Fergusonian Impact*. (Vol. 2). Mouton, 237–43.

MACKEY, WILLIAM F. & CARTWRIGHT, DONALD G., 1977, 1979, Geocoding Language Loss from Census Data In BONIFACIO P. SIBAYAN & ANDREW B. GONZALES (eds), *Language Planning and the Building of a National Language*. Manila: Linguistic Society of the Philippines. 60–87. Reprinted in *Sociolinguistic Studies in Language Contact* edited by W.F. Mackey & Jacob Ornstein. The Hague: Mouton 1979, pp. 69–98.

MACKEY, WILLIAM F. & VERDOODT, ALBERT (eds) 1975, *The Multinational Society*. Rowley, Ma.: Newbury House.

MCRAE, KENNETH (ed.) 1974, *Consociational Democracy: Political Accommodation in Segmented Societies*. Toronto: McClelland & Stewart.

SAVARD, JEAN-GUY & VIGNEAULT, RICHARD (eds) 1975, *Multilingual Political Systems: Problems and Solutions*. (ICRB Publication A-9) Quebec: Presses de l'Université Laval.

TAYLOR, D.R.F., 1977, Graphic Perception of Language in Ottawa-Hull. *The Canadian Cartographer* 14 (1977) 1: 24–34.

—— (ed.) 1980, *The Computer in Contemporary Cartography* (chap. 9) New York: Wiley.

VALDMAN, ALBERT (ed.) 1979, *Le français hors de France*. Paris: Champion.

WILLIAMS, COLIN H., 1977, Ethnic Perception of Acadia. *Cahiers de géographie de Québec* 21 (1977): 243–68.

—— 1981, On Culture Space. *Etudes Celtiques* 18 (1981): 273–96.

—— (ed.), 1982, *National Separatism*. Cardiff, The University of Wales Press.

WREDE, F., MITZKA, W. & MARTIN, B., (eds) 1953, *Deutscher Sprachatlas*. Marburg: Elwert.

3 Language, Geography and Social Development: The Case of Norden[1]

THOMAS LUNDÉN
Director for Education and Research,
The Swedish Institute, Stockholm, Sweden

In traditional descriptive geography, language is regarded as one spatial distribution as all others and treated as a distinctive feature, often unrelated to all other phenomena. It will be argued in this chapter that linguistic distributions can be analysed and explained only in connection with the social, political and technological development of the territory in question. The test area for this argument is the Norden countries, i.e. Iceland, Norway, Denmark (including the Faroes), Sweden and Finland (including the Åland islands). In addition, the German part of Schleswig will also be discussed, as it is related historically to the development of the Danish state.

Norden may be regarded as a "security-community"[2] (Lindgren, 1979), defined as an area whose inhabitants are unlikely to fight each other in warfare. Such a community reflects the relatively high level of interaction between individuals across state boundaries, eased by linguistic and cultural proximity. In aggregate, the states have very much in common, a fairly long tradition of stable democracy, problems of a harsh but reliable climate and nature, dependence on foreign markets and on foreign power. However, clear structural differences may be noted within the community. Both Sweden and Denmark are old colonial powers, having governed their northern neighbours and introduced laws, customs and linguistic forms which retain an influence within Norway, Iceland

47

and Finland, all of which gained their independence only in this century. Also Russia and Germany have exercised a formal and functional influence on their smaller neighbours.

As a linguistic territory, Norden contains many types of conditions and relations, ranging from the dominance of accepted standard languages like Swedish and Danish to multi-faceted relations, as between the dialects and the two written forms of Norwegian and the clear-cut but social and territorially problematic distinction between Germanic and Finno-Ugric speech in eastern Norden. Danish and Swedish belong to the eastern branch of the Nordic languages, Norwegian, Faroese and Icelandic to the western one, although it is Norwegian, through its Danish influences, which has become the best medium of interaction between all Nordic language speakers. Finnish and Samic (Lappish), both belonging to the Finnish group of Finno-Ugric languages, are unrelated to Germanic speech. Finally, West Germanic German, Low German and Frisian are spoken in the border region of Germany and Denmark, Schleswig.[2]

The Nordic minorities comprise a varied pattern in their spatial distribution and physical environmental context. The *Sami* (Lapp) territories cover a vast area stretching along the Swedish Highland ranges from 61°N, into the Swedish woodland region and the Norwegian coastal area before arching into Northeast Finland. Here, nature offers a varied, but harsh ecosystem suited only for an extensive and differentiated land use; half-nomadic reindeer breeding with fishing and agriculture being the main pursuits. Even within their own areas the Sami today, being divided into distinct geolects, constitute a minority. Of an estimated total population of 35,000, some 20,000 Sami live in Norway, 10,000 in Sweden, 2,500 in Finland and 1,500 in the USSR.[3] The autochthonous *Finns* in Sweden (30–50,000) inhabit the western bank of the fertile agricultural valley of the Torne River (Tornionjoki) and its tributaries, together with the meagre wooded areas around Gällivare (Lundén, 1966: 98–102). The *Swedish*-speaking population of *Finland* (c. 300,000) lives in three coastal stretches. The first, in the north, forms a flat, agricultural strip along the shallow Bothnian Gulf. The second extends from the fertile coastal area around Turku/Åbo[4] and its associated archipelago, toward Helsinki/ Helsingfors and eastward for a further 70 kilometres. The third area is composed of the autonomous Åland islands and the archipelago between Åland and Turku/Åbo (Klövekorn, 1950).

The Nynorsk (New Norwegian) standard written version of Norwegian is official in municipalities forming a distinct highland and fjord area in the southwestern "bulk" of Norway, exclusive of the major coastal

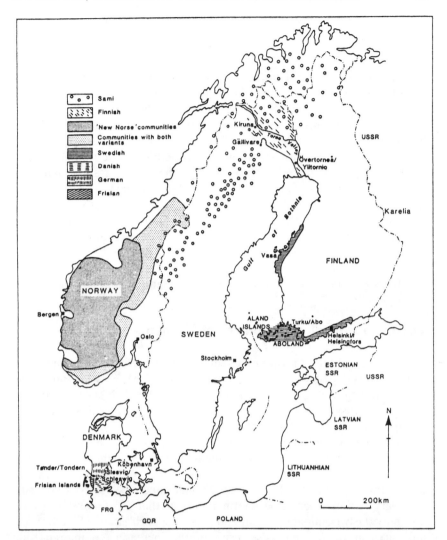

FIGURE 3.1   *The linguistic regions of Norden*

towns. As will be explained later, there is no simple relation between the two written standards and the spoken forms of Norwegian, and thus little reliable data on how many people choose Nynorsk as their written language. However, it is estimated that about half a million people currently use Nynorsk.[5]

Iceland (200,000) and the Faroes (40,000) both have homogeneous populations using the autochthonous languages, although there are still some Danish administrative personnel in the Faroes.

The Danish-German borderland is a wide isthmus with an undulating, fjord-like Baltic coastline, ideal for its main commercial ports (in contrast with the very flat North Sea coast) and a lowland with an associated chain of sandy islands. The German side of this coastal plain is the North Frisian area where, of the 40,000 Frisians, about a quarter speak North Frisian, which is in turn traditionally divided into five rather distinct dialects.[6] In the remainder of Schleswig, there is a gradual but very complex shift from different sociolects of Low German and/or German speech and German sentiment in the south toward Danish speech and association in the north, the state boundary forming a "fault line" of standard language influence. However, on both sides of the boundary are minorities of 20–40,000 people claiming affiliation with the neighbouring state's respective ethnic majorities. Even so, neither of these minority situations evinces a direct relation between ethnicity and speech.[7]

The sociopolitical development of Norden

In the middle of the nineteenth century, Norden's geopolitical situation was dependent on the nearness of the Great Powers and on the new technologies employed in nation-building. On Denmark's southern boundary, Prussia was emerging as the leader of a number of small states. Railway and canal developments served to open up the rich coal and iron areas of central Germany and had a massive impact on the northern, largely agricultural periphery, including the northern duchies of Schleswig and Holstein. These duchies, both members of the German Confederation, were formally owned by the King of Denmark and constituted a linguistic boundary region where Low German was at that time making inroads into previously dominant Danish and Frisian speech areas. High German influences grew stronger as a result of the increased commercial and transport contacts, but Denmark sought to counteract this pressure by integrating Schleswig into its kingdom and reducing its claim on the wholly Germanized Holstein. Prussian and Austrian opposition to this policy led to war which ended in 1866 with the successful incorporation of Schleswig into the expanding Prussian state. There followed a period of rapid urbanization and of closer commercial and industrial integration into the German state. This modernization process not only threatened the Danish language (which was defended by several organizations), but also eventually threatened the viability of the non-written geolects and sociolects of Low German (spoken by several million people) and of North Frisian (with some 10,000 speakers) (see Fink, 1954).

In the Danish possessions, Iceland and the Faroes, Danish was the only official language. In Iceland, the old written language, which had been rendered partially obsolete in the preceding decades, was resurrected as a literary language, whereas in the Faroes an orthography was invented in the same way as had been done in Norway. In both areas, however, these attempts were made at a time when many visitors predicted the death of these Norse languages, along the pattern established in the Shetlands and the Orkneys.[8]

Finland became a Grand Duchy under Russia in 1809 and retained the main characteristics of the former Swedish reign, including the official non-recognition of the 85% Finnish-speaking majority, clustered mainly within the lower social strata. The capital was transferred from the partly Swedified town of Turku/Åbo with its native Finnish-speaking population to its present location at Helsinki/Helsingfors within the Swedish language area (Allardt, 1977; Allardt & Miemois, 1979). The Swedish language group covered all social classes, but was particularly dominant within the upper classes. Within a small group of intellectuals there arose a demand to pursue Finnish unilingual policies, but this was suppressed by the hierarchical regime in power. However, Finland achieved a measure of regional autonomy within the more liberal political climate of the 1860s which was characterized by a period of elementary educational development and the introduction of municipal political activity. Both of these factors served to mobilize the language question as a central political issue. Clerical and agrarian leaders championed the Finnish-only movement, whilst Swedish-speaking intellectuals and liberal industrialists defended the bilingual option.

In 1886, the Russian Imperial authorities decided on a policy of official bilingualism, the majority language in each municipality becoming the local official language. High school education was to be in the dominant local language, which constituted a persistent threat to the upper-class Swedish-speaking minorities living outside the autochthonous Swedish area. Around the beginning of this century, State Agencies operating throughout the country were granted the freedom to choose their own working languages for administration. A period of Russification served to reconcile Swedish and Finnish nationalisms in order to promote the furtherance of the Finland fatherland. This was followed by a radical restructuring of the form of government from a four estate diet to a single chamber democratic parliament in 1907, where the two Swedish-dominated estates almost unanimously agreed to this reform, resulting in a reduction of the number of Swedish Members of Parliament to their proportion of the population, around 12%. This political development was preceded by economic change. Helsingfors grew into the industrial town of Helsinki, generating a massive immigration of workers comprising mainly former peasants and crofters from the Finnish-speaking areas.

In Sweden, the vast herding lands used by the Sami and gradually claimed by the Crown were being lacerated through the intrusion of Swedish and Finlandic settlers. For their part, the Sami were accepted either as herders able to exercise their traditional land use and water rights so long as they did not interfere with the spatially insignificant areas of settlement, or they were accepted as settlers (see Cramér & Prawitz, 1970; Mörner, 1979). In many instances local courts were sympathetic to Sami land claims and allowed them to maintain their existing patterns of socio-economic behaviour. However, the development of the centralized state authority resulted in a policy of more permanent settlement patterns. In 1867 a formal settlement limit was established, partially preventing further inland colonization. This limit, however, was drawn almost at the ecological limit of colonization. Some of this area had, by the end of the century, experienced limited industrial penetration. Initially the vast but slow-growing forest was parcelled out to the settlers and farmers, who in turn often resold it to the sawmill companies. Eventually, the state realized its resource value, imposing restrictions on the herding of forest Sami. Railways were constructed in the area, its water power was harnessed for the needs of industrial southern Sweden and the first sprinkling of a tourist trade occurred. Each of these centralistic and large-scale influences posed a threat to the traditional Sami culture, but they also laid the foundation of local economies.

In the Finnish-speaking northeast of Sweden the new boundary with Finland/Russia meant that new parish centres and churches had to be built on the Swedish side of the Torne river, which previously had served to unite this fertile valley. For a long time the few signs of state power, essentially ecclesiastical affairs, were conducted in Finnish. After 1870 Swedish was introduced in the schools and the churches largely "at the request of the population". This was the beginning of a rapid process of linguistic pressure. New mining and smelting techniques, together with the deeper penetration of the railway network, resulted in the exploitation of the rich ore field of Gällivare-Malmberget (a Swedish word, meaning "Ore Mountain") and of Kiirunavaara (Swedified into Kiruna). Industrial and mineral activity necessitated the introduction of a proletarian work force of navvies, miners and officials into this harsh land populated by a thinly scattered distribution of Sami and Finns.[9] In spite of a considerable number of Finnish-speaking miners, Swedish soon became the undisputed means of communication. In the Torne Valley, however, this did not happen "by itself". In the nationalistic climate at the turn of the century, the boundary situation was used by local Members of Parliament and state officials as a reason for material and cultural support in the area. The Germanization of Schleswig was used as a warning against the alleged spread of Finnish (and Russian) nationalism into Sweden and as a pretext for spreading Swedish nationalism into its Finnish-speaking population. By 1920, a complete de-Finnification of local and state administration, including all schools and libraries, had been achieved.[10]

Norway became separated from Denmark in 1814 and became united with Sweden in a double monarchy, whilst retaining a specific and very progressive form of government. The language of the upper classes and state bureaucrats was a spoken form of southeastern Norwegian very much accommodated to the Danish written language, and which became an established medium during the new regime. Despite this, a number of language reform movements were initiated. One, the Nynorsk movement, was an attempt to revive the old Norwegian language or, rather, recreate a new written standard by using the "unspoilt" dialects of south western Norway. Different ways of creating a common language were tried, all based on purist and anti-urban sentiments. As a reaction to these attempts, the defenders of the Dano-Norwegian speech undertook to revise the written language in order to make it more congruent with contemporary oral usage in Norway. From the 1870s both groups became strong enough to make language a significant political issue; but whereas there was a west–east spatial bias (the west and rural areas favouring Nynorsk, and the east and urban areas favouring a revised Dano-Norwegian, Bokmål), both forms were championed by the radical Left. In the 1880s schoolteachers were instructed to use the "local educated speech" — but this served only to accentute the problem of the language gap between spoken Norwegian and the still-official, written Dano-Norwegian. Soon, every municipality was given the right to decide on its own language preference, which in turn inaugurated a period of language conversion into Nynorsk, and incidentally sharpened language tensions. Bokmål, which was reasonably adaptive to the needs of urban and south eastern Norway, became an officially reformed language, a reflection of Norway's emergent nationalism consequent to its separation from Sweden.[11] In northern Norway, a settlement policy was adopted which favoured Norwegian-speaking inhabitants. Place names and surnames were made Norwegian, and, in the pursuit of national unification, no consideration was given to the fact that the "local educated speech" insisted upon by school laws was Sami and not Norwegian (Eidheim, 1971). This characterization can also be applied, in part, to the Swedish Sami policy of the same time, which was perhaps a little more paternalistic. As landowner, the Swedish State acted both as the protector of economic rights and as an advocate of mining and water power exploitation.

Because of its national integration policies, pastures on Finnish territory were closed, initially to Norwegian Sami and subsequently to Swedish citizens also. The traditional migration of Swedish herds into Norwegian summer pasturages also became regulated after 1905. A further interference with the traditional, delicate human and natural ecology of the reindeer nomads was the establishment of mining settlements (Svensson, 1976).

Language and nationalism in independent Norden

Changes brought about by World War I directly and indirectly altered the geopolitical situation of the Nordic linguistic groups. A national referendum was organized by the League of Nations to decide on the future of the Danish–German boundary area. As a result of a clear and predictable pattern of voting, a line was drawn north of Flensburg and the Island of Sylt, leaving the whole Frisian group and some Danes in German territory. A somewhat larger minority of about 25,000 Germans was left in the territory returned to Denmark, forming local urban minorities of craftsmen and merchants and more sizeable agrarian majorities along the border. Long-standing commercial and administrative contacts within the now-partitioned Schleswig were terminated by the new boundary (Weigand, 1966). On the German side the minorities were almost forgotten, with the Frisians' claim to a distinct ethnic identity being denied by the influential German minority organizations and by German officialdom.[12]

In Denmark the international depression, shared by the whole of Norden, was aggravated by agricultural decline and by the imposition of a new southern boundary. There occurred a progressive favouring of German nationalism which facilitated organizational work for "German" landownership in agriculture. In spite of this, Danish sentiments were so overwhelmingly dominant, even in the last democratic elections of 1939, that Nazi Germany refrained from supporting local German claims for frontier revision, preferring instead a policy of "Germanic Union of Nations" by recognizing an undiminished Danish territory (Tägil, 1970).

The end of World War II brought about another new situation. As the last territory under German rule, and being a rural area largely undisturbed by bombing and other war efforts, South Schleswig was chosen for the resettlement of thousands of refugees from what had become East Germany. This, and the radical change in both ideals and economic power, led to an enormous national political, and partly linguistic, re-orientation among the native South Schleswig population. Demands for frontier revision in favour of Danish annexation were now prominent. In the face of a negative British administration and a reluctant Danish government, the question was postponed until after the dispersal of the refugees to southern Germany and the emergence of the Bundesrepublik had reduced pro-Danish nationalism into a recognized minority's right to language and culture. The Frisians had long since been divided into a pro-Danish group, using a written standard of North Frisian, and a German group which conceived of the language merely as a "respected dialect". Facing the threat of linguistic extinction, the groups adopted a compromise solution. Compared with the rapidly vanishing Low German language, Frisian had shown a somewhat stronger resistance. This was probably due to the distinctiveness of Frisian culture and economy in contrast to the widespread and diversified dialects of Low German, which are often treated as a German "patois" (Kloss, 1978).

In Finland, Russian suppression increased during the First World War, and many Finlanders actively supported Germany. When post-revolutionary Finland became an independent state in 1917, most of the Swedish-speaking officials joined the "white" side in the subsequent civil war. After the "white" victory a liberal regime took power, establishing a package of laws relating to official bilingualism and instituting municipal bilingualism wherever the minority exceeded 10%. In the Åland islands, the new republic was not regarded as the fatherland. Old ties with nearby Stockholm were revived whilst an unofficial referendum showed an almost unanimous support for their inclusion into Sweden. After Finnish–Swedish negotiations, the matter was brought to the International Court, which favoured the more forceful demands of the young Finlandic state. The area was, however, given far-reaching autonomy, including a Swedish-only language legislation and an exemption from military service.[13]

Throughout the rest of Finland, legislation did not help to bring about peace in linguistic relations. Finnish territorial and linguistic nationalists heavily attacked remnants of Swedish over-representation in the administrative and educational institutions. This, of course, hit the position of Swedes in the capital, whose autochthonous Swedish population had been turned into a minority. They now lost even their majority occupational status amongst administrative officialdom, partly through the optional Finnification of bilingual families (Allardt, 1977). After the Second World War, linguistic tensions were eased, partly because Swedish could no longer be regarded as a real threat to Finnish culture and partly because nationalistic aspirations had been muted by Soviet annexations. In the resettlement of refugee farmers from areas annexed by the USSR, lands in Swedish-speaking areas were exempted in order not to threaten their local culture and language. The Swedish-speaking Finlander is now well protected by law in all official administrative matters.

Sweden, Denmark and Norway remained neutral in World War I. In northern Sweden, the policy of Swedification of the Finns continued, aided by reports about popular support. A few Finnish nationalists, urging the incorporation of northeastern Sweden and Soviet Karelia into a Greater Finland, stirred up a reaction of fear and hatred among the local population, eager to show their sentiments. Such claims were further exaggerated by the Swedish (partly Finnish-language) local press, almost creating a situation of mass hysteria. In the 1930s the government and some Stockholm newspapers pleaded for some recognition of the Finnish language, but this met with very heavy protests from local spokesmen, defending a "Swedish-only" policy, while keeping Finnish as a "natural" local dialect. The declining state of Finnish in northeastern Sweden was not really recognized until about 1960, when some small steps were taken towards an official recognition of Finnish at a time when the local speech was rapidly deteriorating, partly turning into a "wild dialect". Even local denunciation of official bilingualism withered (Jaakkola, 1976; Hansegård, 1968).

In the Samic areas, the exploitation of natural resources made reindeer breeding more difficult. On the Norwegian coast, industrial fishing eventually became a threat to the local mixed economy. In 1923 a Norwegian–Swedish agreement was reached which considerably curtailed the ancient rights of Swedish Sami to use Norwegian pasturages. Many families had to resettle in faraway pasturages. They were taken care of by the state, but naturally it was difficult for them to understand the geopolitical situation which caused them to leave their old lands (Svensson, 1976; Uppman, 1978).

The Norwegian "schizoglossia" developed with language reforms intended to harmonize the two linguistic standards. This did not meet with complete success as it was opposed by ardent defenders of what they saw as pure, rural Norwegian, and equally ardent defenders of traditional Danish forms or southeastern upper class speech. Politically, Nynorsk had its strongest support from amongst the religious, teetotaller farmers of Western Norway who favoured centre parties. Labour party affiliates, workers and peasants in the main, favoured a popularized standard language using elements from both norms. During and after World War II, Nynorsk was severely weakened by urbanization and by the growth of formal communication, especially the development of a popular press and mass advertising. Regional planning also became a threat as Nynorsk areas were increasingly integrated into municipalities and counties with Bokmål standards, notably in the Bergen area.[14]

Iceland, gaining functional independence in 1918, and the Faroes, practically autonomous since World War II, gradually ousted Danish as an administrative language, keeping it as their main foreign language (Jonsson & Poulsen, 1977). In both countries, especially in the Faroes, specialization and new technology implies a conscious planning of vocabulary to keep alien influences in language at a tolerable level (Carlsén, 1978).

Contemporary social and linguistic behaviour and the relations of Nordic minorities

In their daily behaviour, members of minorities react to stimuli created by the cultural and physical environment as portrayed above. Some of the Nordic groups have been well investigated, and as they represent very different cases of national and linguistic allegiance, some of these findings will be presented below.

The Germans in Denmark (like their Danish counterparts in Germany) diverge from other Nordic minorities because of the fact that their identity is defined more in terms of ethnic allegiance than in terms of linguistic behaviour. In this respect they form one extreme of an axis whose other extreme is the Finland Swedes, identifying with the country but diverging in speech.

Svalastoga & Wolf (1963) present four "musts" among the Danish majority in their behaviour in the ethnically mixed town of Tønder/ Tondern:

- Danish must be used when talking to minority members
- children must be sent to Danish schools
- there must be no relations with associations or institutions of the minority
- land, particularly agricultural land, must not be sold to minority members.

Although there is no formal shibboleth of being "German", everyone in the area knows the nationality of his neighbours. Language is more a question of deliberate choice by the parents. When speaking to their children half the German families use High German, the other half speak a local Danish dialect. German has a stronger position as a church and school language, while all official matters on municipal and state levels are carried out in Danish. Consequently, all Germans are functionally bilingual, while about one third of Tønder Danes do not feel competent in German. In fact, Germans in Denmark are far more fluent in Danish than are most members of the Danish minority south of the boundary (Høgh in Svalastoga & Wolf, 1963).

In their social position, Germans and Danes do not differ remarkably but in Tønder top rank, two thirds of the Danes have administrative jobs, whereas the same is true for only one third of the top rank Germans, dominated by large landowners. This difference in functional association with the Danish state is found in the whole territory (see Elklit, Noack & Tonsgaard, 1979). Social mobility also is different in Tønder, Danes being more upwardly mobile, while German women show a remarkable downward mobility. This may reflect the important fact that, in this case, national allegiance may also be the *result of* social mobility. Nothing is known about change of nationality, however.

As the target for mass communications, Schleswig is an interesting mixture of local and state-wide media. "Ordinary newspapers" in both states inform about the local areas on an intimate level and about the state territory on a more general level, leaving a blank area across the boundary. The existence of (a) a German language, German-minded newspapers in Denmark, (b) the Danish-Danish "Flensborg Avis" issued in Flensburg, Germany, but spread on both sides and (c) a German language, Danish-minded paper in Germany account for a rather intense coverage of news from all territorial and national sides. But these papers (with the exception of Flensburg Avis in Denmark) are clearly confined to readers belonging to the national minorities.[15] German television has a broad audience extending far up into Denmark, thanks to its many channels and expensive programmes. The effect of this is uncertain. However, the German language is no longer associated with the stereotype of a hated minority group, as once it was. The general picture of the German minority is of a group which identifies more with the local area, rather than with Germany, whereas the Danes represent all conditions from local allegiance to "general Danishness". This is reflected in migration patterns, selection of mass media, recreational patterns and in group perceptions. When asked to estimate the social distance from their own group, the most extreme "Danish sentiment" group put local Danes closest to themselves (Score 0.14), followed closely by Copenhageners (0.26), followed at a distance by local Germans (0.88) and finally, almost considered together were Bavarians (1.57) and foreign guest workers (1.79). The most extreme "German sentiment" group put local Germans (0.08) and local Danes (0.13) almost together, followed by Copenhageners (0.66) and Bavarians (0.92) with a pronounced social distance between them and foreign guest workers (2.13) (Elklit et al., 1979).

Functionally integrated into Denmark, but emotionally attached still to Germany, the German minority's homeland is Schleswig. This territorial identification, which is very difficult to measure, is an important but little known part of the European minority dilemma and deserves to be more widely studied.[16]

The autochthonous Finns in the Swedish part of the Torne Valley represent a very different group with a weak feeling of ethnicity and, by definition, a strong but complicated relationship to their native language. A typical trait in their linguistic behaviour is diglossia, a functional differentiation in the collective use of the local Finnish dialect and of "High Swedish", combined with an intermediary state of individual bilingualism in an historical transition process from Finnish to Swedish. This behaviour should be interpreted in the light of a century-old tradition of official "Swedish-only" policy. Jaakkola (1973, 1976) chose one central municipality, Övertorneå/Ylitornio, with an intermediate number of Finnish speakers (66% in 1957). Test areas in the urban centres and in the peripheral villages were selected. The number of refusals was very high compared with an identical survey in the like-named neighbouring municipality in Finland, probably reflecting the delicacy of the issues raised by the survey and by the fact that it was a Finnish sociologist studying the language complex. Even people speaking Finnish more fluently than Swedish generally chose the Swedish questionnaire to complete. In terms of language ability, there is a clear spatial — hierarchic factor with Swedish dominating the linguistic character of the urban centres. This rural–urban continuum is paralleled in such spheres as education, occupation and recreation and is much stronger than any effects of distance from the river which forms the international boundary. At the individual level, there is a scale of intimacy ranging from the mother–child relationship and religious meetings in which the use of Finnish is dominant, to an intermediate position where, for example, both languages are used in everyday social contacts, to the sphere of administrative officialdom where the use of Swedish is dominant. Even in the local social clubs and cultural associations Swedish is used habitually, except during the coffee breaks. After a long period of exclusion from use in schools and libraries, Finnish is now being introduced as an optional language. However, it is still mainly regarded as a useful foreign language of a neighbouring state.

Now these very marked situational differences in language use can be related to the structural environment. In the Swedish part of the Torne Valley, which is a depopulated area with a male surplus, marriages with Finnish women are both common and natural. This pattern of international marriage has to some extent kept the language alive.[17] In the public sphere, there has been a lack of popular interest in promoting the language, in spite of the passive support given to the minority language by the central authorities. This can be explained by the massive indoctrination of the period 1870–1920s, and by the very weak possibilities for protest at that time. In contemporary democratic Sweden, 30,000 people in the Far North constitute too small a minority to enforce their claims. The irony is that were they to do so, they would probably get much better recognition of their claims. However, so far there has been negligible local support for such claims, not even a native protest (see Lundén, 1966). Given a gloomy economic future, the Torne Valley seems to be heading for a continuation of depopulation patterns and linguistic assimilation in the 1980s.

The Finland Swedes form another variant of linguistic and national allegiance. Under Swedish and Russian rule, Swedish was the language of the upper classes, irespective of their origin or location within Finland. In addition there were also "Swedish" territorial enclaves which covered the whole spectrum of social strata. Those two different Swedish-speaking groups had little in common. Growing democracy and the simultaneous redistribution of population and occupations as a result of industrialization made non-territorially concentrated Swedish-speaking groups disappear. Today the Swedish speakers do not differ markedly from Finns in terms of their occupational distribution patterns. As with all other declining minority groups their age structure is biased in favour of the elderly. In the light of this, the somewhat higher percentage of Swedes with a university education is more remarkable. Because of the language legislation, Swedes in the administration generally have to have a superior educational background, as almost all administrative areas are bilingual or monolingual Finnish (Miemois, 1978a).

The former preponderance of Swedes in urban areas has now been reversed, mainly because of the growth of Helsinki and its related suburbs (Miemois, 1978b). Urban Swedes are in constant daily contact with Finnish speech and its associated cultural symbols. The number of mixed-language marriages is now very high, around 45% of all urban Swedes marrying Finnish women (in rural areas this figure declines to around 15 to 20%) (de Vries in Allardt, 1977). Although Swedish has more status than its numerical strength would suggest, Finnish is chosen as a common medium in those sociocultural environments where it is the local majority language. Among bilingual Swedes, Swedish or Finnish is used according to the demands of the speech situation, ranging from the home or school milieu, where Swedish is predominant (with Finnish as an important subject). In "high" culture, Swedish is also important but so is Finnish, and the individual is likely to choose to watch a play or opera in either language. Popular culture is bilingual, with Finnish dominating television and sports coverage. At the workplace, Finnish is the main language, except for those occupations, such as agriculture, fishing and forestry, which are territorially concentrated in the smaller Swedish communities. However, irrespective of their right to use Swedish, and of the right to be served in the native language, many Swedes use Finnish in their contacts with official agencies, mainly as a result of the ease and convenience of such language shifting to achieve a satisfactory answer.

In the daily life of Helsinki's Swedes, many of the language situations are readily predictable. For example, the percentage of Swedes who start a formal communication in Swedish ranges from an estimated 53% in banks, 36% in government offices, 23% in shops and 16% in taxis and buses. In most cases, a member of the minority knows from past experience which language to anticipate using. In other words, he has a linguistic mental map of the city. People also regard services in the native language as more or less important depending on their character; thus service in Swedish at hospitals is considered more important than a similar service in post offices and libraries. In everyday life convenience is the factor which most determines which language will be used, irrespective of the very strong legal provisions which stipulate under which conditions use of the minority tongue will be obligatory.

Helsinki Swedes do not form a readily identifiable group, either in terms of their settlement pattern or in their networks of social relationships. When asked about their opinion on which type of grouping characteristic they find most important, common language and common region came out fairly equal in their appraisal. Young people stress language more than middle-aged people do, and whilst this may in part reflect the Swedish school environment before the Finnification process of the labour market, it may also reflect the growing feeling of affiliation with other Swedish groups in Finland where the fragmentation of an homogeneous Swedish culture has not gone so far as it has in the capital (Allardt,

1973: 129–37; 1977). In the northern area of Österbotten, there is even a certain "local Swedish nationalism", in spite of, or in fact because of, the rapid advances of Finnification in industry and administration, and of emigration to Sweden. Here, as in the Åland islands, the influence of television and radio emanating from Sweden is an important factor (Berg, 1968). In general, Swedes in Finland do not form an irredentist minority anxious to be incorporated into Sweden. With the partial exception of the Ålanders, Finland Swedes are a specific group of Finlanders serving as a cultural bridge between Finland and Sweden. Seen in a long perspective, however, this may be a step between former dominance and future "disappearance or fight".

Amongst the Swedish Sami population there is an important dividing line between reindeer-breeding families and other Sami. Reindeer breeding is in fact the only official recognition of the Sami's separate ethnicity, being the foundation of important and exclusive Sami rights. Relative to the ecological base and the number of reindeer per family, from an economic optimizing viewpoint the number of herding families is far too high. This is especially true of the North, where economic, social and linguistic traditions have survived far longer than in the South. Recently the introduction of technical equipment such as snow-scooters and two-way radios has three clear implications for their group organization, namely:

(a) an increased efficiency of the herding operation,
(b) a reduction in the number of people required for such operations;
(c) a new dependency on the non-Samic, outside world.

In their attitude toward their situation, the reindeer breeders show a faith in co-existence with the Swedish majority, but a resentment towards the patriarchic state policies. In relation to education and modernization, they are willing to enter modern society, whilst at the same time maintaining their Sami culture. This is not to say that they do not recognize the inherent conflict between these two desires. With a diminishing number of reindeer breeders, Swedish Sami are rapidly losing their cultural and linguistic base. Equal rights to education involve a preparation for life outside Sami Ätnam, their native territory. Today, Stockholm has a larger number of Sami inhabitants than any other town. The same situation prevails amongst the Sami in Norway and Finland, although the Norwegian Sami have a wider occupational basis (in fishing and agriculture) which has led to a certain split in their ethnic-political cohesion. In the last few years, however, co-operation between the three Sami groups has proved rather successful with the estabishment of a Nordic Sami Institute in Kautokeino, Norway, within the Samic core area. Samic claims have become more ardent, especially concerning the Crown Lands question, where the Swedish Sami are claiming their traditional supremacy over their territories which were gradually expropriated by the state. Even if their case should ultimately fail, the old semi-colonial situation in the north of Norden is certainly on the wane. It is doubtful, though, whether this will help safeguard the Sami from total assimilation into their respective state systems.

Language and societal development

The history of languages in Norden may at first glance seem bewildering. Some small tongues like Faroese and Icelandic have developed into official languages, others, such as Low German and Samic, have been severely eroded by modernization, whilst the relationship between socially prestigious languages and common vernaculars has almost been reversed, as in Schleswig or in Finland. In order to fully comprehend these developments it is essential that the "natural" living conditions of the language groups be related to the sociopolitical geography of the area which they inhabit.

In common with all other areas of the world, Norden has experienced a process of specialization. Development must be seen in a literal sense: new, precisely delimited occupations have been unfolded upon society, which as a corollary has become more dependent upon communication between specialists. From the initial stages of food collection as hunters and gatherers, men have developed their spheres of specialization such that we have specialists in livestock management, in plant growth, producers of manufactured goods (industry), exchangers of goods and materials (commerce and transport), creators and directors (administration, education, art and communication). This development takes place in society and space. Areas and groups at different levels of development encroach one upon the other. Social groups become inter-related in new and diverse ways, involving among other things linguistic and nationalistic rearrangements; *linguistic*, in the sense that languages are differentially prepared for development, partly in their vocabulary and grammar, but mainly in their vernacular equipment (e.g. the immediate possibility of using technical devices for communicating in the language — and this with profit) (see Dahlström, 1973; Pelto, 1973; Lundén, 1979); *nationalistic*, in the sense that territories and groups have different possibilities of forming nation states, i.e. states comprising a people identifying itself with an area. In this respect the island territories of Norden have an advantage over other territorial groups such as the Sami.

A typical confrontation of different development occurred between the colonists and the Sami. Because of different kinds of land use, colonists could invade the pasturage areas without any immediate dangerous repercussions on Sami life. As the economy developed, the Sami were gradually marginalized. This refers also to their language, which is very well suited to the local ecology, but like all other languages, not directly applicable for use in the new technical life. In fact, the total number of Sami is insufficient to necessitate a technical vocabulary in Sami speech, let alone the problem of the low intelligibility between the various Sami dialects (or geolects).

In the seventeenth and eighteenth centuries, the language of administration and the language of the people could exist in parallel because of the small amount of interchange between them. Sweden rapidly changed the official language of former Danish–Norwegian areas annexed in 1658, and Russia persisted in using Swedish in Finland even in areas where the peasantry could not understand it (see Jaakkola, 1973; Ohlsson, 1978). With the transformation of the agricultural sector (now run according to the principles of capitalism) and with industrialization, both education and communication became increasingly necessary. The development of a rail and telegraph network made nation-building a planning goal (Deutsch, 1953). All over Norden, the question of language was raised – not by the people but by the intelligentsia, often speaking the old official language better than their conservative opponents. Danish eventually lost its formal status in three territories, Swedish in one territory. At the same time, a change took place from a fairly homogeneous settlement and linkage pattern of self-sufficient agriculture into patterns of rural–urban interdependence. This greatly influenced the language boundaries. Commercial contacts were now formalized, exclusively in the language of the town. Consequently even rural schools and municipalities had to accommodate. With the presence of an active official interest, the situation became even more acute, as in northern Sweden and Prussian Schleswig, where the urban areas acted as the spearheads of official language penetration into the surrounding rural areas. Extra stress in this new pattern of linguistic contact was occasioned by the differences in the ecological bases for development. Some of the minority language areas were suited to the demands of new technology, others were not. In Finland, for example, the southern mainland area was an ideal landscape for the development of railways, ports and water-powered industry, whereas the adjoining archipelago was unsuited both for this and for other new, specialized occupations demanded by a technological society.[18] For the Swedish Finlanders, this meant that part of their territory developed faster than they could manage to control because they were such a small group, whilst in the archipelago the Swedish culture and language survived until the last inhabitant left.

The contemporary situation

Modern society depends on world-wide relations and communications. Despite this, most people identify more with their national society, i.e. they are more influenced by intra-state information than ever before.[19] The local and regional levels have declined in importance, so that most intra-state communication normally reaches the citizen through mediation in his capital city. There is a spatial pattern partly resembling the hierarchy of central-place theory.[20] Finnish-speaking villages in the Swedish Torne Valley are related to bilingual local towns, which in turn form the link to the outside world. Urban areas thus tend to form the "holes in the Swiss cheese" of minority speech. At each step in the hierarchy there is a set of technical devices at an economical population range. Television and broadcasting stations, dailies, weeklies, libraries, books and opera houses have typical threshold levels, working in favour of large, and spatially concentrated, consumer groups.

The principle of a central place hierarchic pattern is paralleled at the occupational level also, reflecting further development in specialization in large cities. In order to survive as a territorial entity, minorities must fulfil the occupational requirements of the area. This implies a very delicate balance between the supply of occupational skills and the demand from the people. Applicants must be occupationally appropriate as well as ethnically acceptable. In most modern, democratic Western-type states, this form of occupational and territorial planning does not seem feasible. Large industrial concerns, when located within minority areas, necessitate an influx of alien personnel. This has happened in the past in the Swedish iron ore and water-power producing districts. Today in Finland, pulp mill and nuclear power stations are being located in the Swedish language coastal area, with the immediate consequence of substantial alien immigration. Similarly Norway's high technology aluminium plants are situated in the traditional West Norwegian dialect areas. In the Frisian and Danish areas of Germany, tourism has developed substantially and with its seasonal labour demand most of the personnel have to be imported from distant regions. Another example could be given at the community level. Consider the needs of the Faroesian population for eye care: with a threshold level equalling the actual number of inhabitants, the only ophthalmologist capable of being sustained on the Faroes represents a small scale example of the individual occupation-language matching process. Will it be possible to foresee the future need for his successor in order to prepare for the medical education of a Faroese student? (communication from Jóhan Hendrik W. Poulsen).

The Åland islands offer a good example of the beginning of an "alienation" process which is occurring at both the upper and lower levels of the occupational strata. As a result of the flourishing shipping and tourist industries, owned and managed by local concerns, well-paid jobs are available to Ålanders with little formal education, who can now afford to refuse the low-paid seasonal jobs in tourism. The vacancies are filled by unilingual Finns from the mainland. Key administrative positions for which knowledge of Finnish is expected, although not necessary, are often taken up by mainland Swedish Finlanders. To the linguistically-sensitive Ålanders this combination suggests a future similar to that of the rest of Swedish Finland, that is, a gradual accommodation in which Swedish is officially recognized, but where all economic and social contacts work in favour of the majority language of the state.[21]

Concluding observations

The total social situation of Nordic minorities can be portrayed from a number of different viewpoints:

History

Conceived as transmitting previous occurrences, it is only of importance insofar as it is used as a basis for present thoughts and actions. Present-day attitudes of Finns and Swedes in both countries towards Finnish Swedes and Swedish Finns often reflect the minorities' *former* social position, much to the detriment of the minorities. This difference between actual circumstances and "lessons from History" is still more conspicuous in Schleswig.

Geography

The actual location of minority groups is of interest only if related to other spatial distributions. The attractiveness of the Frisian sandy islands can only be understood against the background of Germany's massive population and limited coastal area. The Sami problem is partly a geopolitical one of a territorial partition between all four big powers in the region, each with a very distant core region and capital which directs and steers events in the Sami periphery of the country.

Economy

The local base for economic development is one of the main determinants of the social position of minority peoples. A strong economic base is not necessarily the best guarantee for protection, however, as it may lead to an influx of socially or economically stronger population groups.

Politics and Law

"Law" is more a confirmation of social norms than a prescription for behaviour. Similarly, the territorial and hierarchical divisions of politics are more a reflection of situations that have occurred than of democratic decisions. The Swedes in Finland are well protected by law, but should Helsinki's Swedes insist on the full implementation of what the law prescribes, then surely the laws would be revised and their rights restricted. Likewise, the implementation of official language rights by the Swedish Finns would in all probability not be fully realized by that group, given their current sociobehavioural circumstances. Laws and state territories do, however, have important effects upon minorities, even if their role has been exaggerated when compared with other factors, such as economic and technological considerations.

Technology

New technology is often the precursor of social change. Almost every innovation has changed the relationships between ethnic and linguistic groups. The intricate balance between ecology and communal economy in pre-industrial times was gradually disturbed by the introduction of new methods involving the expansion of communication networks within which nearly everybody was forced to participate.

Sociology

The total outcome of group relations is thus determined by a host of factors. Without being too deterministic, it must be said that the spatial economy of minority group areas has been overlooked as an explanatory factor. Minorities are not protected by good laws, but through a conscious process of planning for jobs, infrastructure, land use and education, carried out by the minority group itself, in order to preserve its territory and language. This is certainly not an easy task. There is, in fact, an inherent conflict between the concept of an ethnic group with strong inter-relationships and the concept of parliamentary democracy, based upon the will of the political majorities within delimited territories. Without denying the overwhelmingly positive effects of democracy in Norden, it must be said that minorities are now in a less favourable situation — as minorities — than they were before the Industrial Revolution.

Acknowledgements

This paper is mainly based upon works of Nordic Social Scientists, Geographers and Linguists. Where possible, reference has been made to English or German language works which provide reference to original works in the Nordic languages. I am very grateful for the generous advice and assistance given by Dr Colin H. Williams, North Staffordshire Polytechnic and by Fil. Kand. Eric Clark of the Department of Human Geography, The University of Stockholm.

Notes to Chapter 3

1. For a general description see Sømme (1960). Greenland, being part of North America, has not been included in this article.
2. This concept has been discussed by Lindgren (1959).
3. For a linguistic survey of the development of the languages in Norden see Haugen (1976).
4. In this chapter, Finlandic place names are written in their Finnish/Swedish forms. Åland is monolingually Swedish, å being pronounced like au in Austin.
5. Nynorsk and Bokmål are the official names of the two written standards of Norwegian. See Haugen (1966).
6. See Århammar (1975: 129–45), and for North Frisian Language planning and politics in Nordfriesland, No 28 (1973) and 30 (1974).
7. There is a vast literature on the Schleswig question, mainly in Danish and German. A summary of the social history of the region is provided in Svalastoga & Wold (1969).
8. For a general description of linguistic development in Iceland and the Faroes, see Jonsson (1977). See also West (1972).
9. Citation refers to the impression mediated by the official report, Betänkande och förslag rörande folkskoleväsendet i de finsktalande delarna av Norrbottens län, (Stockholm, 1921). The mining colonization is described in Forsström (1975). See also Jaakkola (1976).
10. The state policy and parliamentary debate on the Finnish population in the Torne Valley is described in Slunga (1965).
11. Haugen (1966). For a radical, pro-Nynorsk view, see Vikør (1975).
12. For the German opinion on the question of Frisian nationality, see e.g. Ethnopolitischer Almanach 1930–32 (Wien, Braumüller).
13. Barros (1975). For a general treatment from the standpoint of International Law, see Modéen (1965).
14. See Kristiansen (1977: 41–57). The threat of regional integration is discussed in Nysaether (1971).

15. For a comparison of the spatial coverage of items in boundary newspapers see Ax *et al.* (1972).
16. This problem is further elaborated in Gubert (1976) and in Lundén (1978). See also Allardt (1979).
17. A general sociological survey of the Torne Valley is to be found in Haavio-Mannila & Suolahti (1979: 11–22).
18. The detrimental effects on the Åland-Åboland archipelago economy of a gradual turn-over from vertical to horizontal linkage is discussed in Jaatinen (1978: 83–100). A more general background is given in Mead & Jaatinen (1975).
19. For a Nordic perspective on this see Lundén (1973: 147–61) and remarks by Bruce Russett in Strassoldo (1973).
20. In Christaller's classic formulation the theory and analysis is clearly more important than the geometrical model. Christaller (1967).
21. Communication from Bjarne Lindström, Dept of Human Geography, University of Stockholm.

References

ALLARDT, ERIK, 1973, Samhörighet och tvåspråkighet bland Finlands-svenskarna, *Nordisk tidskrift*, nr. 54.
—— 1977, Finland's Swedish-speaking minority. No. 17, *Research Group for Comparative Sociology.* Helsinki: University of Helsinki.
—— 1979, *Implications of the Ethnic Revival in Modern Industrialized Society.* Commentationes Scientiarum Socialum 12. Helsinki-Helsingfors, Societas Scientiarum Fennica.
ALLARDT, ERIK & MIEMOIS, KARL-JOHAN, 1979, Roots both in the centre and in the periphery: The Swedish-speaking population in Finland, No. 24, *Research Group for Comparative Sociology.* Helsinki: University of Helsinki.
ÅRHAMMAR, NILS, 1975, Historisch-Soziolinguistische Aspekte der Nordfriesischen Mehrsprachigkeit, *Zeitschrift für Dialektologie und Linguistik* No. 42.
AX, TORBJÖRN *et al.* 1972, *Tre gränstidningars täckning av nyheter.* Kulturgeografiska inst, Stockholms Universitet. Mimeo.
BARROS, JAMES, 1975, *The Åland Islands Question: Its Settlement by the League of Nations.* Newton Abbot: David & Charles.
BERG, ULF, 1968, *Radiolyssnande och tv-tittande i svenska Finland.* Exponeringens omfattning och genomsnittliga längd. Oy Yleis-radio Ab, LSP-Unders. 1/68. Helsinki.
CARLSÉN, ULLA, 1978, *Nyord i färöiskan, Ett bidrag till belysningen av språksituationen på Färöarna.* Stockholm.
CHRISTALLER, WALTER, 1967 (1933), *Central Places in Southern Germany.*

70   LANGUAGE IN GEOGRAPHIC CONTEXT

Englewood Cliffs, N.J.: McGraw-Hill.

CRAMÉR, TOMAS & PRAWITZ, GUNNAR 1970, *Studier i renbeteslagstiftning.* Stockholm: Norstedts.

DAHLSTRÖM, EDMUND, 1973, A Lappish minority in Sweden: A macrosociological study, *International Journal of Sociology.* Vol. 111, No. 3–4.

DEUTSCH, KARL W. 1953, *Nationalism and Social Communication.* Cambridge, Mass.: MIT Press.

DE VRIES, JOHN, 1973, *Local Homogamy and Linguistic Endogamy in Finland 1951–1967.* mimeo.

EIDHEIM, HARALD, 1971, Assimilation, ethnic incorporation and the Problem of identity management. In H. EIDHEIM (ed.), *Aspects of the Lappish Minority Situation.* Oslo: Universitetsforlaget.

ELKLIT, JØRGEN, NOACK, J.P. & TONSGAARD, O., 1979, *Nationalt tillhørsforhold i Nord-Slesvig.* Århus, Acta Jutlandica XLIX Samfundvidenskabelig Serie 14.

FINK, TROELS, 1954, *Rids av Sønderjyllands Historie.* København.

FORSSTRÖM, GÖSTA, 1975, *Malmberget.* Luleå: Norrbottens Museum.

GUBERT, RENZO, 1976, *L'identificazione ethnica.* Udine: Del Bianco.

HAAVIO-MANNILA, ELINA & SUOLAHTI, KIRSTI, 1971, *Studier kring gränsen i Tornedalen.* Nordisk utredningsserie 7. Stockholm: Nordic Council.

—— 1974, Adjustment problems and willingness to migrate of the farm population in the Tornio Valley. In ERIK BYLUND (ed.), *Ecological Problems of the Circumpolar Area.* Luleå: Norrbottens Museum. 277–96.

HANSEGÅRD, NILS, 1968, *Tvåspråkighet och halvspråkighet.* Stockholm: Aldus.

HAUGEN, EINAR, 1966, *Language Conflict and Language Planning: The Case of Modern Norwegian.* Cambridge, Mass.: Harvard University Press.

—— 1976, *The Scandinavian Languages: An Introduction to their History.* London: Faber & Faber.

JAAKKOLA, MAGDALENA, 1976, Diglossia and Bilingualism among two minorities in Sweden, *The International Journal of Sociology of Language*, No. 10. 67–84.

—— 1973, *Språkgränsen: En studie i tvåspråkighetens sociologi.* Stockholm: Aldus/Bonniers.

JAATINEN, STIG, 1978, Identitet och överlevande i en insulär miljö – ett exempel från en Nordåländsk utskärgård, *Regional Identitet.*

JONSSON, BALDUR, 1977, Isländskans situation. In BENGT SIGURD (ed.), *De nordiska språkens framtid.* Stockholm: Esselte.

KLOSS, HEINZ, 1978 (1952), *Die Entwicklung neuer Germanischer Kultursprachen.* München: Pohl.

KLÖVEKORN, MARTIN, 1950, *Die sprachliche Struktur Finnlands 1880–1950*. Helsinki/Helsingfors: Finska Vetenskaps-Societeten.

KRISTIANSEN, BJARNE, 1977, Språkstrid og politikk. In BENGT SIGURD (ed.), *De nordiska språkens framtid*. Stockholm: Esselte.

LINDGREN, RAYMOND, 1959, *Norway – Sweden: Union, Disunion and Scandinavian Integration*. Princeton: Princeton University Press.

LUNDÉN, THOMAS, 1966, The Finnish-speaking population of Norrbotten, *Europa Ethnica*, Vol. 3. Vienna.

—— 1973, Interaction across an International Boundary. In R. STRASSOLDO (ed.), *Regions and Boundaries*. Trieste: Lint.

—— 1978, Regionen inklämd mellan nation och hembygd, *Regional identitet och förändring i den regionala samverkans samhalle*. Acta Universitatis Upsaliensis, Symp. Univ. Upd. Annum Quingentis Celebr. 11. Uppsala: Almqvist & Wiksell.

—— 1979, Language Minorities in a World of Communications. In WILLIAM F. MACKEY & JACOB ORNSTEIN (eds), *Sociolinguistic Studies in Language Contacts*. The Hague: Mouton.

MEAD, WILLIAM R. & JAATINEN, STIG H., 1975, *The Åland Islands*. Newton Abbot: David & Charles.

MIEMOIS, KARL JOHAN, 1978a, Changes in the social structure of the Swedish-speaking population in Finland, 1950–1970, No.19, *Research Group for Comparative Sociology*. University of Helsinki.

—— 1978b, *Language Use in the Finnish Administration: The View of the Minority Client*. Paper presented at the IX World Congress of Sociology, Uppsala.

MODÉEN, TORE, 1965, *Om de folkrättsliga garantierna för bevarandet av Ålandsöarnas nationella karaktär*. Ekenäs.

MÖRNER, MAGNUS, 1979, Native land rights: A comparative historical study of Swedish Sami and Spanish American Indians, *Samerna och Omvärlden, Samernas Vita Bok V:1*. Stockholm: SSR.

NYSAETHER, EGIL, 1971, Målsaka og Vestlandsplanen. In JAN ASKELUND (ed.), *Mål og Makt*, Oslo: Orion.

OHLSSON, STIG ÖRJAN, 1978, *Skånes språkliga försvenskning*. Lund: Ekstrand.

PELTO, PERTTI, 1973, *The Snow Mobile Revolution: Technological and Social Change in the Arctic*. Menlo Park, California.

POULSEN, JOHAN HENDRIK W., 1977, Det Faerøiske sprogs situation. In BENGT SIGURD (ed.), *De nordiska språkens framtid*. Stockholm: Esselte.

RUONG, ISRAEL, 1967, *The Lapps in Sweden*. Stockholm: The Swedish Institute.

SLUNGA, NILS, 1965, *Staten och den finskspråkiga befolkningen i*

Norrbotten. Tornedalica. Luleå.

SØMME, A. (ed.) 1960, *A Geography of Norden.* Oslo: Scandinavian University Books.

SVALASTOGA, KAARE & WOLF, PREBEN, 1963, *En by ved graensen.* København: Gyldendals Uglebøger.

SVALASTOGA, KAARE & WOLF, PREBEN, 1969, A town in Danish Borderland. In NELS R. ANDERSON (ed.), *Studies in Multilingualism.* Leiden: Brill.

SVENSSON, TOM G., 1976, *Ethnicity and Mobilization in Sami Politics.* Stockholm: Liber.

TÄGIL, SVEN, 1970, *Deutschland und die Deutsche Minderheit in Nordschleswig.* Stockholm: Scandinavian University Books.

UPPMAN, BRITT, 1978, *Samhället och samerna.* Umeå.

VIKØR, LARS S., 1975, *The New Norse Language Movement.* Oslo.

WEIGAND, KARL, 1966, *Stadt-Umlandverflechtungen und Einzugsbereiche der Grenzstadt Flensburg und anderer zentraler Orte. Schr. des Geogr. Inst. der Univ. Kiel*, Vol xxv, Kiel.

WEST, JOHN F., 1972, *Faroe, the Emergence of a Nation.* London: Hurst.

4 Assessing the Authenticity of a Supra-National Language-Based Movement: La Francophonie[1]

WILLIAM WALTER BOSTOCK
Department of Political Science,
The University of Tasmania, Australia

One of the great problems of politics is to assess the authenticity or genuineness, validity and entitlement to acceptance of the various movements, groups, organizations and even nations which make claims on behalf of themselves and their adherents. Many long and most tragic of wars have been fought on the basis of incorrect evaluations of authenticity.

It is thus a legitimate concern of political scientists and practitioners of related disciplines to attempt to assess the authenticity of movements claiming to represent millions of adherents across many national boundaries on grounds of common language-use, and regardless of race, ethnicity, religion and ideology, i.e. the supra-national language-based movement.

Although there are a number of such movements in existence today, working through such languages as Spanish, Portuguese, Dutch and Bahasa-Malaysia-Indonesia, the furthest developed is francophonie,* the movement which claims to represent all of the populations of the world which speak French. The term 'francophonie' is believed to have been coined by a French geographer, Onésime Réclus, in the late nineteenth century (Deniau, 1983: 7).

73

At a time when world maps were divided into units of nation, colony and race, Réclus wanted a new term that would describe populations that spoke French, and thus introduced *francophonie* from the Latin *Francus* (French) and the Greek *phone* (sound). Thus his definition linked people by language rather than state, nation, race or ethnicity. However, the term fell into disuse until it was revived in the 1960s, specifically with the publication of a special edition of the intellectual revue *Esprit* on the subject of French in various parts of the world as discussed by a select group of prestigious writers. About the same time, a number of important political leaders, notably President Leopold Sedar Senghor of Senegal, began agitating for the formation of an international movement of francophone peoples.

Dictionaries and encyclopaediae began soon afterwards including the term *francophonie*, the first being *Quid* in its 1968 edition, and today the term has official recognition in that it is used by governments such as those of France, Canada and Belgium. It is also becoming recognized and used in the English-speaking world and could be defined as follows:

> *francophone* (adjective) French-speaking
> *francophonie* (noun) the conglomeration of those parts of the world
>   where French is spoken

To denote the organization of those nations, provinces, regions and communities where French is spoken, the term *la Francophonie* (with a definite article and capitalization) may be used. Although it is today a clearly recognizable movement, it is one with a number of constituent organizations, whose adherents are variable in the degree of their adhesion (which is one of the grounds on which doubts as to authenticity have been expressed). Another factor to note is that the type of French spoken in the various regions is variable, though less so than with nearly all other languages. Standard French has some degree of universality among francophones, unlike for example English, Spanish or German (Clyne, 1984). Standard French remains the prestige form, even where considerable variations exist (Bourhis, 1982).

The distribution of French

As is clear from the map, French has a truly global spread, but it is impossible to state with any certainty the total number of francophones, and in any case, as an exercise in linguistic demography, it is beyond the scope of this monograph. As a working figure, most estimates of the total number of francophones world wide are around 90 million (le Gentil, 1978: 8–13), although the number may be slightly less.

> "... the real number of francophones, those from France included, probably does not reach 90 million people, which is little in comparison to the 350 million anglophones, 200 million hispanophones, 120 million arabophones and 116 million lusophones." (Roger Cans, *Le Devoir*, December 10 1979, quoted by Old, 1984: 12–13).

Another estimate is that of Salon (1983: 72) who distinguishes francophones by mother-tongue (69,520,000) and by education (15,920,000), giving a global total of 85,440,000 persons, somewhat lower than the figure of Deniau of "about 100 million" (1983: 45). Another writer, Malka (1980) suggests that the number of persons to whom French is a second language could be considerably higher, taking the total to around 180 million, but on this criterion Deniau suggests a figure of 264 million or 6.5% of the world's population (1983: 45), while another estimate by Turcotte (personal communication, 1984) is 100 million for all categories, that is, mother-tongue, second language, or French as a foreign language. For Europe and North America, accurate survey information is not available, and for developing nations personal estimates are all that exist in relation to many countries and regions, although work is currently being carried out by researchers from Laval University.

In reality, actual numbers will never be known, but 90 million seems a suitable working number, revealing francophonie as a substantial worldwide language-based movement.

The raison d'être of francophonie

In the eighteenth and nineteenth centuries French was the sole language of international diplomacy, but lost its position to English in a process which reached its climax just after World War I. In 1919, on the insistence of President Wilson of the USA and Lloyd George, the Prime Minister of Great Britain, the Treaty of Versailles was drawn up in English *as well as* French, thus representing a departure from the previous exclusivity of French (Rickard, 1974).

At the end of World War II, when the foundation of the United Nations Organisation was being undertaken in San Francisco (April–June 1945) only English, Spanish and Russian were proposed as working languages and French was admitted only after energetic protests and with

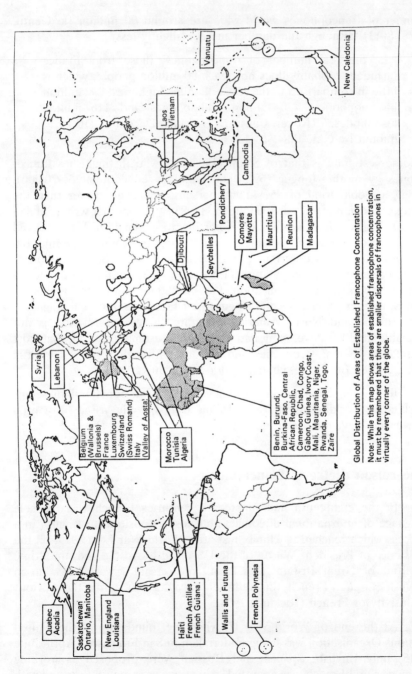

FIGURE 4.1 *Global distribution of areas of established francophone concentration*

a majority of only one. Then in December 1967 a special debate was needed before *equal* publication of communications in French and English was secured (Rickard, 1974: 150–151).

Since those times, and as a result of carefully planned, systematic and sustained efforts, French has made a dramatic comeback, such that today it is not only an official language of the UN, but also its subsidiary agencies of the United Nations Education, Scientific and Cultural Organisation, and the World Health Organisation. It is also a working language in the International Labor Organisation, the Organisation of Economic and Cultural Development, and even the North Atlantic Treaty Organisation (of which France is not a member). French is the most commonly used language of the European Economic Community and French shares equally with English the same position in the Council of Europe in Strasbourg.

French is also a leading language in the Red Cross, the International Court of Justice, and the International Standards Organisation. It is the only official language of the Universal Postal Union, such that in all member states, all documents concerning international postage are written in French as well as English or another language.

The Vatican has chosen French among other languages as a language of its diplomacy, and it uses French in its training courses for missionaries. The Universal Jewish Alliance uses French in its schools alongside Hebrew. However, this organization, which is of nineteenth century French Jewish origins, appears to be in decline. Its purpose was to spread French language and culture among Sephardic Jews of the former Ottoman Empire and other non-Ashkenazic areas. (Anonymous reader, 1985). French shares with Arabic the position of an official language of the Islamic Conference and the Arab League (Salon, 1976: 301–302).

Although French is now second to English as an international language, its position as an international language retains considerable power.

The major organizational forms of la francophonie

As early as the nineteenth century some people saw a need to organize a world-wide movement based on the French language. The Alliance Française, an organization dedicated to the promotion of French language and culture but without reference to ideology, race or religion, was founded in 1883, and included in its initiating committee such figures as de Lesseps and Pasteur (Bruezière, 1983). So far-reaching and enduring were its efforts that the Alliance Française could be described as the forerunner of La Francophonie, which as a movement gained an organizational form only after World War II.

The organization of francophonie at supranational level was not the result of a single initiative; rather, it was a continuing process which is still evolving today. This process is one of re-evaluating existing roles and creating new ones by various participants. When France fell in 1940, France and its language underwent a catastrophic decline in prestige. A small aspect of this with considerable implication for francophonie was that the centre of French language publishing had to be shifted to Canada (Deniau, 1983: 49). After World War II, France was keen to re-establish its colonial empire and recover its prestige, only to suffer a humiliating military defeat in Indo-China in 1954, and was forced to wind-up most of its empire elsewhere and today there is strife in Mayotte, New Caledonia, and some of the Overseas Departments. Some notable French statesmen realized that the future lay in a voluntary organization based on co-operation. Though fully aware of this need, and having facilitated the independence of Algeria, President de Gaulle preferred to let the concept of francophonie develop of its own accord, probably through fear of stamping it with the mark of neo-colonialism, an accusation which is still being frequently made. Deniau reports that de Gaulle only used the term once, and that was in 1968 when hearing of the death of his friend, the Quebec Prime Minister Daniel Johnson,

"Thus a great loss for francophonie"* (Deniau, 1983: 54)

The nature of this low key and unobtrusive role by France has been continued today, although President Mitterand has declared himself as "passionately in favour of francophonie"* (Deniau, 1983: 56).

Though for the greater part of its history neglected by France, the province of Quebec, Canada's only province with a francophone majority, has also re-evaluated its role. Traditionally Quebec has distanced itself from France. In two World Wars there was significant opposition in Quebec to Canadian participation, not only through anti-British feeling but also through lack of identity with France but through some support for Mussolini's concept of a "corporate state" linking Church and State. Even in the post-1945 period, Quebec has shown ambiguity in its view of and support for France.

From the French side, recognition of and sympathy for the cause of Quebec was dramatically stated by the French President General de Gaulle when he gave voice to the slogan of the Quebec separatists in

1967, thus marking a turning point in the evolution of franco-Quebec relations, which are subtle, complex and far from straightforward even today, and are the product of affection, pride and jealousy from both sides. The two largest cities of these two concentrations of francophonie, Paris and Montreal, are foci of cultural and linguistic generating activity but by no means to the exclusion of other centres.

At the organizational level, some of the first steps were the Association of French Language Journalists (A.I.J.L.F.) and in 1954 of the French Cultural Union, in 1958 the International Association of French-language Sociologists, and in 1970 the Association of Partially or Wholly French-language Universities (A.U.P.E.L.F.). In the founding of these organizations most of the initiative was taken by Quebecers. In the field of broadcasting, co-productions became a common line of development for finance, production and distribution, and while Canada at first found reluctance on the part of the French authorities, willing partners were found in Belgium and Switzerland, and with the spectacular success of several ventures the French authorities re-evaluated their position and successfully joined (Personal Communication with a senior Canadian Broadcasting Corporation officer). In 1984 TW5 Francophone Television commenced broadcasting through the ECS R Satellite, thus providing another cultural outlet for francophonie.

At official level, the first francophone contact was in 1960; when a conference of Ministers of Education from France and Africa and Malagasy states was convened, followed soon afterwards by a similar conference of Ministers of Youth and Sports. Within France, a High Committee for the Defense and Expansion of the French Language was created on December 1, 1965, while in 1967 the first Biennale to discuss francophonie took place at Namur, Belgium, under the chairmanship of Professor Guillermou (Deniau, 1983: 52).

Developments were not confined to the European and North American region, however. In 1965 a number of African nations joined to form the Organization of the African and Malagasy Community (O.C.A.M.), following the inspiration of three francophone African leaders, Léopold Sédar Senghor of Sénégal, Habib Bourguiba of Tunisia, and Hamani Diori of Niger. Bourguiba's concept envisaged a "Commonwealth à la française", African unity, and rapprochement with France. O.C.A.M. defined francophonie as a "spiritual community of nations which use French". This ambitious plan to link all the francophone nations was not to be realized, and failed to gain from within the African continent the support of Algeria and Morocco. During this time of African activity, France maintained a "discreet silence" in the words of Xavier

Deniau, who was at that time a parliamentarian at the heart of negotiations (Deniau, 1983: 53).

France was at this time still re-evaluating its attitude, in a process that led to the historic signing on November 23, 1965 of a Cultural Agreement between itself and Quebec, the first agreement ever when France would agree to share the responsibility for its language. Article 1 of this Agreement stated

> "The Government of the French Republic and Government of Quebec will closely co-operate in the promotion and diffusion of the French language".*

The signing of this agreement, probably more than any other, marked the birth of La Francophonie, the organizational form of francophonie. It showed at once the perspicacity of French and Quebec leaders, the French in sharing their patrimony, and the Quebec in awareness of the difficult nature of the task ahead of preserving and securing francophone identity, particularly in view of the Quiet Revolution taking place in Quebec and transforming 300-year old cultural patterns and leading to a secular state, with all of its problems for language and culture maintenance.

Other developments were also taking place, though. In 1967 the International Association of Parliamentarians of the French-language was created, and this in turn led to the creation of the Agency of Cultural and Technical Co-operation in 1970, which was to become the central organizing body of la Francophonie.

Within France, the legislators were anxious to encourage francophone developments. Article 2 of the Superior Education Act of 1968 provided for universities to "take the necessary steps to develop international co-operation, notably with partially or wholly francophone universities".*

In 1973, a Committee for Francophonie was established, and a year later an Interministerial Committee for Francophone Affairs, while within the Ministry of Foreign Affairs, a Francophone Affairs Section was also established.

In January 1973, a French law for the first time recognized a "French linguistic and cultural entity". Law 73.42 of January 9, 1973 (Code of Nationality) recognized such an entity for the purposes of granting naturalization, and, in so doing, provided an opportunity for francophone persons to become French citizens.

In Quebec in the 1960s the Quiet Revolution mentioned above took place, based on the concept of *rattrapage* or "catching up" through modernization of the whole of society in Church-State relations, education, technology, administration, and an assertion of Quebec identity. It led in 1968 to the setting up of the Gendron Commission to investigate the position of French language rights and recommended in its report of 1972 the legislative reinforcement of French as official language in Quebec.

In 1969 the Quebec Government passed Bill 63, which enhanced French language rights and set up an office of the French Language. In 1974 Bill 22 was passed, making French the sole official language of Quebec and in 1977 an even stronger Bill 101, the Charter of the French Language, was passed with a view to cementing the place of French in Quebec society for ever (Bourhis, 1984).

But while these legislative measures had been enacted to protect French in Quebec and in France, at the international level a number of organizational steps were being taken.

The first of these was the creation of the International Association of Parliamentarians of the French Language, largely at the instigation of Léopold Sédar Senghor in 1966. This organization, which is actively functioning today, brings together parliamentarians from 47 countries from almost every part of the globe. The value of this organization can be seen from the fact that members join as individual parliamentarians rather than as governmental representatives, such that it provides a forum for francophonie at a high level embracing members from countries which may or may not wish to formally align themselves with the movement.

From the meetings of the International Association of Parliamentarians of the French Language came an initiative to create a formal organization to unify la Francophonie at governmental level. In 1969 at Niamey, Niger, the representatives of 28 francophone nations assembled and agreed upon the foundation of the Agency for Cultural and Technical Co-operation. At that Conference the French Minister of Culture, André Malraux, committed his nation's full support, thus indicating that France had overcome its fears of a loss of hegemony in francophone Africa (Gordon, 1978: 87).

The original aims of the Agency as set down at the Conference were: to facilitate cultural and technical exchanges between member states; to standardize and simplify administrative and educational practices, in, for example, civil service training programmes; to provide mutual technical assistance in, for example, education and health; to share information; and to provide for cultural exchanges. The French language was of course to be the working languge of the organization, but the indigenous languages, cultures and sovereignty of each member state were to be respected, and on questions of ideology and politics, the Agency was to observe strict neutrality. The Agency was to collaborate with all existing international and regional organizations and take account of all existing forms of development assistance. The permanent headquarters of the Agency were to be located in Paris, and general meetings were to be held at least every two years in cities of the different member states.

It has today 30 full member-states, 7 associated states and 2 participating governments.

The member-states are

Belgium	Ivory Coast
Benin	Lebanon
Burkina-Faso (formerly	Luxembourg
Upper Volta)	Mali
Burundi	Mauritius
Canada	Monaco
Central African Republic	Niger
Chad	Rwanda
Comores	Senegal
Congo	Seychelles
Djibouti	Togo
Dominica	Tunisia
France	Vanuatu
Gabon	Vietnam
Guinea	Zaïre
Haïti	

The associated states are

Cameroun	Mauritania
Egypt	Morocco
Guinea-Bissau	Saint Lucia
Laos	

The participating governments are

New Brunswick
Quebec

Thus, of the world's wholly or partly francophone states, all but three (Algeria, Madagascar and Switzerland) are members or associates of, or participants in, the Agency, a remarkable indication of the acceptance of a body in only 15 years of existence. It should be noted, though, that in the case of some members, links with francophonie are tenuous. Guinea-Bissau is lusophone, and in Vietnam, French is nearly extinct. Privately, considerable doubts were expressed as to the wisdom of allowing Vietnam to join, and, as a member, Vietnam has criticized the place of French with the Agency. (Private communication, senior French administrator, 1984).

This difficulty notwithstanding, the future direction of its development is to establish and strengthen contacts with other organizations, both governmental and non-governmental, that have some links with the movement. There are in addition a number of other bodies which are concerned with specialized areas of francophonie, most notably the International Council for the French Language, which specializes in linguistic questions. There is also a grouping of francophone nations in the United Nations, in which some 30 delegations have been meeting regularly since 1966, and a number of organizations representing a diverse range of francophone activities, from writing to science, education, medicine and law. The total collectivity of organizations of governments, associations and private individuals thus constitutes a truly supra-national language-based movement. How genuine, durable and valid is that movement?

The assessment of authenticity

There is no single reliable test that can be used in the assessment of authenticity. The ability to withstand destruction through genocide, war, hardship or assimilation is a valid criterion over a sufficient period of time. La Francophonie and its instrumentalities have all been accused of lack of authenticity, and it is a vitally important exercise to examine the arguments that have been brought forward.

Many of the criticisms have been aimed specifically at the Agency of Cultural and Technical Co-operation, but some critics have also discussed the movement as a whole. The criticisms could be listed as:

(1) francophonie is neo-colonialist
(2) member governments lack a genuine commitment
(3) French is not the authentic language of many of the populations whose adherence is claimed
(4) the French language does not possess the intrinsic qualities claimed of it and

(5) *francité* is a movement of greater authenticity, where *francité* means the quality of possessing ethnically or genetically French origins. These criticisms must be examined in turn.

(1) The conception of la Francophonie as a vehicle of neo-colonialism was one made from the outset. At the first Niamey Conference the Foreign Minister of Madagascar, Jacques Kabenmananjara, expressed the contrary view that francophonie was a vehicle of protest against colonialism and a medium in which to express black identity (Gordon, 1978: 89). Certainly Senghor saw no contradiction between francophonie and *la négritude* (black identity): the concept was in fact one which he and two other intellectuals had introduced. The idea that France would dominate la Francophonie was first expressed by Jacques Berque in 1967, and is a view with which some senior French civil servants are reported to be covertly in agreement (Gordon, 1978: 94n). As has already been noted, de Gaulle was sensitive to these criticisms and chose not to overtly promote a French role in la Francophonie, preferring to foot the bill to the extent of 45% of its total budget, a proportion still roughly the same today. (Agence de Co-opération Culturelle et Technique, 1981). The present author's own interviews within both the Quai d'Orsay and the Agency Headquarters in Paris have failed to elicit indications of cynicism of the kind encountered by Gordon, but admittedly this is inconclusive. The fact that its founders were non-French francophones, as are many of its most vigorous promoters today, does indicate some absence, at least on their part, of feelings of neo-colonialism.

(2) The motives of governments or any other type of political actor are notoriously difficult to assess. Colin Old raised these doubts when he wrote in a monograph on Quebec's relations with francophonie

> "... questions are raised as to Quebec's sincerity in La Francophonie ..." (Old, 1984: 3).

Old went on to argue that francophonie was nothing more than a stepping stone in the ambition of Quebec's political leaders to achieve independent statehood

> "Since the P.Q. (Parti Québécois) is dedicated to Quebec becoming sovereign it seems only logical that the government is using aspects of Quebec's external affairs, e.g. francophonie, to promote its independence project" (Old, 1984: 47).

As evidence, Old points to Quebec's multiple role within francophonie and the numerous points of friction that this has created with the

Canadian federal government. Although in the end he concedes that further research is necessary,

"Unearthing the connections between francophonie and the sovereignty issue offers a rich field of endeavour for further investigation" (Old, 1984: 47).

In assessing this argument, it must be noted that a doubt over the sincerity of Quebec's desire to maintain its linguistic and cultural heritage has often been expressed, particularly by English Canadians, and yet that desire has continued to burn unabated for nearly 400 years (Williams, 1980). There does not seem to be a contradiction between a desire for independence and a desire to participate in francophonie, both desires could be equally genuine, and in fact they could be said to amount to the same desire, specifically, to preserve an identity as expressed in French.

Brian Weinstein also expressed doubts as to the sincerity of some members of the French Government when he wrote

"... the development of such a movement is clouded not only by the diversity of its participants but by the conflict between those who want to build a genuine world force and those who want to use Francophonie to pursue the narrower interests of the French government" (Weinstein, 1983: 167).

In view of the persistence of France's colonial role it is doubtful whether these suspicions as to motives will ever disappear. It is quite probable that such views do exist within the French Government, particularly in defence circles, but to the present they have not been sufficiently in evidence as to invalidate the movement.

(3) That French is not the authentic language of many peoples whose adherence is claimed.

Weinstein does not accept that francophonie is an authentic expression of peoples other than those of France, Quebec, Wallonia, Romand Switzerland and several other small areas. Outside these areas he sees French as a language of élites intent upon maintaining their position of power not only against "Americanism" but also against local nationalism (Weinstein, 1976a: 266–7).

He has pointed to the fact that *Mouvement Militant Mauricien* (M.M.M.), which claims to speak for the masses of Mauritius, demands a cultural revolution, including the replacement of French and English by Créole (or Kreol), and to the leaders of the student revolt of May

1972 in Madagascar who demanded the use of Malagasy in education and government (Weinstein, 1976a: 295).

In evaluating these criticisms, a number of points can be made. The élitist nature of the dispersal of francophonie in the developing and ex-colonial nations has never been denied. Senghor estimated the percentage of francophones in the black African francophone countries at between 8 and 10 (le Gentil, 1976: 12).

But many writers from the developing world have expressed appreciation of the value of French as a medium of international communication. For example, the Arabic writer Tahar ben Jalloun stated in an article in *Le Monde*

> "If I had written in Arabic, this debate would not have taken place ... I would have had to wait until the year 2000 to be translated into French, to be read and discussed".* (Tahar ben Jalloun, 1982: 2)

In addition, many other nations have found it necessary to rely upon an international language, as well as having a "national language". For example, India has had Hindi as national language since 1950, but still is forced to rely upon English as *lingua franca* and "Associate Official Language" (Le Page, 1964). In the Republic of South Africa denial of instruction in English as part of a policy of divide and rule has been practised (Brooks, 1968: 59). It would seem unlikely then to believe that in those developing nations affiliated with francophonie there would be reluctance on the part of the masses to maintain an identification with an international language such as French, particularly when it provides access to the outside world as well as facilitating development aid, famine relief and co-operation in the form of field visits by experts.

(4) The French language does not possess the intrinsic qualities claimed of it. A number of figures have written in very lyrical form as to the properties of French, among them Charles the Fifth of France, Rivard and Voltaire. It is beyond the scope of this work to attempt to assess these comments, but Weinstein questions the properties of clarity, precision, harmony and logic which have widely been attributed to the French language; he questions the actual numbers of effective francophones, which he notes has been stated to be as high as 200 million; he questions the international standardization of the French language, quoting the Belgian writer Pol Vandromme, who accused francophonie of masking a "totalitarian conservatism or a subversive movement ... which everywhere serves the French political empire by dividing nations such as Belgium or Canada" (Weinstein, 1976a: 274). Weinstein also

questions the often expressed view that French has instrumental value, considered already under (3), particularly in relation to African nations, in that it opens communication with the outside world and allows greater access to science and technology.

(5) *Francité* is a movement of greater authenticity than francophonie. The concept of francité is one that could constitute a competing alternative to that of francophonie. C. Ph. Bodinier (1984: 9) believes that the term made its first appearance in a novel, *Aller et Retour*, by the Swiss writer H. de Ziegler in 1943, and did not appear again until 1957 when it was used by Roland Barthes when he spoke of the "pommes-frites as the culinary symbol of francité"*. Later the Belgian writer J. Boly spoke of "our spiritual vocation: francité: our world-wide expression: francophonie"* while later Xavier Deniau stated that "francité is the soul of francophonie"*. (Deniau, 1983: 13).

Francité can thus be described as the "totality of characteristics of French civilisation"* as in *le Grand Larousse* (quoted by Deniau, 1983: 13). However, it also has another meaning applied with increasing frequency to it, and that is that francité refers to a set of ethnic or genetic characteristics, described by Old as:

> "The French ethnic community where French is the mother tongue of the population; primarily associated with Europe and Canada." (Old, 1984: iii)

This was clearly not the original sense of francité, as used, for example, by Senghor when he gave an address at the Université Laval in 1966 stating that:

> "... the spirit of the civilisation, or the French culture is that which I will call francité."* (Deniau, 1983: 13).

In this sense, Senghor as an African could himself possess francité; in the second sense of French ethnicity, where French genes are required, he could not. Thus, in the second sense of francité, francophone Africans, Arabs, Asians, Inuit, Polynesians, etc. must be excluded. In effect, this situation has found institutional expression in some recent organizations that have been created. There is for example a Conference of French Ethnic Communities (*La Conférence des communautés ethniques de langue française*), which is a non-governmental assembly of European and North American French ethnic communities (Old, 1984: 27). This conference has direct contacts with some grass-roots organizations in Quebec according to Old. Another account of a meeting of the Conference in Quebec City reported that it was attended by Wallonie Libra, Jura

Libra, several organizations from the Val d'Aosta, the Federation des francophones hors Quebec, and a few New England organizations. All were white and of more or less French descent, and, although the political battles of each group had little in common, it was an emotional experience (Anonymous reader, 1985).

It is therefore legitimate to ask whether francité has become synonymous with ethnic and racial exclusivity, that is, a "francophonie for whites only"? There are undoubtedly such strands of thought in France and in Quebec, and an analogy has been made between Quebec nationalism and Afrikanerdom, the expression of another former colonial minority. Roger Omond, for example, has written that:

"René Lévesque and his Parti Québécois might be Afrikaner Nationalists" (Omond, 1981: 9)

and goes on to refer to similar attempts to form a new society, opposition to integration, job reservation and some other similarities, though, of course, in attitudes to indigenous peoples there is an acute difference.

However, Bodinier believes that the first sense of francité (civilization) is the prevailing one:

"As for French ethnicity, and the absurd suspicions of 'racism' (race depends on anatomical characteristics), it is nothing more than a 'community of French language'" (Bodinier, 1984: 9)

If, as has been suggested, the majority of the populations of the greater number of francophone nations do not have an authentic attachment to francophonie, it being nothing more than a manipulation by élites, then in the long term francophonie may come to be co-terminous with francité (in the sense of ethnicity). Even here, there are difficulties in making francophonie co-terminous with francité as Luxembourg is a white European country with a political commitment to francophonie, but which is not part of francité, and similarly the Bruxellois are a heterogeneous mixture, mainly of Flemish origin, who are more less assimilated to French and thus are part of francophonie but not francité.

If, at some stage in the future, francophonie and francité are to become co-terminous, the above exceptions notwithstanding, then the ideal of a multiracial and multicultural francophonie as espoused by Senghor, Bourguiba and many others would have failed, and French would revert to the status of a regional and ethnic language.

Conclusion

Probably the only true test as to the authenticity of a movement based on language, culture or any other dimension of human attachment is the test of time, that is, the durability of such an attachment through great adversity. While the organizational forms of la Francophonie are comparatively new, francophonie is not. On the North American continent it has in Quebec survived a rigorous testing in the universally understood knowledge that with language goes identity. As a former Quebec Prime Minister has written

> "Being ourselves is essentially a matter of keeping and developing a personality that has survived for three and a half centuries. At the core of this personality is the fact that we speak French ... To be unable to live as ourselves, as we should live, in our own language and according to our own ways, would be like living without a heart." (Lévesque, 1968 (1977): 14–15).

Whether this sentiment extends beyond the areas of *francité* remains to be seen. Even one of its most critical observers, Brian Weinstein, is prepared to concede that

> "... Francophonie could become an important transnational actor in world politics." (Weinstein, 1983: 167)

In the light of the various arguments considered and evaluated — neo-colonialism, lack of government commitment, lack of commitment to the French language, the nature of that language, and the competing claims of francité — it would appear that none of these is of overwhelming force. By contrast, it would appear that la Francophonie has not been used for colonialist aims, that governments do find it useful, and that the French language is a valid and valuable instrument of communication in over 30 nations. Only in the threat of racism in the form of a "francophonie for whites only" or *francité* does there seem to be a question mark over the future of la Francophonie. But until such an alternative movement is to fully develop, one is reasonably entitled to assess this particular supra-national language-based movement as authentic.

Acknowledgement

I wish to gratefully acknowledge the comments of an anonymous reader. All responsibility for opinions and any errors rests with me.

Notes to Chapter 4

1. Where English language translations are available I have referred to these. Those translated by myself are marked with an asterisk (*).

Bibliography

(*Note*: Where English translations are available, these have been cited).
AGECOP LIAISON, (Periodical) Paris, Agence de Co-opération Culturelle et Technique.
AGENCE DE CO-OPÉRATION CULTURELLE ET TECHNIQUE, no date, *Convention et charte*. Paris: A.C.C.T.
—— 1981, *Action Internationale de l'A.C.C.T.* Document 5. Paris: A.C.C.T.
ASSOCIATION INTERNATIONALE DES PARLEMENTAIRES DE LANGUE FRANÇAISE, 1982, *Bulletin de Documentation*. Paris: AIPLF.
BENGTSSON, SVERKER, 1968, *La Défense organisée de la langue française*. Uppsala: Almqvist and Wicksell.
BEN JALLOUN, TAHAR, 1982, Les P.M.A., *Le Monde*, (20 mars) 2.
BODINIER, C.-PH., 1984, Chronique de la francophonie, Du français dans l'air. *Construire*, édition Genève, (novembre 21), 9.
BOSTOCK, WILLIAM W., 1979, The Rose and the Fleur-de-Lis: The Conflict of Cultures in Canada. *Dyason House Papers*, 6, 2, (December) 155–58.
—— 1980, The Commissioner of Official Languages: A Canadian response to a situation of ethno-linguistic cleavage. *Ethnic and Racial Studies*, 3, 4. (July) 415–26.
—— 1981, Review of *The French Language and National Identity* by David C. Gordon, *Language Planning Newsletter*. 7,1,6.
—— 1983, Review of *Minority Languages Today* by EINAR HAUGEN, J. DERRICK MCCLURE & DERICK THOMSON (eds), *AUMLA*, 59, (May) 161.
—— 1985, *Francophonie: Organisation, Co-ordination, Evaluation*. Melbourne: River Seine.
BOURHIS, RICHARD Y., 1982, Language policies and language attitudes: Le monde de la Francophonie. In E. BOUCHARD RYAN & H. GILES (eds), *Attitudes Towards Language Variation*. London: Edward Arnold.
—— (ed.) 1984, *Conflict and Language Planning in Quebec*. Clevedon: Multilingual Matters.
BROOKS, EDGAR H., 1968, *Apartheid – A Documentary Study of Modern South Africa*. London: Routledge & Kegan Paul.

Bruezière, Maurice, 1983, *L'Alliance française, Histoire d'une institution.* Paris: Hachette.

Cans, Roger, 1979, 'Qui parlera français en l'an 2000?' *Le Devoir,* December 10–12.

Clyne, Michael G., 1984, *Language and Society in the German-speaking Countries.* Cambridge: Cambridge University Press.

Conseil International de la Langue Française, no date, *Status.* Paris: C.I.L.F.

—— 1981, *Rapport d'Activités.* Paris: C.I.L.F.

Deniau, Xavier, 1983, *La Francophonie, Que sais-je?* paris: Presses Universitaire de France.

le Gentil, Claude, 1978, Ici on parle français. *France Information,* 96, (September), 8–23.

Gordon, David C., 1978, *The French Language and National Identity* (1930–1975). The Hague, Paris, New York: Mouton. Contributions to the Sociology of Language 22.

Kloss, Heinz & McConnell, G., 1974–81, *Linguistic Composition of the Nations of the World,* Vols. 1–3. Quebec: Les Presses de l'Université Laval.

—— 1981, *Linguistic composition of the Nations of the World.* Vol. 4. Quebec: Les Presses de l'Université Laval.

Le Gentil, C. 1978, Ici on parle français. *France Information,* 96 (Sept) 8–23.

Le Page, R.B., 1964, *The National Language Question: Linguistic Problems of Newly Independent States.* London: Institute of Race Relations.

Lévesque, René, 1977, *An Option for Quebec.* Toronto: McClelland and Stewart. (First Edition 1968).

Malka, Victor, 1980, Talking about the French Language. *Le Courier Australien.* (October).

Old, Colin, 1984, Quebec's Relations with francophonie: a Political Geographic Perspective, *Carleton Geography Discussion Papers,* 1.

Omond, Roger, 1981, Quebec's Afrikaner Nationalists. *Rand Daily Mail.* (January 13), 9.

Québec, 1984, *Charter of the French Language, Revised Statutes of Quebec,* Chapter c-II. Québec, Editeur officiel du Québec.

Revue des parlementaires de langue française (periodical), Paris: Association International des parlementaires de langue française.

—— 1980, *A propos de la communauté organique, francophone et dialectique.* Paris: A.I.P.L.F.

Rickard, Peter, 1974, *A History of the French Language.* London: Hutchinson.

SALON, ALBERT, 1976, Le Francais langue de communication internation-
ale. In M. BLANCPAIN & J. REBOULLET (eds) *Une Langue: Le
Français*. Paris: Hachette.
—— 1983, *L'Action culturelle de la France dans le monde*. Paris: Fernand
Nathan.
VIATTE, AUGUST, 1969, *La Francophonie*. Paris: Larousse.
WEINSTEIN, BRIAN, 1976a, Francophonie: International languages in
politics. In A. VERDOODT et al. (eds), *Language in Sociology*.
Louvain: Peeters.
—— 1976b, Francophonie: A language based movement in world politics.
International Organisation, 30,3, 1976, 485–507.
—— 1983, *The Civic Tongue, Political Consequences of Language Choices*.
New York: Longmans.
WILLIAMS, COLIN, 1980, The desire of nations: Quebecois ethnic separatism
in comparative perspective, *Cahiers de Géographie du Québec*, 24,
61, 47–68.

5   On Measuring Language Border Areas

C.H. WILLIAMS and J.E. AMBROSE
Department of Geography and Recreation Studies,
North Staffordshire Polytechnic
Stoke-on-Trent, U.K.

Introduction

Geographers have long been fascinated with the pressing, if difficult, need to identify and demarcate border regions, frontier zones and boundaries at a variety of scales. In its imperial heyday Europe gave full employment to the geo-political cartographer whose skills were often an essential element accompanying the colonial drive and the conquest of far-flung territories. Legitimization of such territories within international law followed long established guidelines which have served as a precedent for the resolution of boundary disputes in more recent times.

In this chapter we shall concentrate upon the relevant methodological issues which are raised by the various attempts to measure language border areas at both the international and nation-state level in Europe. Having highlighted several key contributions to geolinguistic analysis from this field, we shall provide a more detailed illustration of the problems and pitfalls involved in measuring one longstanding border area, the Breton language divide of western France.

Why border areas?

Geographers, such as Ratzel (1897), have interpreted the border zone as a surrogate for the general condition of the whole territory, arguing that the border/frontier acted as a thermometer by which one could gauge the general health of the state. Although Ratzel's organic growth theory of state development is no longer central to human geography, several of the related concerns which animated his work remain as the subject of much intense research. One such concern was the means by which people identified with a particular territory, and sought to dominate surrounding areas by the extension of their power and influence within a culture region.

Oscillating at times between the environmental determinist and possibilist viewpoint of nineteenth-century geography, there gradually emerged a model which sought to explain the formation of culture regions. These regions were deemed to capture the essence of a particular culture group, its personality and identity. Meinig (1969) has suggested that under ideal conditions, interpreted by Zelinsky (1973) to be relative isolation for a long time, freedom from interference from others, and the opportunity for unhindered territorial expansion by a cultural group, three broad cultural geographic zones would emerge. Initially one would be able to identify a core area, defined as the centralized zone of settlement where the most virulent characteristics of the culture under review would be displayed. Here also would be located the chief decision-making institutions and groups, and locus of the most intense group socio-economic activity and social organization. Moving out from the core we have a secondary zone of settlement which Meinig terms the Domain. This refers to areas in which the original culture is still dominant, but where the bonds of connection are fewer and more tenuous, and where regional peculiarities are evident. Finally, there is the Sphere. This represents the zone of outer influence, and often of peripheral accultur-ation, wherein the culture is represented by only certain of its elements, or where its people reside as minorities among those of a different culture. At the outer edge of the sphere is the border area, whose zone of sovereignty is terminated at the frontier with the neighbouring culture region. It is this interface region, the cultural zone of transition, which is the principal concern of this chapter's argument.

In essence Meinig's model (Figure 5.1) is an application of core-periphery theorizing to cultural phenomenon. Its assumptions are couched in the language of diffusion theory, involving competition between cultures over space and through time. The culture area concept has received much criticism, especially the tendency to reify culture on behalf of several researchers. Hudson has crystallized the essence of this tendency as detailed below:

"The Culture Area is a classic example of the pitfalls of inferring temporal processes from maps. It is also a good example of the kind of generalizations that result when essentially discontinuous phenomena are grouped areally and characteristics are ascribed to the resulting regions instead of to the phenomena used to define the regions."

(Hudson, 1972).

Despite this general criticism the tripartite division suggested by Meinig has the merit of focussing attention upon the differential intensity and organization of culture within various territories of the polity.

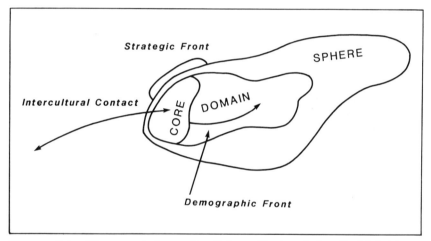

FIGURE 5.1 *The morphology of a Culture Region (after D. Meinig)*

The international context

Clearly one cannot discuss the position of border language communities without reference to the historic forces which have shaped their destiny. The "territorial–bureaucratic" state is central to the welfare of minority language communities as other chapters in this volume amply demonstrate. The centralizing state is vital because it sets the limits of freedom of action for its constituent groups, and through its increasingly interventionist role serves to favour some groups and their culture at the expense of others. Many authors have increased our understanding of the state as an ethnic-defining instrument; our present emphasis will be upon those who have adopted the core-periphery perspective. Of the many variants on this theme, the most comprehensive explication is provided by Stein Rokkan's "Conceptual Map of Europe" (Rokkan & Urwin, 1982; Allardt, 1981). In examining the processes of state-formation and nation-building, Rokkan adopts a Parsonian scheme incorporating four functional prerequisites — economy, political power, law and culture. These elements separate from each other in time, and provide institutional domains within which competitive élites vie for influence at various junctures in the process (Allardt, 1981: 259). The originality of Rokkan's interpretation is that he ties these functional attributes to the constant tension between core and periphery in European state development, producing central co-ordinates for his conceptual map. Broad in design and catholic in execution, Rokkan's four interactive requisites of economy and culture, core and periphery, structure the development of the modern European state system and help locate the ethnic identity of Europe's people within a social and spatial order as shown in Figure 5.2 (Williams, 1985).

When these attributes are translated into territorial realities we may display the tensions and processes inherent in the state-building histories of Europe as shown in Figure 5.3. This composite map is derived from the work of Rokkan (1980), Parker (1983) and Williams (1980), and illustrates the central strategic role of the "Lotharingian Axis", the principal European axis of trade and communication. Control of this vital corridor of power and commerce has been a persistent feature of modern European history, and a strategic target in most continental warfare since the Thirty Years' War (1618–1648). The map brings into sharp relief the dynamic pressure exerted by expansionist states such as France and England in the west, and by Germany in central Europe. It also illustrates the marginalized position of peripheral minority groups, such as the Celts on the fringe of empires and developing world states. However, this apparently simple core-periphery tension at the European scale does not necessarily imply a permanent dependency situation for such groups in the European economy and state system. Euskadi, Catalonia and Scotland, though geographically distant from their respective core territories, have good grounds for being classified as well-integrated regions within the economic expansion of advanced capitalism.

In geolinguistic terms these processes suggest three important influences upon the development of linguistic territories. The first is the obvious recognition that successful states can impart great power to a language by institutionalizing it within a burgeoning economic and political system, a feature which is well documented in the literature (Weinstein,

	SEAWARD PERIPHERIES	SEAWARD EMPIRE-NATIONS	CITY BELT	LANDWARD EMPIRE-NATIONS	LANDWARD BUFFER TERRITORIES
CENTRE FORMATION:	WEAK	STRONG	WEAK	STRONG	WEAK
CITY NETWORK:	WEAK	STRONG	STRONG	WEAK	WEAK
WEST TO EAST:					
NORTH TO SOUTH					
ARCTIC PERIPHERIES	Iceland Faeroes Finnmark			Norrbotn	Lappland
PROTESTANT TERR.	Norway Scotland Wales	DENMARK ENGLAND	Hanse Germany	SWEDEN PRUSSIA	FINLAND Baltic Terr.
MIXED/ NATIONAL CATHOLIC TERR.	Scots Highl. Ireland Brittany	FRANCE	NETHERLANDS Belgium RHINELAND GERM. SWITZERLAND		Lithuania Poland
COUNTER REFORMATION	Galicia Navarre Basque	SPAIN PORTUGAL	Rousillon Catalonia	AUSTRIA	Hungary Croatia
MEDITERRANEAN PERIPHERIES	Andalucia Estremadura		Balearic Islands Southern Italy		Dalmatia Albania

Note: Territories sovereign before 1789 are in capital letters.

Source: F. H. Aarebrot, 'On the Structural Basis of Regional Mobilization in Europe' in B. de Marchi and A. M. Boileau (eds.), *Boundaries and Minorities in Western Europe* (Franco Angeli Editore, Milan, 1982).

FIGURE 5.2 *Rokkan's Conceptual Map of Western Europe: Principal Features*

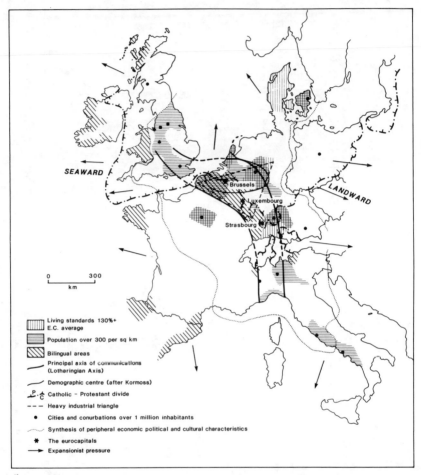

FIGURE 5.3   *State-building in Europe: Tensions and processes*
Reproduced with permission from Williams (1985), after Parker (1983).

1983; Smith, 1986; and Gordon, 1978). The second is that expanding multi-ethnic empires engineered population movements as a means of strengthening their hold upon threatened frontier regions. The ethnolinguistic maps of the Ottoman, Tsarist and Austro-Hungarian Empires are replete with the often tragic results of forced migrations, mass expulsions and geopolitical re-locations of minority populations (Kann, 1974; Sugar, 1977; Kann & David, 1984). The third implication is that for many autochthonous groups, who did not share in the successful establishment of nation-states, their future has been decided by the dominant host group(s) of the sovereign state. Free market forces alone might well have created several beleaguered minorities in a modernizing world. When one considers the awesome power exercised by the uniform bureaucratic state in its search for "national integration", it is little wonder that some minorities feel themselves to be the victims in the historic drive toward the attainment of cultural homogeneity. In the past many have argued that relative geographical isolation helped maintain the separateness of the Welsh, Bretons and Frisians. In an age of instant mass communication, and state socialization, it is less likely that geographic factors, such as isolation, topography, and distance from a core area, will be invoked as a defence against the pressures of assimilation.

Boundary studies

Scandinavian geographers and historians have been in the forefront of boundary contact studies. Sven Tägil and his co-researchers at Lund have developed a general theory for explaining boundary conflicts which lays emphasis on "resources" and "barriers" in boundary areas. Their case studies, drawn from a variety of European border locations, such as Schleswig, Eupen-Malmedy, Danzig, East Prussia, Hultschin and Teschen, illustrate a long-debated problem of border conflict, namely how to accommodate ethnic overlapping in border regions. In this case the core-periphery model assumes quite different proportions dependent upon which state or political-administrative unit one recognizes as the relevant context. As Tägil suggests:

"In one sense — administratively, for example — an entire population in a border area may be regarded as the periphery in relation to the center of the same state, while at the same time, for example, in cultural respects, the same population may in view of ethnic heterogeneity recognize different centers as their superiors. Spatial and social center/periphery relationships thus need not coincide." (Tägil et al., 1977: 87).

This lack of congruence has often fuelled language-related conflict in border areas. Perhaps we should say, it has fuelled material and ideological conflict which has used language as a marker of group differentiation and sociopolitical mobilization. European history is too well endowed with such examples to allow us to ignore the potentially explosive nature of language in political conflict. The many case studies in Strassoldo (1973) testify that such conflicts are too deeply woven into the fabric of bi- and multi-cultural regions throughout Europe to be regarded as either ephemeral or insignificant (Strassoldo, 1973; Stephens, 1976; Krejci & Velimsky, 1981).

Given these factors it is vital to be able to demonstrate the effect which living within a border region has upon the attitudes, behaviour and loyalties of frontier communities. The remainder of this chapter will seek to address two related aspects of this concern. The first is to examine the activity patterns of citizens living within an international border zone, the second is to examine the significance of informal boundary delimitation for the claims of a minority group to possess an historic homeland within a nation state. The first demonstrates the integrative power of the state's social communication system, whilst the second illustrates the difficulties which arise when a minority's claim to a specific homeland is denied by the modern state.

Behavioural dimensions

The international language border

Thomas Lundén's research on the activity patterns of individuals within an "open" border region of the southern Swedish–Norwegian boundary is a comprehensive illustration of the methodologies employed by geolinguists interested in trans-border contacts. His research focuses on two inter-related processes which operate at two different scales: a) the integrative processes of nation-state consolidation, and b) the behaviour of local residents on either side of an international boundary in adjusting to their position as border zone dwellers. Lundén (1982) distinguishes between three levels of social organization: a) the state as a system and territory; b) the more diffuse level of voluntary associations and regions; and c) the level of the individual citizen who forms the basis of social organization. Each level of analysis implies its own related set of behaviours combining to form a complex whole. It therefore follows that actions and reactions in the border area have to be seen as part, not only of the constituent state system, but also in terms of the wider geopolitical milieu. Thus:

> "a boundary is a secondary phenomenon in relation to the binding power and the bounded objects. To understand the meaning and impact of boundaries we therefore have to look at those systems which end and meet at the boundary and those which overlap or are translated at the boundary." (Lundén, 1982: 151).

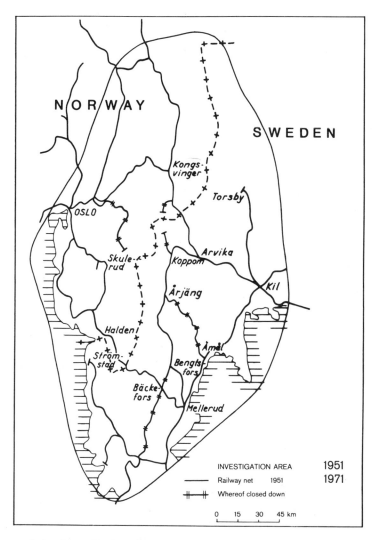

FIGURE 5.4   *Investigation Area*

In an impressive empirical exercise, Lundén measured the state integrative forces of education, mass communication and political directives which so powerfully bind people into the national communities of Norway and Sweden respectively. His study area is peripheral to both Norwegian and Swedish core areas (Figure 5.4). But it is relative location which is paramount in differentiating between the two cases, for while "only 8% of Sweden's population live within 100 kilometres of the boundary the corresponding figure for Norway is 4%. This may be one of the reasons why Norway is just one of Sweden's neighbours while Sweden is *the* neighbour of Norway" (Lundén, 1973a: 194).

By measuring patterns of individual spatial behaviour in the boundary region (Figure 5.5), the incidence of trans-border co-operation and contact via telephone calls (Figure 5.6) he was able to demonstrate how communities either side of the boundary relate to their co-national, rather than to their physical neighbours across the open border. This trend is reinforced by the decision to locate public facilities, such as high schools, state-supported churches, health clinics and the like, in specific locales which serve a central place function for the region.

Norway and Sweden have long propounded a social philosophy of state intervention to reduce inequality between regions and individuals. Paradoxically, however, this equalization process results in growing inequality in the border area, for example, in accessibility and place utility, and in a decrease in trans-border contacts over time.

Lundén's field-work methodology involved asking sample populations drawn from Töckfors, Sweden (600 inhabitants) and Örje, Norway (1200 inhabitants) to record their trans-border movements. Both samples of a hundred respondents live within 6 kilometres of the boundary, along the route of the E18 highway. They were asked to record in a one-week diary all their activities and contacts with others outside their immediate locality. The resultant maps of their activity and contact fields indicate the high proportion of total trips from Töckfors to Örje for shopping and the relative absence of Norwegian contacts with Swedish locations (Figures 5.7a, 5.7b and c). Lundén concludes that this pattern is dependent upon the network of communication in this particular sphere and confirms the fact that the state boundary is also a communications boundary. Note, however, that there is no distinct dialect boundary (Lundén, 1973b: 150). In a situation he describes as "semi-communication", it is the cultural attitudes, rather than the actual linguistic differences, which make Norwegians "more open to heterogeneity in linguistic communication" (p. 150). It is also a reflection over time of a realistic assessment of the relative power and attraction of their respective state languages, and must surely encourage a predisposition on behalf of the weaker language community to master the language of the stronger national community at the international scale.

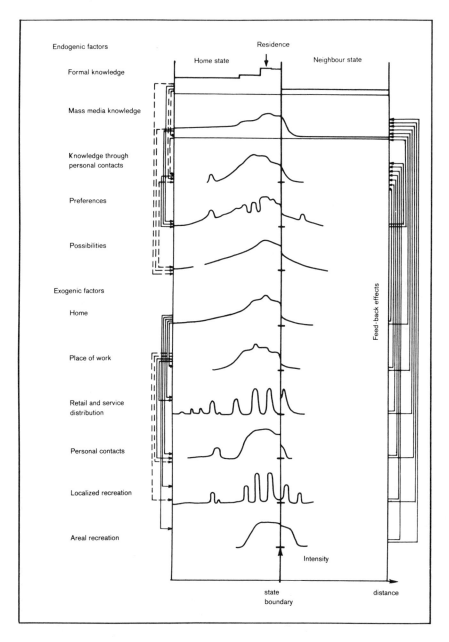

FIGURE 5.5 *Individual spatial behaviour in a boundary area*

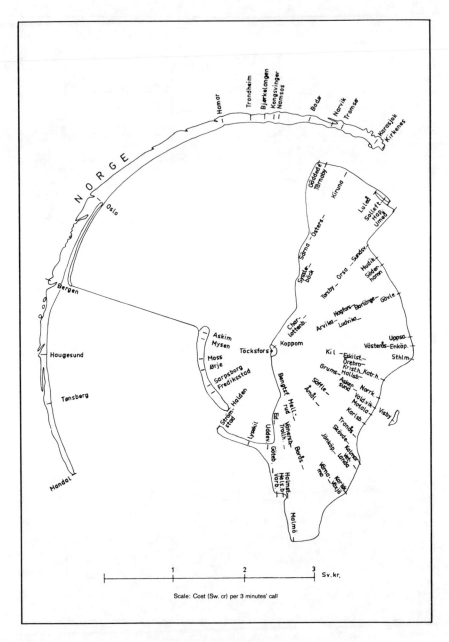

FIGURE 5.6   *Map of telephone costs from Töckfors, Sweden*

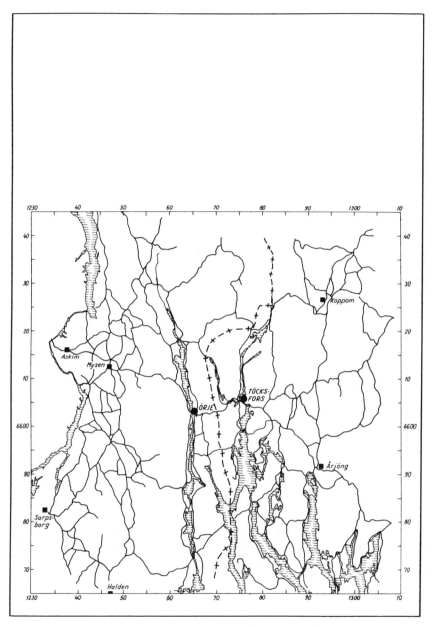

FIGURE 5.7A   *Area of the research on actual activity and movement patterns at the boundary*

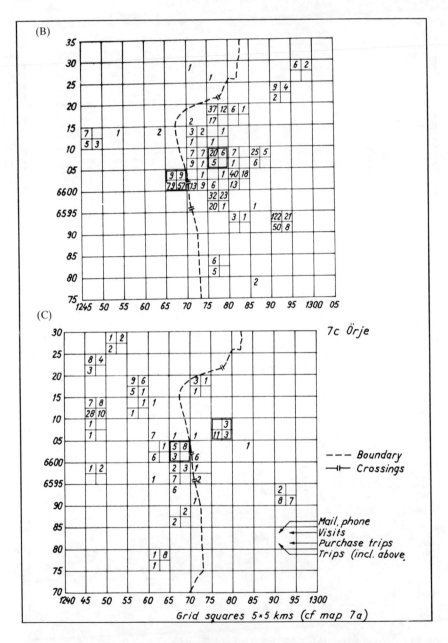

At the more immediate local scale the decrease in trans-border co-operation over time is a function of the success of the respective states in incorporating this periphery into the national space economy. The growth of national congruence (that is, the attempt to make nation and state co-extensive entities) affects both individual spatial perception and the re-orientation of community activities in response to cues and promptings which emanate from deep within the respective political system (Williams, 1986). The scale paradox of inter-state transactions between the two states having increased whilst the "relative external exchanges" at the border have decreased, leads Russett (1973) to extrapolate that if this trend were to be repeated for the whole of Western Europe, it would have severe implications for the ideal of European integration at the cutting edge, namely within communities in border regions.

Lundén's behavioural approach is a useful corrective to much of the earlier work undertaken by geographers on language and social communication. Their over-reliance on state census data, government policy and the operation of formal agencies in border regions led to a clear understanding of the institutional barriers to inter-group interaction, but left out the dynamism of individual and communal action. By returning to the individual scale of activity, and relating such actions to the functioning of borders as both opening and closing mechanisms, Lundén has provided a signal service to geolinguistic analysis.

The language border within the state

The Breton language and its borders

Lundén's work alters the focus of the study of language borders to the social, behavioural systems operating at the scale of local communities in his study area. The presence of the state boundary, with associated pressures for assimilation of local communities into the state territory, is clearly a complicating factor, having the effect of producing what might loosely be termed a sociocultural "fault-line" which traverses his study area, as Figure 5.4 demonstrates. The occurrence of language borders and political boundaries in close proximity is common in Europe; but so, too, is the language border entirely enclosed within the state. While that does not mean that state influences on the minority language are reduced (indeed, it may imply the opposite), it does at least have the effect that state pressures are more consistent on each side of the language border, and thus makes the study of the border slightly more straightforward.

A second case study follows, intended to illustrate the character of such internal language borders. It is based on a behavioural field-study of linguistic change at the eastern fringe of the Breton language area (Ambrose, 1979). This example has the additional purpose of suggesting some of the practical approaches to the detailed measurement of language borders — as well as illustrating a number of the attendant successes and failures which such methods produce.

Any such act of measurement has first to set out a general framework of reference. What follows, the briefest of backgrounds, cannot do justice to the complexity of the Breton culture area, but is intended to provide some anchor-points for later discussion.

Shared cultural traits between the British Isles and the "Little Britain" of the Armorican peninsula seem to date at least from the third and fourth centuries AD. A variety of influences, generally presumed to include population pressure in the British Isles, tribal warfare and perhaps also Roman efforts to defend Armorica against attack, combined to produce a migration, including a disproportionately large number of migrants from Wales, Cornwall and Devon, into the peninsula. (Markale, 1985: 21 *et seq.*). The conventional interpretation is that the newcomers brought with them not only the Brythonic language inheritance which was the basis of modern Breton, but also other cultural traits such as a political and administrative system based upon a number of mainly small, autonomous kingdoms, and a strong Christian culture identified, not with the towns, as in Gaul, but with the rural economies and societies which were characteristic both of the region itself and of the incoming culture groups. (It should also be stated that there is an alternative interpretation, expressed, for example, by Falc'hun (1962), that the Brythonic links owe more to Gaulish origins than is normally acknowledged.) Whatever the origins, few question that the Celtic links were reinforced by further waves of migration from the British Isles, until the eleventh century. From the ninth century onwards, however, the Breton language began to lose territory to French (Chadwick, 1965; Markale, 1985).

The Breton language border has remained far from static during the centuries which have followed (see Figure 5.8), and has been pushed progressively westwards by the political and economic forces which lend power to the French language. While it has been mobile, it has, on the other hand, been a border which has suffered comparatively little political disturbance, a feature which is beneficial in the context of the present study. Much scholarly work, documented through the use of historical, toponymic and other evidence, traces this process of withdrawal. (See, as examples, Falc'hun (1963 and 1970) and Chadwick (1965).)

One consequence of the retreat of the language border has been its separation from the Breton culture area more generally, until it has become the convention to view Brittany as having two linguistically quite separate societies: in the west *Breizh Izel*, or *Basse Bretagne*, has been seen as a generally Breton-speaking area, with only a few enclaves where French was generally known, whilst in *Breizh Uhel*, (*Haute Bretagne*), to the east, Breton was represented to an equally small extent. Many authors hasten to qualify this generalization, and are at pains to point out the considerable linguistic and cultural variety existing to the west of the language border. (See, for example, Flatrès (1986: 13–17).) On the other hand, the same author describes the strong feelings of group cohesion and identity amongst the people of *Breizh Izel*, together with their communal view of *Breizh Uhel* as being separate and different, and having more in common with the remainder of France than with their own culture. What is more, he claims, these feelings of cultural separation have broader, regional planning implications:

"In Central Brittany it is very difficult to unite, for planning purposes, people from either side of the linguistic frontier." (Flatrès, 1986: 14)

While it may be doubtful whether, during recent centuries, the division has ever been quite as clear as is often implied, it has been accepted as a useful general means of estimating the size of the Breton-speaking population. Until the end of the nineteenth century, at least, it has been considered possible to gauge the number of *bretonnants* merely by enumerating the population of *Breizh Izel* (Stephens, 1976: 362). More precise evidence, at the scale of the language area as a whole, is difficult to assemble, since students of the geography of the Breton language find themselves entirely unencumbered by even the most general of census data or other official statistics on the survival of Breton.

The balance of evidence seems to be that the border between the French and Breton languages, as expressed in terms of the local usage of either language, has been one which has tended towards sudden transition. Two reasons suggest themselves: first, that the relative rapidity of the territorial retreat towards the western core of the language area is likely to have reduced the opportunity for the evolution of a series of zones of gentle gradation; and secondly (following to some extent the ideas of Hémon, 1947: 54 and more recent re-statements such as those of Rousseau, 1986), that the predominant socio-economic pattern of life in inland Brittany has continued the long-standing cultural tradition of locally self-sufficient, mainly agricultural communities, with a reduced need for east–west contact across the languge border.

This background may also be instrumental in explaining another notable feature: the eastern edge of the Breton language area is not reflected by parallel changes in topography or other environmental features. Musset (1937: 162) says of the border:

"... by historical chance, it passes through a landscape of striking uniformity; nothing changes, when one crosses it, except the language itself."

The abruptness of the transition seems, in the case of the Breton border, to merit that somewhat abused description *"linguistic divide"*. This term is common in geolinguistic study, especially for small-scale (i.e. highly-generalized) depictions of linguistic borders (Pryce & Williams, this volume, Chapter 7). Divides have commonly been used to show the Breton language border; for example, Figure 5.8 shows that drawn by Sébillot as early as 1886. In some circumstances, as a means of measurement of the language area, such divides can lead to confusion because there is no general convention about what stage of transition across the language boundary they are seeking to outline. Amongst the possible stages the following could be cited: (a) the area where Breton is the only, or (b) the preferred everyday language of the majority; (c) the line at which French asserts itself as the usual language for the majority of people; (d) the edge of the area where only a minority of people can speak Breton, or (c) where they do so in a reduced selection of circumstances; and (f) the point at which French becomes the only everyday language. From Sébillot's accompanying comments it is clear that his divide is a line depicting the edge of the monoglot Breton area and, given the conditions already mentioned and the date of his work, it is perhaps not too unrealistic to conceive of a sharp, almost linear transition. Other applications of the concept are more ambiguous; for example, another divide, shown on Figure 5.9, was discovered in Béchard (1968) and, while it may represent stage (c) on the earlier list, is undefined in terms of the stage of transition it portrays. Its use is thus limited, even if it does provide a clue to the general position of the language border.

This failure to define clear units of measurement is, however, only one of the problems accompanying the concept of the divide as a way of defining language borders inside the state. There is another, still more important one: that such a linear feature fails to recognize the range of processes which take place *across* the language border, and increasingly do so in the modern world. Many authors (for example, Gwegen (1975), Stephens (1976)) describe the new pressures on the Breton language, rising from a combination of internal factors such as selective local ageing

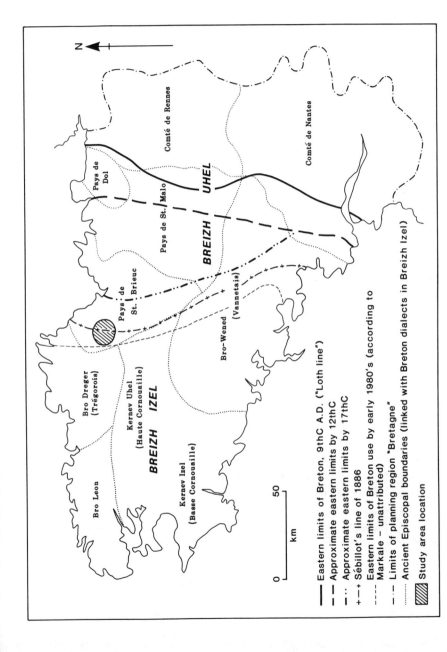

FIGURE 5.8 *Breton cultural identities*

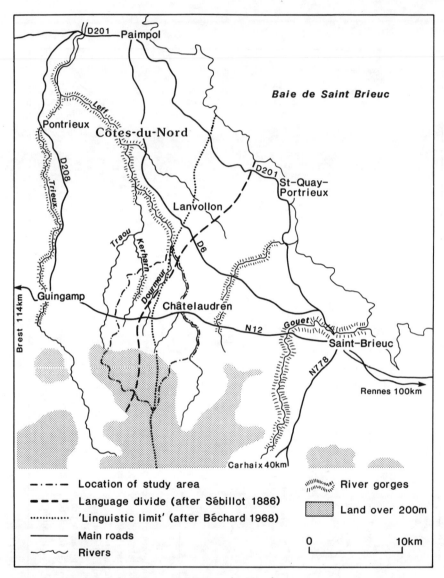

FIGURE 5.9   *The study area in Côtes-du-Nord*

of the *bretonnant* population and the changing balance between the agricultural and other sectors of the economy of *Breizh Izel,* and also external pressures such as the influence, status and economic power of French. There are also alternative arguments, exemplified by Gicquel (1986), that Breton is in a position to benefit from the economic transformations under way, and should be seen as a positive resource for development in Western Brittany. It must be said that such arguments seem to ring hollow in the face of the apparent continued decline of nearly the whole of the language area *in situ*, and the impression given by Markale (1985: 14) is that in the past decade — even in the period since the fieldwork reported here — there has been a further westward retreat of the language area as a whole, to the point indicated on Figure 5.8 (though he does not provide substantive evidence for this). What is clear is that whereas, a century ago, one might have expected to pass, within the distance of a few kilometres, from the area of habitual French usage to that of monoglot Breton speaking, to encompass that transition now, if it could be done at all, might involve a study area covering the whole of *Breizh Izel*, as far as the furthest points of Finistère.

Pryce, writing of late eighteenth-century Wales, sees fit, even for that period, to substitute for the linguistic divide the concept of a transitional "buffer zone" between English and Welsh, in the context of an increasingly mobile, industrializing society (Pryce, 1975: 88). In the present day, the linear divide must be much more open to question. Is it simply to be replaced by the idea of the decline of the language area as a whole, with no notion of transitional change? Evidence from elsewhere indicates not; for example, census data and fieldwork from the periphery of the Welsh language area point to the presence of a "zone of collapse", where the decline of Welsh may be documented not only in numeric terms but also in the frequency and range of usage of the language. It is as if there is a crisis of confidence in the language's viability, a sudden and decisive disintegration of the fabric of its use and, critically, that crisis appears to express itself in spatial, transitional terms (Ambrose & Williams, 1981).

To what extent does a similar, transitional zone of collapse affect the Breton language area? To answer that question requires a change of scale, and the use of a local study area. Using the somewhat intuitive method of focusing on the area where linguistic divides such as those defined by Sébillot and by Béchard bisect the main Paris–Brest road (a point of assumed incursion of Francophone influence into the Breton area) a case-study area of approximately one hundred square kilometres has therefore been defined, a little to the west of Châtelaudren, in the département of Côtes-du-Nord, central Brittany. The area is intended to provide a context in which a number of different measures of the location and strength of the language border can be applied. The location may be seen on Figure 5.8 and is shown in more detail in Figure 5.9.

The act of measurement, when applied to language strength and distribution, is far from straightforward, both in the selection of units and in the process of applying the measures themselves. At the scale of the language area as a whole, Mackey's (1973) work on the comparative "power" and influence of languages at the world scale is an original and innovative contribution, of particular relevance in the present context because it shows the strong position of French. On a number of Mackey's criteria (for example, the population size and wealth-creating capacity of its speakers, and also a range of additional indicators such as annual book publications and broadcasting) the French language emerges as one of the world's most influential. On similar criteria, Breton would fare badly. This relatively poor position is compounded by what can only be called an unenlightened state attitude to the Breton language, exemplified by a derisory allocation of broadcasting time, a poorly-developed legal and administrative status and an education system which treats the language as a second-class qualification, if it acknowledges it at all (Sérant, 1965; Gwegen, 1975; Markale, 1985).

While a knowledge of such general conditions is clearly a most useful prerequisite to measuring the language border at the macro-scale, when it comes to examining its more local form, measures such as those used by Mackey are a less feasible starting point. That is particularly so in the case of Breton, where there is an apparent absolute refusal to gather census data or other statistics which would help to document both its general situation and its more local state of survival. Instead, it is a matter of relying upon a collection of estimates and more and less informed guesses. Table 5.1 is a summary of some of the better-known of these.

Geographers working on other aspects of France, particularly on aspects of national and local economic geography, would generally confirm the admirable thoroughness and currency of statistical information available from *I.N.S.E.E.* and other official agencies, a fact which makes the comparative neglect of minority language data appear to be a reflection of official policy, rather than simple accident. To those studying language borders in other areas of the world, where such data are available, the task of pin-pointing a suitable study area is one which could be undertaken with at least an element of confidence. Here, as already described, it is more a matter of informed guess-work, based upon the sometimes ageing literature on the divide, with the help of more general estimates (for example that in Bozec, 1974) and very occasional local studies such as that of the commune of Trédarzec, quoted in Gwegen (1975). "First, find your figures" is the rule in Brittany.

TABLE 5.1   *Estimates of Breton-speaking population numbers during the nineteenth and twentieth centuries*

Source	Date	Population estimates and comments
Coquebert de Montbret (quoted in Stephens, 1976)	1806	967,000
Sébillot	1886	1,300,000
Unattributed source (quoted in Stephens, 1976 and Gwegen, 1975)	c.1914	1,300,000 (90% of population of *Breizh Izel*)
Hémon	1929	c. 1,000,000 (based on language of church catechism; figure represents 75% of population of *Breizh Izel*)
Gourvil	1960	700,000 "who used French only in case of necessity"; 300,000 "who were able to speak Breton if the need arose"
Bozec	1974	685,250
Denez	1983	("I wonder who, today, would give a fair guess? Between the 20,000 given by the Préfecture and the 700,000 given by the Breton activists there is bound to be a lot of wishful thinking.")

Criteria for measurement of the language border

The devotion of much time to the consideration of suitable scales at which to work is perhaps one of the hallmarks of the geographical approach. The efforts are warranted, for the choice of an inappropriate scale, particularly one which is too generalized, can mask or distort the understanding of the subject under study. Figure 5.9 shows the restricted size of the study area chosen in this case — the district surrounding the small town of Châtelaudren and its neighbouring village of Plouagat, in Côtes-du-Nord. The study area size may seem inappropriately small in view of the fact that it was only being speculated, a few paragraphs ago, that the scale of transition across the language border might by now have widened to cover much of western Brittany; but it represents the kind of compromise which frequently has to be made in geolinguistic study, and the restricted extent was not without its compensations. It allowed a focus on the processes operating in a small locality, and made it realistic to study the role of the individual speaker and to construct a picture of local patterns of Breton use. Such a focus on the precise nature of the individual unit is surely one of the essential features of the process of measurement.

As to the nature of the precise criteria for measuring the border, they, too, were partly dictated by the lack of any other data, and had to be of the most straightforward kind. Two measures were finally chosen: first, the "potential" for Breton speaking, in numeric terms; and secondly, the use of the language in practice, as shown by indicators of frequency and versatility (see below).

The first of these criteria, the "potential" for Breton speaking, was thus combined with an element of exploration at the line of the linguistic divide, in search of areas where field investigation first encountered sufficient numbers of people able to speak Breton to make it apparent that a numeric border had been reached. That is not so straightforward as it sounds, for Breton appears increasingly to be a language of the home and the fields, long absent from many of the towns and increasingly deprived of the public usage which would make its observation easy (Stephens, 1976: 399–400). The method employed, despite these difficulties, was a house-by-house survey, asking: "Is there anyone in your house who is able to speak Breton?". The initial suspicions produced by the question often made the task a difficult one, requiring the diplomatic help and advice of a few "key" figures such as local clergy, school teachers and one particularly helpful local postman. The data obtained, though not by any means a complete record, were used to produce Figure 5.10, which has been "smoothed" by the use of a floating circle technique, to increase its legibility. (For further details see Ambrose (1979: 87–9).)

Figure 5.10 turns out to have a surprising degree of transition, confirming that this very straightforward question did allow the location of the edge of the language area, and elicited the first of what was hoped would be a number of clear bases for the measurement of stages of transition in this locality. A slight compromise of scale must immediately be pointed out, however, in that the incompleteness of field data meant that the unit finally adopted for this stage of investigation was the household, rather than the individual speaker. This also means that the map gives the impression of a rather stronger eastward survival of Breton than is the case, because in the typical "Breton-speaking" household it

Percentage of households with one or more members able to speak Breton, 1972

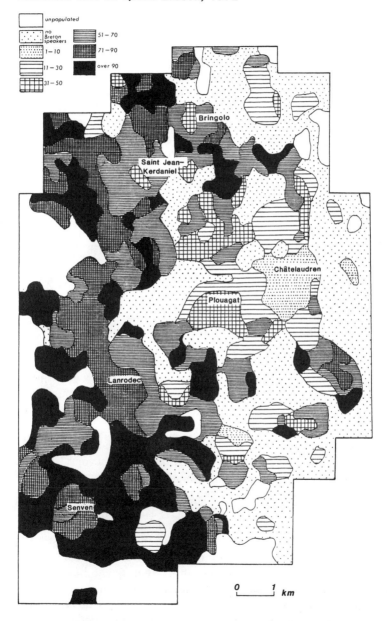

FIGURE 5.10 *Breton speaking: A measure of potential*

was one or two of the members who knew the language, rather than the whole family, and there was thus a factor of "speaker isolation" which would be likely to have an effect upon use of the language in practice. In addition, the Breton-speakers also prove to have a disproportionately large representation in the older age-groups (Ambrose, 1979: 135–38), an observation supported by Gwegen (1975: 58) in the commune of Trédarzec, some 50 miles north of the study area, and in Brittany more generally (Bozec, reprinted in *Télégramme de Brest*, 1974). This factor would lead to a gradual decrease in the mobility of the Breton-speaking population, and mortality in the decades since the survey was conducted is likely to have made large inroads into this section of the population.

As an associated measure of the "potential" for Breton speaking, a later stage of the investigation asked a selection of Breton speakers to state the place where they had first learned the language. It could be contended that this is a useful indicator not only of the language border but of the health of the language area in general, since it allows the identification of areas where the language is "generated", before the process of recent or lifetime migration has modified the pattern. Applied in this locality (Figure 5.11), it confirmed the general extent of the language generation area, but was, of course, a retrospective measure, showing the process as it had functioned over the whole of the previous century. It must be remembered that the eldest of those included in the sample would have been alive at the time of Sébillot's survey, when the edge of the language area was possibly located further to the east than at present. The very restricted numbers of younger Breton speakers discovered (including only three pre-school children) would indicate that as a generator of the language, the area has ceased to function almost completely, and the area of generation has retreated an unknown distance westwards.

On the whole, in its methodology if not in the information obtained, this first step of the exercise was reassuring, producing clear transitions and offering encouragement to proceed to the next stage — the measuring of the use of language in practice, rather than just the numeric potential for speaking it. This is a process which is always likely to suffer from problems of subjectivity and inconsistency. One way to reduce these problems is for the field-worker to observe, listen to and make an accurate record of the language use of individuals or groups *in situ* over a fixed period, and under some circumstances that might be a valid way of measuring linguistic behaviour in border areas. But even such a rigorous procedure tends to bring with it its own problems of intrusiveness and atypical respondent behaviour, as well as being time-consuming and thus reducing the sample size greatly. In the present case, it was important that responses were obtained from large numbers of respondents, over

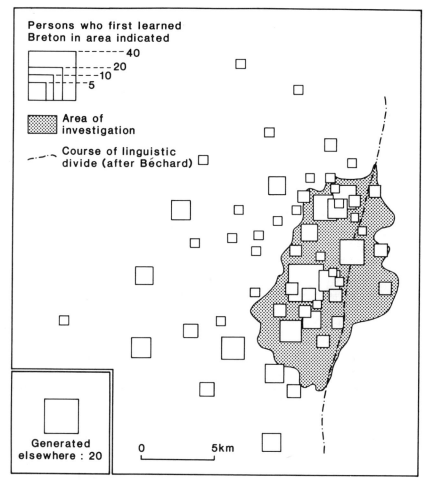

FIGURE 5.11   *Breton language generation*

the whole area. Thus it was that they were asked to make a self-assessment of their use of the Breton language, and the questions were phrased more simply than might have been ideal, in order to keep up the response level. Two aspects of language use in practice were chosen: "frequency" and "versatility" of use.

Taking the generalized zonation, proposed earlier, as a guide, the "frequency" measure was based on two working hypotheses: that increasing language potential would result in an increased frequency of use of Breton; and that, on that basis, further into the language area, there would be a greater reported frequency of its use. The frequency measure was assessed by the straightforward choice of a number of verbal descriptions of use, ranging from "speaks only Breton" to "knows Breton, but rarely or never speaks it". A standard procedure of allocating a score to each description followed, with scores for individual speakers being plotted at their home location. After the superimposition of a grid over the area and the averaging of scores for each grid square, to improve legibility, the information could be illustrated (Figure 5.12). On the basis of the scores used, areas with a score of between 2 and 3, indicating a regular or frequent use of Breton, could be said to be those where the language was in a healthy state of survival.

Nowhere in the study area achieved that score. The highest average for any square was 1.7, in an isolated corner of the south-west. Several interpretations present themselves. First, that the respondent sample was biased, in some way, against frequent speakers of Breton, and answered by disproportionately high numbers of infrequent users. Second, that there was some interpretation of such words as "frequently" or "rarely" which escaped attention in the phrasing of the frequency descriptions. Third, and more possibly, that the external factor of "power" or "status", referred to earlier, exerted an influence on speakers, causing many to understate their use of the language, because of its connotations with rurality, unsophistication and an old-fashioned, subsistence life-style. This attitude was quite frequently encountered during casual conversations with people in the area. A fourth reason for the low rates seems most probable of all: that is, that speakers really did find their frequency of usage to be low, especially when they compared it with the past, and that the Breton language in this locality was approaching the point of extinction, as an everyday medium of conversation.

Thus the potential for Breton use was not converted into practice, if this measure is to be believed. The "speaker isolation" of elderly people, offering reduced opportunities to meet and to use the language, could have lain at the root of the problem, especially under conditions of scattered farming settlement, a difficult communications network over much of the area, and lack of supporting structures as adequate broadcasting, newspapers and library services. Perhaps the very proximity to the border played a part in the process, by reducing the threshold number of Breton speakers on whom any individual might draw, or just by making continuance of the language seem not to be worthwhile. Only in one locality of the far south-west of the study area would it seem possible to see the local state of language survival in anything other than a profoundly pessimistic light. There, despite the stated rarity of Breton use, there remained a sufficiently large number of speakers, to judge

Average frequency scores for Breton speaking

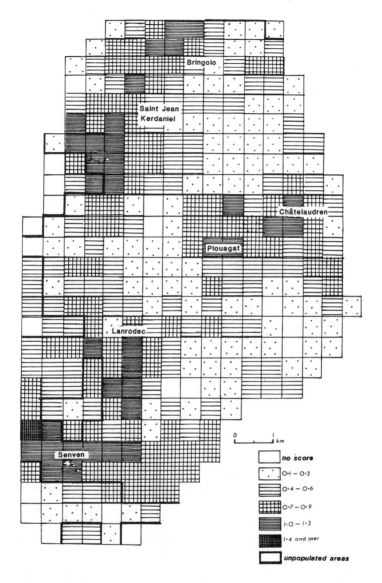

FIGURE 5.12 *Self-assessed frequency of Breton use*

from the response rate, to form a viable speaking group for everyday Breton use. Perhaps this corner of the study area was in a different zone of border transition, one step further towards the centre of the language area.

What of the second measure of use in practice, the "versatility" of Breton use? This measure has its origins, dating back at least to the 1930s, in the copious sociolinguistic literature which has attempted to relate language choice to environment. One of the best known examples is the work of Fishman (1965) looking at *"dyads"* (intra-household roles and language choice), but perhaps a closer approximation to the measure here is the concept which he discusses in a slightly later work (Fishman, 1971): the *"domain"* (for example, the home, school or church) as an influence on language choice of bilingual individuals. This time, the working hypothesis was that further across the language border there would tend to be an increased variety of domains in which Breton was used.

Figure 5.13 selects four from the rather larger number of domains used for the original work. The domains are arranged in increasing order of formality and decreasing order of privacy. For the home locations of speakers, the maps show their reported patterns of use of the language. For further details of the method, see Ambrose (1980).

It is clear, from Figure 5.13, that different domains did prompt differing degrees of Breton use, and that patterns of use also varied quite strikingly between domains. So often during fieldwork was the truism encountered that "Breton is a language of the home", that it was scarcely surprising to find that household use far exceeded that in the other domains (5.13b), though use in the immediate neighbourhood (5.13c), presumably an extension of home use, was also relatively common, in spatial terms if not in frequency. The shopping environment, even that of Châtelaudren, usually prompted an immediate switch to French (5.13d), and even the Catholic Church, with a good reputation for the preservation of the language throughout Brittany, seemed not to prompt a great response (5.13e). One local village *recteur* stated that he occasionally used the language for some parts of the Mass, but that, afterwards, conversation in the churchyard was invariably in French. Experience in the area more generally was that it was extremely rare to hear snatches of Breton in public places, except for two particular cafés — and even they might be regarded to some extent as extensions of the home domain.

To return more precisely to the earlier hypothesis, about versatility as a measure of the border, it can be seen from the summary diagram

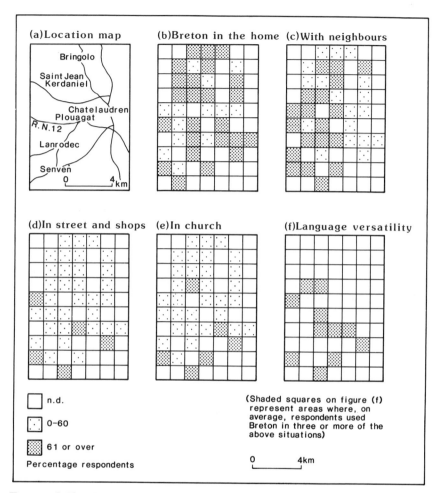

FIGURE 5.13 *Domain-related use of Breton*

(5.13f) that perhaps a limited amount of credence may be attached to the idea that further into the language area (at least, the south western corner of this study area), speakers were prepared to use the language in a greater variety of places. On the whole, however, the evidence is not substantial, and the measure could perhaps be tried out over a more extensive study area before being worthy of any stronger acceptance.

Taken overall, the measures of Breton use in practice did not live up to the promise in the strong pattern of transition on Figure 5.10, though there is some evidence of their validity, in purely methodological terms. The need for a broader study area, and a great deal more time to investigate usage within it, is perhaps the clearest conclusion to be drawn from this exercise in empiricism.

If, however, as the evidence indicates, the fate of Breton speaking in the area has been to pass from the status of vernacular tongue, the habitual language of most of the district, to that of relict feature, the preserve of a small group of mainly elderly, isolated people in a few remote corners, all within the lifetime of the oldest inhabitants, then a change in the geographical character of the border has clearly occurred. From being a well-demarcated language divide, it had evolved, by the 1970s, into a "zone of collapse" of the kind mentioned earlier (Ambrose & Williams, 1981), with all the linguistic confusion and uncertainty which accompanies such a process. Small wonder, perhaps, that the language was in such obvious spatial and social retreat within the study area.

Under such circumstances the attitudes and perceptions of local people, concerning the use of the French and Breton languages and the location of the language border, seem likely to have played a central role in the changes which have occurred. A final stage in this illustration of ways in which language borders can be measured and assessed therefore involved a brief excursion into the realms of cognitive mapping. If attitudes to the border were as important as implied, did they have a spatial expression, and could they be used to assess language border location?

The language border as mental image

Cognitive mapping examines the mind's ability to absorb, process and recall information about places. The use of such an approach implies a contrast with the assumed objectivity of positivist approaches, but it is perhaps best seen as a way of complementing them rather than supplanting them. Having gained rapid popularity in some areas of geography in the late 1960s and early 1970s, cognitive mapping has been the subject of increasingly frequent dissatisfaction in more recent times, often on the grounds that it can give the impression of being little more than a geographical game, of limited and uncertain significance in the understanding of processes at work (Tuan (1974), quoted in Downs (1981: 96); Pryce & Williams, this volume, Chapter 7).

The decision to make use of it here raises the possibility of criticism on just the same grounds. In this case, three goals were intended for it: the first was to seek for reasons why the study area should show such an apparent shortfall of Breton use in practice; the second, drawing on a theme discussed at the beginning of this chapter, in the international context, was to look specifically at the concept of "territoriality" at the edge of the language area, this time at the local scale; and the final aim was to make an assessment of the reliability of local opinion as a way of measuring the strength of Breton language survival in this area. If this opinion were to show itself to be internally consistent and capable of interpretation, and to accord with any of the previously-measured aspects of language in the area, then in the absence of official data it might be possible to use such cognitive methods again, elsewhere in Brittany, to make a diagnosis of the health of the language.

As an approach to measurement, however, the technique must, from the very outset, recognize a problem. Downs (1981: 106) is sharply to the point in asking:

"How can you measure a cognitive map? Or, as some would phrase the question, can you measure it?".

Perhaps all that could be expected of the procedure, in this case, is that it would act as a means of refining and assessing the reliability of the previous measures, rather than being as a measure in itself.

Difficulties also surrounded one of the aims, that of examining the concept of territory and its possible effects on language at the border. Earlier discussion of the shrinkage of the Breton-speaking territory over time had involved the scale of the whole of the language area; but subsequent evidence pointed to the disproportionately important role of the home and neighbourhood domains in keeping the language alive. This implies a different kind of territory — the local preserve of Breton speaking, an extension of the idea of personal space. Gold (1980: 89) confirms the distinction between scales of territory, also quoting the work of Altman (1975), which interprets the concept, instead, in terms of three levels of privacy and exclusivity: "primary", for example the home; "secondary", less exclusive territory, for example the neighbourhood; and the wider, "public" territory. From all this, the question emerged: would local Breton speakers, if they had a recognizable pattern of response, be more preoccupied with local patterns of use, or would their cognition reveal a wider image of the language area as a whole, perhaps reflecting linguistic divides or the broad division between *Breizh Izel* and *Breizh Uhel*?

Of all the potential pitfalls occurring at this stage, perhaps the greatest of all is that underlying the use of the word "map". It is one with which a geographer ought to be most familiar but, as used, for example, in the term "mental map", it gives rise to all kinds of misconceptions, frequently being intended merely as a synonym for "image". The two are not the same. A map ought to have a recognizable and consistent orientation and scale, to be free from ambiguities and, if its aims are reputable, should seek to tell a clear and accurate story, without over-generalizing or biased selection of material. In an individual's mental image, one could not expect any of these virtues. To present a person with a local map and to ask him or her to trace upon it the locality of the language border would not only bias the sample in terms of "cartographic literacy" but would invite the indulgence in all kinds of spatial prejudices, deliberate or otherwise, about the nature and location of the language border. While these are an undoubted part of every perception, the method used relied instead upon the use of names of localities within the study area, and the respondent sample selected from a series of verbal descriptions of the role which Breton played in each of the localities (see Figure 5.14). Only at the next stage were the descriptions converted into map form.

It could be argued that this was simply exchanging one source of bias for another, particularly in the use of the vague word "important" in the descriptions (for example *"Breton plays a very important part"*). It was a deliberate choice, made in an effort not to restrict the interpretation of the role of Breton just to "functional", day-to-day purposes, but to incorporate more traditional aspects of its place in the life of people in the area (such as the *festoù-noz* — evenings of folk song), or even less identifiable, but still influential, "spiritual" roles of the language, such as a feeling of continuity, belonging and identity with the locality. The drawback was that "bretonnants" and non Breton-speakers might interpret the word rather differently, the second group attaching a less abstract meaning to it, and thus suggesting a different pattern of usage. Such problems typify the doubts expressed by Downs in his earlier comment. It is possible to measure the results of such a process of enquiry, but not, in any totally reliable way, to measure the feelings which prompted those results.

In the face of all these doubts, one year after the first stages of the survey, another group of respondents, from the whole age range and including Breton and non-Breton speakers, answered a follow-up questionnaire, relating to a somewhat wider study area than previously. Figure 5.14 (a) was compiled from the results and, as anticipated, it immediately posed problems of interpretation. That some major change of opinion, concerning the role of Breton, occurred across the area was clear, and for simplicity of analysis, the modal description was taken as the basis for drawing the analysis map (5.14b). The logic of that is not

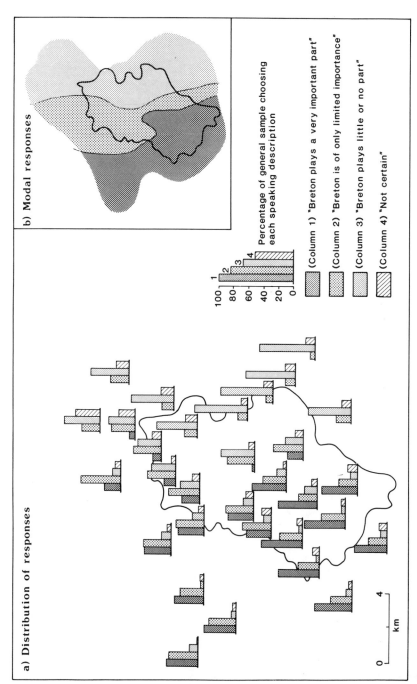

FIGURE 5.14 *Group image of the Breton language border in part of Côtes-du-Nord*

beyond dispute (since there does not seem to be any compelling reason why a non-modal description should not be most in accordance with reality), but the impression of linguistic transition was confirmed to exist in the minds of the respondent sample. The modal (and in some places the absolute majority) description that "Breton plays a very important part" picked out the south-west of the study area as being at a distinctly different phase of transition from the remainder. While that was hinted at on earlier maps, it goes almost without saying that the impression of a high degree of Breton-speaking activity given by this description is strictly at odds with the patterns of usage indicated by the first stage of the survey. That, in turn, must cast doubts on the accuracy of one or other of these sets of measures. Given the detailed fieldwork on which earlier evidence was based, together with all the more casual signs of linguistic collapse, it seems fair to conclude that in the case of this particular study area, the reliance on cognitive maps of local opinion as a guide to the location of the language border would be misguided indeed!

Perhaps such a map has other functions, however. With this in mind, the next step was to disaggregate the total sample into some of its component parts. Earlier observations, on the increasingly ageing nature of the "bretonnant" population (Bozec, 1974), and upon their feelings of cultural separation, provided two obvious sub-groups for such a division of the sample (Figure 5.15). The first was the elderly (over-60) people, over whose lifetime much of the erosion of local Breton speaking had taken place, and the second was the "Breton speakers", (represented by people who claimed an ability to speak the language, rather than those who did so in practice).

The first pair of maps (5.15a and 5.15b) shows the variation in opinion between age groups. Differences are not dramatic, in terms of areal contrast, and it seems fair to conclude that in this locality, at the time of the study, the language area was being eroded more quickly than its image was. Those who had the longest familiarity with the area maintained a group cognition of something which, by chance or otherwise, bore a close resemblance to Sébillot's or Béchard's divides, or to the assumed extent of *Breizh Izel*. For the youngest people in the area (many of whom came from families with a strong tradition of Breton speaking), the point where the main RN12 road crosses the area seemed to signal a greater acknowledgement of the influx of French influence, particularly in the village of Plouagat, whose degree of Breton retention seemed to occasion much local disagreement, but which was now almost completely francophone in the eyes of the young.

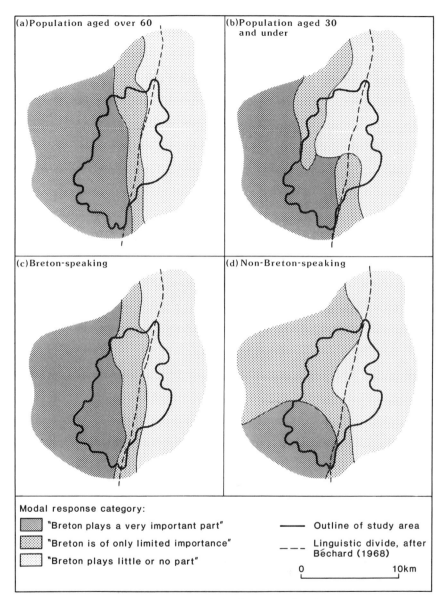

FIGURE 5.15 *Sub-group images of the language border*

The division by age groups was, of course, tantamount to dividing the population into Breton and non-Breton speaking cohorts, but that is done more directly in Figures 5.15 (c) and 5.15 (d). The map for Breton speakers confirms a strong sense of linguistic "territory", according more with tradition than practical usage, while that of the remainder of the population is a more graphic illustration of decreased Breton influence in almost the whole area. Looking back to Figure 5.14, it can be seen that even in the west of the area a section of the respondents steadfastly maintained that "Breton is of only limited importance", adding weight to the suspicion that non-speakers of Breton perhaps attached a rather different meaning to that description, interpreting it in terms of what they saw as the language's limited value in the economy and regional development of the new Brittany.

A look at individual responses inside the general pattern of cognition reveals two interesting aspects of the response patterns of individuals. First, there was a frequent occurrence of what is sometimes called the "over-the-hill reaction". (*We do not use the language here, but go over the hill. There you will find it.*") Most individuals, if they considered that "Breton played a very important part", tended not to use it for their own locality, but for those at some distance away — presumably on the assumption that it must be in a stronger state than in their own corner of the study area. Second, though responses on individual points varied, almost every respondent had in mind a clearly-demarcated transition, with a series of zones running generally parallel to the lines of the linguistic divides (or, more appropriately, perhaps, to the line of distinction between *Breizh Izel* and *Breizh Uhel*). Impressions were an idealized view of the broader linguistic and cultural divide, rather than of local details.

What interpretation is to be put upon this, if any? It seems appropriate to recall what is, to date, perhaps one of the most thoughtful (and, incidentally, critical) appraisals of "mental mapping" exercises: that of Tuan (1975). Aiming his comments at geographers generally, he calls into question the whole compatibility of such exercises with the behavioural approach (Tuan, 1975: 205). To interpret his arguments in this context: the behaviour of local Breton speakers may be a key to understanding the fortunes of the language; but what evidence is there that mental images are the key, in turn, to understanding their behaviour? They may hold two quite separate images: that of where the language area is and that of where they would like it to be.

In connection with this, one unexpected response should be reported: quite spontaneously, some local respondents — a small number, compared with the total sample — volunteered their opinion that the line (*sic*) of the language border did indeed run through this area, and that "it followed this wood", or "ran the other side of that village", or "along that particular river gorge". In view of the early dismissal (outside the context of the political frontier) of the applicability of the concept of a line as the division between linguistic groups in twentieth-century Europe, and of its replacement by a postulated "zone of collapse", such images came as something of a surprise. It need hardly be said that there was no consensus on the precise route of the line, but the very willingness to conceive of such a sharp transition and to nominate "landscape markers" for the edge of the language area raises, once again, the spectre of the linguistic divide, together with a multitude of concepts from regional geographies long presumed dead. Tuan's further comments on the definition of the word "image" are of relevance. They include the idea of a "*mental picture in the memory*" and "*a schematic knowledge of place*", rather than an accurate portrayal of current detail. An image, as opposed to a percept, is "*something we see when the environmental stimuli do not appear to justify it*" (Tuan, 1975: 208). It seems clear that what was measured here was a folk-memory, a communal self-assertion, perhaps a self-deception, on the part of some cultural sub-groups, rather than the reality of the language border.

The passage of the relatively short span of years since the study was made seems likely to have been enough to have destroyed what remained of the fabric of Breton speaking in this particular study area, and while the reader may begin to appreciate exactly why so little geographical fieldwork has been undertaken in the Breton language area, there is a critical and pressing need for more micro-scale case-study areas to be examined, in this and other regions of Brittany, if a realistic impression of the process of decline is to be gained, and if a practical strategy for the defence of the language is ever to be evolved.

The sad and frustrating impression gained from this exercise is perhaps best likened to the feelings of one who has arrived at a theatre just in time to witness the closing scenes of a long play. Elsewhere in Brittany, on the border and further west, it seems justified to conclude that similar final scenes are being played out, year by year, apparently before uncomprehending or uncaring audiences.

Bibliography

AAREBROT, F.H., 1982, On the structural basis of regional mobilization in Europe. In B. DE MARCHI & A.M. BOILEAU (eds), *Boundaries and Minorities in Western Europe.* Milan: Franco Angeli Editore, 32–91.

ALLARDT, E., 1981, Reflections on Stein Rokkan's conceptual map of Europe, *Scandinavian Political Studies*, 4, 257–71.

ALTMAN, I., 1975, *The Environment and Social Behavior.* Monterey: Brooks-Cole.

AMBROSE, J.E., 1979, *A Geographical Study of Language Borders in Wales and Brittany.* University of Glasgow: Doctoral Thesis.

—— 1980, Micro-scale language mapping: An experiment in Wales and Brittany. *Discussion Papers in Geolinguistics*, No. 2. Stoke-on-Trent.

AMBROSE, J.E. & WILLIAMS, C.H., 1981, On the spatial definition of minority: Scale as an influence on the geolinguistic analysis of Welsh. In E. HAUGEN, J.D. MCCLURE & D.S. THOMSON (eds), *Minority Languages Today.* Edinburgh: Edinburgh University Press.

BÉCHARD, G., 1968, Les Noms de Lieux en Pays Gallo. *Mouez ar Vro*, No. 2. Rennes: Collège Breton.

BOZEC, J.-C., 1974, Survey of Breton speaking; Results communicated to the *Télégramme de Brest* by R. Laouénan, 21st February, 1974.

CHADWICK, N., 1965, The colonization of Brittany from Celtic Britain. *Proceedings of the British Academy*, Vol. 51. London: Oxford University Press.

COX, K.R. & GOLLEDGE, R.G. (eds) 1981, *Behavioral Problems in Geography Revisited.* London: Methuen

DENEZ, P., 1983, The present state of the Celtic languages: Breton. *Proc. 6th International Congress of Celtic Studies*, University College, Galway, 6th–13th July, 1979. Dublin: Institute for Advanced Studies, 73–81.

DOWNS, R.M., 1981, Cognitive mapping: A thematic analysis. In K.R. COX & R.G. GOLLEDGE (eds), *Behavioral Problems in Geography Revisited.* London: Methuen.

ELEGOËT, F., 1971–2, *La Domination Linguistique en Bretagne: Essai d'Approche à partir d'une Enquête à Grouanec en Plouguerneau, Nord-Finistère.* University of Paris-Nanterre: thesis for Maîtrise de Sociologie.

FALC'HUN, F., 1962, Une Controverse sur les Origines de la Langue Bretonne. *Les Cahiers de L'Iroise*, Oct.–Dec. 1962, 178–84.

—— 1963, *Histoire de la Langue Bretonne, d'après la Géographie Linguistique.* Paris: Presses Universitaires de France.

—— 1966 and 1970, (with B. Tanguy). *Les Noms de Lieux Celtiques* (2 vols.). Rennes: Éditions Armoricaines.

FISHMAN, J.A., 1965, Who Speaks What Language to Whom and When? *La Linguistique*, Vol. 2, 67–88.

—— 1971, The relationship between micro- and macro-sociolinguistics in the study of who speaks what language to whom and when. In J.B. PRIDE & J. HOLMES (eds), *Sociolinguistics*. Harmondsworth: Penguin.

FLATRÈS, P., 1986, *La Bretagne*. Paris: Presses Universitaires de France.

GICQUEL, Y., 1986, Oser Accoupler Culture et Économie Bretonnes. In F. ELEGOËT, *Bretagne 2000*. Plabennec: Tud ha Bro, Sociétés Bretonnes.

GOLD, J.R., 1980, *An Introduction to Behavioural Geography*. Oxford: Oxford University Press.

GORDON, D.C. 1978, *The French Language and National Identity*. The Hague: Mouton.

GOURVIL, F., 1960, *Langue et Littérature Bretonnes*. Paris: Presses Universitaires de France.

G.R.E.L.B. (GROUPE DE RECHERCHE SUR L'ÉCONOMIE LINGUISTIQUE DE LA BRETAGNE) 1986, *Prépublications, 6ème Journée d'étude*, 31 mai, 1986. Brest: Centre de Recherche Bretonne et Celtique, Université de Bretagne Occidentale, Faculté des Lettres et des Sciences Sociales.

GWEGEN, J., 1975, *La Langue Bretonne Face à ses Oppresseurs*. Quimper: Nature et Bretagne.

HÉMON, R., 1929, Enklask Diwar-Benn Stad ar Brezoneg e 1928, *Gwalarn*, 17–19.

—— 1947, *La Langue Bretonne et ses Combats*. La Baule: Éditions de Bretagne.

HUDSON, J.C., 1972, Geographical diffusion theory. *Northwestern Studies in Geography*, no. 19.

KANN, R.A., 1974, *A History of the Habsburg Empire, 1526–1918*. Berkeley: University of California Press.

KANN, R.A. & DAVID, Z.V., 1984, *The Peoples of the Eastern Habsburg Lands, 1526–1918*. Seattle: University of Washington Press.

KREJKI, J. & VELIMSKY, V., 1981, *Ethnic and Political Nations in Europe*. London: Croom Helm.

LOTH, J., 1907, Les Langues Romane et Bretonne en Armorique. *Revue Celtique*, Vol. 28, 374–403.

LUNDÉN, T., 1973a, *Individens Rumsliga Beteende i ett Gränsområde*. Kulturgeografiska Institutionen, B26. Stockholm: Stockholms Universiteit.

—— 1973b, Interaction across an 'Open' international boundary: Norway – Sweden. In R. STRASSOLDO (ed.), *Confini e Regioni*. Trieste: Edizioni LINT, 147–61.

—— 1980, Language, geography and social development in Norden.

Discussion Papers in Geolinguistics, No. 3. Stoke-on-Trent.
—— 1982, Linguistic minorities in boundary areas: the case of Northern Europe. In B. DE MARCHI & A.M. BOILEAU (eds), *Boundaries and Minorities in Western Europe*. Milan: Franco Angeli Editore, 149–63.
MACKEY, W.F., 1973, *Three Concepts for Geolinguistics*. Quebec: International Center for Research on Bilingualism, Publication B-42.
MARKALE, J., 1985, *Identité de Bretagne*. Paris: Éditions Entente.
MEINIG, D.W., 1969, *Imperial Texas: an Interpetative Essay in Cultural Geography*. Austin: University of Texas press.
MUSSET, R., 1937, *La Bretagne*. Paris: Armand Colin.
PARKER, G., 1983, *A Political Geography of Community Europe*. London: Butterworths.
PRYCE, W.T.R., 1975, Migration and the evolution of culture areas: Cultural and linguistic frontiers in north-east Wales, 1750 and 1851. *Transactions of the Institute of British Geographers* No. 65, 79–107.
RATZEL, H. 1897, *Politische Geographie*. Munich: Oldenbourg.
ROKKAN, S., 1980, Territories, centres and peripheries. In J. GOTTMAN (ed.), *Centre and Periphery*. London: Sage, 163–204.
ROKKAN, S. & URWIN, D.W. (eds) 1982, *The Politics of Territorial Identity*. London: Sage.
ROUSSEAU, J.-M., 1986, L'influence des transformations de l'économie bretonne sur la langue bretonne depuis le début du siècle. *Prépublications, 6ème journée d'étude* G.R.E.L.B. (*q.v.*), 1–4.
RUSSETT, B., 1973, Communications and Discussions. In R. STRASSOLDO (ed.), *Confini e Regioni*. Trieste: Edizioni LINT, p. 485.
SÉBILLOT, F., 1886, La Langue Bretonne: Limites et Statistique. *Revue d'Ethnographie*, 1–29.
SÉRANT, P., 1965, *La France des Minorités*. Paris: Robert Laffont.
SMITH, A.D., 1986, *The Ethnic Origins of Nations*. Oxford: Blackwell.
STEPHENS, M., 1976, *Linguistic Minorities in Western Europe*. Llandysul: Gomer.
STRASSOLDO, R., 1973, *Confini e Regioni*. Trieste: Edizioni LINT.
SUGAR, P.F., 1977, *Southeastern Europe under Ottoman Rule, 1354–1804*. Seattle: University of Washington Press.
TÄGIL, S. *et al.* 1977 *Studying Boundary Conflicts*. Lund: Esselte Studium.
TUAN, Y., 1974, Review of P.R. Gould and R. White: *Mental Maps*. In: *Annals of the Association of American Geographers*, Vol. 64, 589–91.
—— 1975, Images and mental maps. *Annals of the Association of American Geographers*, Vol. 65, 205–13.
WEINSTEIN, B., 1983, *The Civic Tongue*. London: Longmans.
WILLIAMS, C.H., 1977, Ethnic perceptions of Acadia. *Cahiers de Géographie de Québec*, Vol. 21, nos. 53–4, 243–68.

—— 1980, Ethnic separatism in Western Europe. *Tijdschrift voor Economische en Sociale Geografie*, 71, 142–58.

—— (ed.) 1982, *National Separatism*. Cardiff: The University of Wales Press.

—— 1985, Minority groups in the modern state. In M. PACIONE (ed.), *Progress in Political Geography*. Beckenham: Croom Helm, 111–51.

—— 1986, The Question of National Congruence. In R.J. JOHNSTON & P.J. TAYLOR (eds), *A World in Crisis?* Oxford: Blackwell, 196–230.

ZELINSKY, W., 1973, *The Cultural Geography of the U.S.* Englewood Cliffs, N.J.: Prentice-Hall.

6 The Geographical History of Gaelic in Scotland

CHARLES W.J. WITHERS
College of St. Paul and St. Mary
Cheltenham, U.K.

Introduction

The geographical and historical study of languages and their change over space and time may involve analysis of the extent of a language area at a given date — the "geography of languages" (Delgado De Carvalho, 1962) — or an assessment of the variation over time and space of the language itself, "word geography", "linguistic geography" or "dialect geography" (Iordan & Orr, 1970). The term "geolinguistics" has also been advanced to describe the analysis of the distribution patterns and spatial structure of languages in contact, and the concern of historical geolinguistics has been the examination of such patterns and structures in the past (Williams, 1980). To be anything more than a narrative of distributional change, however, assessment of language shift in the past should aim at explanation of the patterns and an identification of the mechanics of language shift. This chapter is an attempt to document in broad outline the changing geography of the Gaelic language in Scotland and to explain those changes.

The geographical history of Gaelic in Scotland is largely one of decline. A fall in the numbers speaking the language (Figure 6.1) has been paralleled by the retreat of the Highlands or *Gaidhealtachd* — the Gaelic speaking area — and a decline of intensity of use within the Gaidhealtachd. The shifting position of the language is thus a complex story of social and geographical change not just within the Gaelic areas, but within Scotland as a whole. What follows reviews a number of works upon the place, past and present, of the Gaelic language in Scotland, but is chiefly concerned with an examination of the geography of Gaelic from the late seventeenth century to the present, and an explanation, not just of where and when the language was spoken in Scotland in the past, but also of how and why Gaelic has declined as it has. In conclusion, attention is paid to the contemporary (and future) geography of Gaelic in Scotland using the evidence of the 1981 Census.

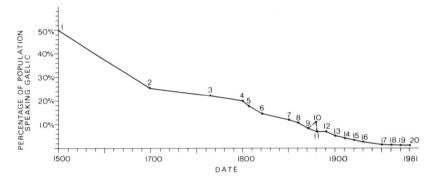

I. From Campbell 1950. 2. Estimate based on Hearth Tax, Poll Tax and 1698 M.P.L.H.P 3. J.Walker c.1765 - c.1769. 4. From Campbell 1950. 5. Earl of Selkirk 1806. 6. Estimate based on Moral Statistics 1826. 7. Estimate based on 1851 Edinburgh Almanac. 8. Estimate based on 1861 Edinburgh Almanac. 9. Estimate based on 1871 Edinburgh Almanac. 10. E.Ravenstein 1879. 11. 1881 Census and C.Fraser-Mackintosh 1881. 12–20. Census evidence 1891–1981.

FIGURE 6.1   *Gaelic speakers as a percentage of Scotland's population, 1500–1981*

Gaelic in medieval and early modern Scotland

Gaelic is a member of the Goidelic or Q-Celtic languages and was introduced to what is now Scotland by the Scottic people of Ireland about the year AD 500 (Bannerman, 1974). Several languages were known and spoken in Scotland in the early sixth century (Jackson, 1953). Gaelic, Cumbric, Norse, Pictish and Anglian were all spoken, each with varying prevalence over others in different parts of Scotland. The processes whereby Gaelic supplanted these other languages was not everywhere the same throughout early Scotland (Watson, 1914–1916), but by the late eleventh century Gaelic had superimposed itself upon rather than replaced, the above languages. The geographical distribution and relative proportion of Gaelic-derived place names throughout Scotland reflects the varying strength of that language: in the areas north and west of the Forth and Clyde valleys Gaelic names predominate. In the south-east lowlands

Gaelic names are not as common and suggest a less permanent and less dense settlement by Gaelic speakers in the past (Nicolaisen, 1964, 1970, 1976). Murison (1974) has suggested that Gaelic attained its maximum geographical spread — from Pentland Firth to the Tweed — by the early twelfth century. Gaelic's territorial advance was not, however, equatable with the wholesale adoption of that language throughout Scotland: at no time in early modern, medieval or even dark age Scotland was Gaelic everywhere understood and spoken for all purposes by all persons (Withers, 1984: 18). By the later twelfth century, Gaelic — known as Scottish — was predominant north of the Forth and Clyde; Norman-French was the commonly-used language of court; Latin was used for documentary purposes and religious duties and Anglo-Saxon was the language of towns, of trade, and, to an extent, of the upper classes (Sharp, 1928). Norse survived in the western isles until the late thirteenth century and in parts of Orkney and Shetland probably until the early eighteenth century (Flom, 1952; Jakobsen, 1928).

Gaelic's "long linguistic retreat" begins from the late eleventh and early twelfth centuries (Duncan, 1975; Murison, 1974; Withers, 1984). Just as the complex over-laying of languages in early medieval Scotland makes it difficult to know in detail the regional variations in intensity of use of Gaelic at that period, so it is also difficult to identify the mechanisms behind Gaelic's decline. Several authors have considered the retreat to begin from the reign of Malcolm III (1058–1093) and his English-born wife, Margaret. Rait (1914) identified nine reasons for the decline of Gaelic from this period: the influence of the Scottish court; the authority of the Roman over the Celtic Church; the transition from tribalism to feudalism within Scotland; the spread of English-dominated trade; the rise in status of the English language among the upper classes; an increased Anglicization in language and in personnel among the ecclesiastical hierarchy; placement of areas of land under Anglo-Norman hegemony; English-speaking merchants living in Scottish burghs; and what he termed "the general shift toward an English way-of-life" (Rait, 1914: 258–59). The movement of Scotland's "capital" or seat of power into the less-strongly Gaelic south east and the frequent wars with England may also have undermined Gaelic's position (MacKinnon, 1974: 21–22; Mitchell, 1900: 195). What is important to note is that these changes were neither sudden in coming nor everywhere equally felt. Gaelic was certainly less used in court and amongst the nobility from this period yet James IV (1488–1513) knew and spoke the language. The growth of Scotland's market economy in this period was not a national phenomenon: it was centred on those areas south of the Forth and Clyde and through the burghs and ports of the eastern coastal lowlands. English rose in importance up the social scale but took centuries to do so. And most critical of all in the light of later patterns of language use is the fact that feudal tenures were largely unknown north of the Forth and Clyde and where they did find expression in that area it was in a limited way along the eastern seaboard. The fact was that feudalism scarcely affected the north and west, the rugged nature of the land in those parts with scanty soils and with a dispersed population distant from the authority of the king and parliament allowing those areas to exist almost untroubled by events in the lowlands. The result, by the late fourteenth century, was the emergence of the Highlands as a distinct cultural and linguistic region in Scotland (Barrow, 1973: 362; Smout, 1969: 39). The areas of north and western upland were synonymous as they had not been before about 1380 with the *Gaidhealtachd* (Joannis de Fordun, 1759). The emergence of the Highlands as a distinct language area and the separation between Highlands and Lowlands in Scotland's geography and culture were paralleled by important changes of status for the Gaelic and English languages.

Throughout the medieval period, those variants of the English language spoken over much of south and east Scotland were known as "Inglis" (Murray, 1873: 41–42). As Scotland developed a national and cultural distinctiveness apart from England, the term "Inglis" used to describe the language of the Lowlands became inappropriate (Nicholson, 1978: 274). As a result of its increasing social and political status, the English language in the Lowlands became known as "Scottis", and Gaelic became known as "Yrisch", "Ersch" or "Erse" in reference to its Irish origins. The fact that Gaelic lost its political associations as the Scottish language and as the language of social esteem at the same time as the Highlands emerged as a separate cultural area are crucial elements in the early history of Gaelic in Scotland. Evidence for Gaelic's loss of status and its cultural alienation in the middle ages is quite well documented, but the same is not true of the evidence available to understand the actual territorial extent of the Gaelic areas. Gaelic was probably extinct as the native vernacular in the central lowlands by about 1350 and only a little later amongst the population of the eastern coastal lowlands from Kincardineshire to Nairn (Barrow, 1973: 363; Grant Michie, 1908: 285). Gaelic continued to be used in the more remote parishes of south west Scotland until the later sixteenth century at least (Armstrong, 1884: IV, 17). By that period and into the 1600s, Gaelic had become the focus of direct political policy.

When James VI and I (1567–1625) addressed parliament in 1604 he spoke of how God had "united these two Kingdoms ... in Language,

Religion and similitude of manners" (Daiches, 1977: 15). The unity was more apparent than real: Gaelic was the language of perhaps half of Scotland's people; the Highlands remained largely apart from the affairs of the English-speaking Lowlands. It was this very separateness and linguistic distinctiveness that those policies initiated in the seventeenth century sought to counter. Gaelic was regarded as culturally inferior: English was considered the language of a civilized nation. An act of the Privy Council, on 10 December 1616, may be taken as illustration: the act termed Gaelic "... one of the chief and principall causes of the continewance of barbaritie and incivilitie amongis the inhabitantis of the Ilis and Heylandis" and equated "the vulgar Inglishe toung" with "civilitie, godliness, knawledge, and learning" (Register of the Privy Council, 1616, X; 671–72). From this period the Highlands became the focus of educational and religious policies aimed at the extension of the English language (see below). And it is through evidence dating from the last years of the seventeenth century that we are afforded the earliest detailed picture of the geography of Gaelic in Scotland.

The past geography of Gaelic, 1698–1981

The earliest picture we have of the nation-wide extent of Gaelic is dated at 1698 (Withers, 1980). In that year, a series of lists was drawn up to assist in the distribution of the Irish Gaelic Bible in the Highlands and these source lists, produced largely on a parish-by-parish basis, have been used to infer the extent of the *Gaidhealtachd* (Figure 6.2). The population of Scotland at this time is uncertain. Estimates have been given at 800,000 for the year 1700 and 1,048,000 in 1707 (Flinn, 1977: 52–53): a more exact figure for the Gaelic areas is impossible given the limited coverage of the hearth and poll tax records for the Highlands. It is reasonable to suggest, however, that the total population of Scotland in the late 1690s stood at about 900,000 of whom perhaps 30% spoke Gaelic.

Of course, the patterns of language use on the ground were much more complex than a dividing line on a map suggests: the varying boundary between the Gaelic and non-Gaelic parishes, for 1698 and later, should be interpreted as shifts of a diffuse zone rather than changes in a firm border. Not everyone in the *Gaidhealtachd* spoke only Gaelic. English was spoken in preference to Gaelic by some and in several parishes nearer the Lowlands was quite widely used for a number of purposes. Gaelic seems to have been particularly preferred as the

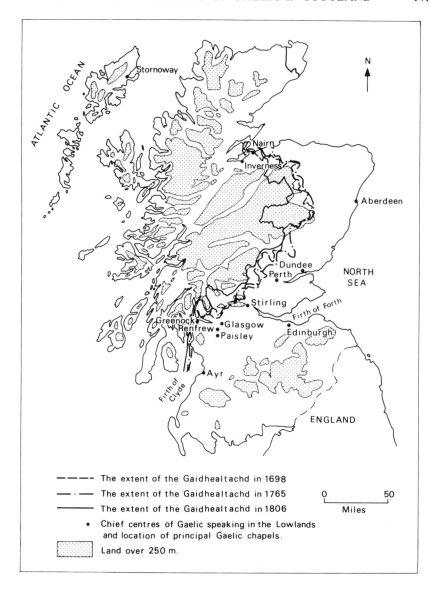

Figure 6.2   *The geographical extent of the Gaidhealtachd, 1698–1806, and chief centres of Gaelic speaking in the Lowlands*

domestic language and for religious uses: as one contemporary source noted, even persons of Highland origin who had lived for some years "in those parts where they speak English have never acquired so much skill in that language, as to be able to understand a Sermon in it". There were also many Gaelic speakers who could "buy and sell in English, who does not understand a Sermon in that language" (Kirkwood quoted in Withers, 1984: 53–54). But the great majority of persons in the Highlands at this period spoke only Gaelic.

By the early eighteenth century, there is some evidence to suggest that English was becoming more widespread in some Gaidhealtachd border parishes. Graham, writing in the 1720s, considered Gaelic the only language in south-west Perthshire at that period (Graham in Mitchell, 1906: I, 335), but a recent evaluation of the situation in one parish in that area has suggested that English was well known and widely used by native parishioners (Withers, 1982). Martin (1703) noted how Gaelic and English were both spoken on Bute and Arran at that time, with Gaelic prevailing on the west of Arran and English on the east (Martin, 1703: 225). In south-west Argyll, English had been known longer and used more widely than in many other areas of the Highlands (McKerral, 1948). Burt (1726) records how Gaelic and English were both used for religious administration throughout the southern half of Argyllshire, although Gaelic was commonly used in most other walks of life. In Caithness and Sutherland at the same period, the language border was established as it had been in 1698 with Gaelic predominant to the west and to the east, Gaelic increasingly displaced for most social uses, except in religion, by English (Bayne 1735 in Donaldson, 1936: 13). John Home, writing in his History of the Rebellion in the Year 1745, noted the difficulties in putting a firm boundary to so fluid a thing as language:

> "the same shire, the same parish at this day, contains part of both, so that a Highlander and Lowlander (each of them standing at the door of the cottage where he was born) hear their neighbours speak a language which they do not understand" (Home, 1802: 3).

These complex patterns are well illustrated in the case of Perthshire, whose physical geography as a county mirrors that of Scotland as a nation and whose linguistic history has been characterized, since the early fourteenth century, by a strongly Gaelic north and west merging through a zone of transition into an English south and east (Withers, 1983). In Perthshire's isolated northern parishes, English was spoken by only 15 to 20% of the population by the 1750s and 1760s, but in several southern and eastern parishes, English was known and regularly employed by over three-quarters of the population.

This evidence is substantiated by that of Walker, which, although published early in the nineteenth century, was collected during the period 1760 to 1786 (McKay, 1980: 8). Walker considered the Highlands those areas where Gaelic was "either preached or spoken by the natives" (Walker, 1808: I, 19); the Highland boundary for the 1760s may be seen from Figure 6.2. Using population tables for the year 1755, it is possible to estimate the numbers speaking Gaelic at that time at about 289,798 persons, a little under 23% of Scotland's population (see Figure 6.1). Evidence is less forthcoming as to how Gaelic and English were actually used in daily life in the Gaelic areas. It appears that Gaelic was the language of the heart and the hearth, and, as we have also seen it to be from the late seventeenth century, much preferred to English as the language of worship. English was used only by a few for religious purposes, although it was becoming more widespread as a result of schooling and through contact with the south (see below). Several Highland "towns" — in reality little more than villages in the eighteenth century — were reckoned chiefly English by contemporary observers (Burt, 1754: I, 40; Lettice, 1794: 339–40), and the extension of spoken English through trade was hastened by the temporary migration of Highlanders to the harvest, fishing, and textile mills in the Lowlands (Durkacz, 1983: 156; Withers, 1984: 108–110).

Many of the statements on Gaelic in the first or 'Old' *Statistical Account of Scotland* (1791–1799) (hereinafter the *O.S.A.*) document social variations in language use and hint at the retreat of Gaelic by the end of the eighteenth century (Price, 1976–1978; 1979). Gaelic was waning in most upland parishes of Aberdeenshire and Banffshire and eastern Ross and Cromarty. In the central and north-western Highlands, Gaelic was still "generally spoken", though there were few parishes where, to quote from the 1792 report on Durness in Sutherland, English was not making "considerable progress among the people" (*O.S.A.*, 1792: III, 581). Argyllshire exhibited complex patterns of language shift at this period: English more common in the villages and towns such as Inveraray and Campbeltown; Gaelic more widely spoken by the old than the young; English being introduced through trade with the south and, understandably, more widespread in the south-east mainland of the county than in the islands; Gaelic widely preferred in spiritual administration and used in most social domains, English increasingly employed in them all (Price, 1979: 246–47).

At the same time as the Gaidhealtachd proper was declining by the end of the eighteenth century, a new geography of Gaelic was emerging with the establishment of communities of Highland migrants and of Gaelic chapels of worship in the cities of the Lowlands. Highlanders had been resident in places like Glasgow and Greenock since the early eighteenth century at least, but not until the later 1700s were they present in sufficient numbers to warrant the construction of separate places of worship. Chapels were opened in Edinburgh in 1769, in Glasgow in 1770 and 1798, in Aberdeen in 1781, Perth in 1787, Dundee in 1791, and in Greenock and Paisley in 1792 and 1793 respectively (Withers, 1984: 185). These chapels provided a focus for lowland-resident Gaels. Several Highlanders had jobs as managers and industrialists, but the majority found employment as porters, chairmen or labourers. In Edinburgh, the Town Guard was largely made up of Gaelic speakers (Arnot, 1779). By the later nineteenth century there were 17,978 Gaelic speakers resident in Glasgow, 4,781 in Edinburgh and 3,191 in Greenock (Census 1891). By 1981, there were more people professing ability in Gaelic in urbanized Strathclyde Region than in the traditional Western Isles "heartland" of the language.

Writing in 1806, Thomas Douglas, the fifth Earl of Selkirk, reckoned the Highlands to be those areas where Gaelic was regularly used in church service (Selkirk, 1806: Appendix V, lvi). The boundary derived from his work reveals, in comparison with the position of the Gaelic–English border in 1698 and c.1765, the retreat of Gaelic in parts of Dunbartonshire, southern Perthshire, and in upland Aberdeenshire and Moray (Figure 6.2). In contrast, Cromarty parish in eastern Ross and Cromarty became increasingly Gaelic owing to an influx of Highlanders to work in the hemp factory there (Mowat, 1981: 137). An estimated 18.5% of Scotland's population spoke Gaelic in the first decade of the nineteenth century.

By the 1830s and 1840s, it is possible to record in some detail the changed situation with regard to language in several Highland parishes. Statements on Gaelic in the *Second* or "New" *Statistical Account of Scotland*, published in 15 volumes between 1831 and 1845, may be used in comparison with those in the *O.S.A.* 50 years before. Consider the case of Comrie parish in central Perthshire. In 1794, the sources record "The common language of the people is Gaelic" (*O.S.A.*, 1794: XI, 186): by 1838, we were told "The English language is generally spoken, and has gained ground greatly within the last 40 years" (*N.S.A.*, 1838: 10, 586). Similar change had occurred along the Gaelic–English border in other counties, and even in the more strongly Gaelic north and west, English was much more widely known and regularly used in the 1840s than it had been in the 1790s. Although we must allow for variation at and within the scale of the parish, it is clear that the patterns characterizing the border parishes in the 1790s were apparent in the less isolated parts of the north and west Highlands by the 1830s and 1840s and that, by that period, parishes nearer the Lowlands had become chiefly English in language.

This geographical retreat of Gaelic was mirrored in the "purity" of its use. Just as Gaelic has long been spoken more widely in the north and west in the past, so it also appears to have been spoken more correctly and with less admixture of English words and idiom. Martin (1703) and Walker (1808) both reckoned the Gaelic of Eriskay in the Western Isles to be very pure on account of its isolation, but in the transition zone of central Perthshire, Marshall, writing in the 1790s, recorded how Gaelic spoken there was marked by "the Lowland accent, the tone and many of the provincialisms of the Lowlands" (Marshall, 1794: 233). These patterns of "language interference" (Weinrich, 1953: 1) were themselves characterized by age and sex differences in the use of Gaelic or English. Gaelic seems to have been longer retained and more properly used by the elderly: the young, and particularly the men, were more familiar with English. When they did employ Gaelic, their use of it was often marked by borrowings from English or by switching from Gaelic to English (Withers, 1984: 75–76).

By the 1870s, the decreasing intensity in use of Gaelic was widespread throughout the Gaidhealtachd. The Gaelic border as understood by Murray in 1873, and Ravenstein in 1879 (Figure 6.3), embraced an area very similar in extent to that of 1698 (Figure 6.2), but it was an area much less strongly Gaelic. Murray's Gaelic boundary delimited the *outside limits* of the Gaelic ". . . that is, every district is included in which Gaelic is still *spoken by any natives*; regardless of the fact that English may be spoken by the majority of the people" [original emphasis] (Murray, 1873: 232). In several districts, Gaelic was spoken only as a result of incoming Highland migrants: in others, English-speaking immigrants had introduced that language to parishes that had been chiefly Gaelic fifty or a hundred years earlier. Ravenstein's survey of the numbers speaking Gaelic throughout Scotland re-affirms what earlier evidence has suggested. The retreat of Gaelic by the later 1870s was very marked along the border parishes and even in the more isolated parts of Ross and Cromarty and Inverness, Gaelic was less and less widely used. Gaelic was still widely used in church services, but was not used by the young as much as it had been in earlier generations and was seldom used as a school language (Ravenstein, 1879: 592–599). Many of these patterns are reflected in the census statistics on Gaelic, begun in 1881.

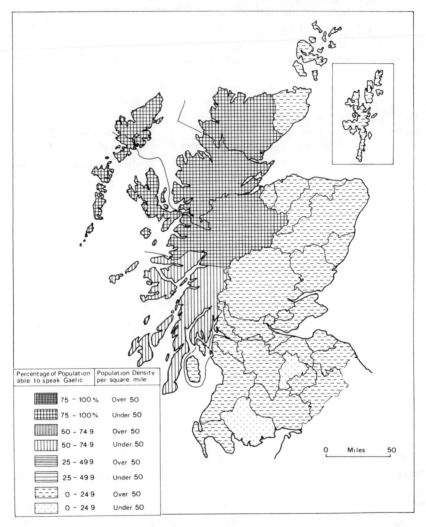

FIGURE 6.3   *Gaelic speaking in relation to population density, by county*
1881
(For key to counties, see Figure 6.6)

  The census is an important aid to an examination of the geographical
and social shift of Gaelic. Its evidence reinforces the picture provided by
earlier sources on the regional variation in intensity of language within
the Highlands and, in so doing, brings the geographical history of Gaelic
up to date.

THE GEOGRAPHICAL HISTORY OF GAELIC IN SCOTLAND   147

A total of 231,594 persons were recorded as Gaelic speakers in the census of 1881, a little over 6.7% of Scotland's total population (Census, 1881: I, iv). There is some evidence to suggest that this figure underenumerates the total Gaelic population, by perhaps 5,000 persons (Fraser-Mackintosh, 1881: 438–41). Later censuses also present difficulties. The 1891 census was the first to ask questions about ability in Gaelic and English, not just Gaelic. The difference in the questions asked and the likely under-representation of a decade earlier are responsible for a registered increase in Gaelic speakers from 1881 to the 1891 total of 254,415 persons (Census 1891). From 1901, and in all censuses thereafter, only those three years of age and over were enumerated. Examination of the percentage of the county population speaking Gaelic (monoglots and Gaelic and English speakers) over the period 1881 to 1971 shows the Gaelic "core area" to lie in the counties of Argyll, Inverness, Ross and Cromarty and Sutherland, with a "fringe" made up of the counties of Bute, Nairn, and Caithness. The figures also reveal a consistent decline in the Gaelic population (Table 6.1).

Underlying these figures and the changing intensity in Gaelic speaking in relation to population density (Figures 6.3–6.6), is a fall-off in Gaelic-only speakers, and by the 1970s and 1980s, the virtual disappearance of the monoglot Gaelic population (MacKinnon, 1974; 1975). This element of Gaelic's language shift is reflected in the census figures on age and sex variations in the use of Gaelic. The Gaelic-only population has traditionally been made up of children of pre-school age and the elderly, particularly women. As education introduced the young to English and the older generation died to be replaced by persons speaking Gaelic and English, so the monoglot Gaelic population has declined. Older age groups are proportionally "more Gaelic" than the young and comparable age groups less and less Gaelic over time (Withers, 1984: 239).

Figures on ability to read or write Gaelic were first asked in 1971 (Gaelic Report 1975 [Census 1971]: iv). About two-thirds of the bilingual population in Inverness and Ross and Cromarty could read the language, and this proportion varied little with age. The ability to read or write Gaelic did fall with age, from about 60% in the 10–19 age group to a little under 50% at age fifty, to less than 25% in the over-75 age group (Gaelic Report, 1975: xii–xiii).

In 1981, a distinction was made between ability to speak Gaelic, read Gaelic or write Gaelic. Of the 82,620 persons recorded as speaking, reading or writing the language in 1981, 3,313 claimed an ability to read or write Gaelic but not to speak it. The rise in Gaelic speaking between

TABLE 6.1   Gaelic speaking population as a percentage of county population, 1881–1971*

	1881	1891	1901	1911	1921	1931	1951	1961	1971
SCOTLAND	6.76	6.84	5.57	4.56	3.47	2.97	1.98	1.64	1.78
Aberdeen	0.25	0.59	0.48	0.38	0.30	0.26	0.26	0.21	0.65
Angus	0.24	0.57	0.50	0.42	0.29	0.27	0.18	0.19	0.56
Argyll	65.25	60.88	54.35	47.06	34.56	33.17	21.69	17.20	13.72
Ayr	0.33	0.89	0.73	0.58	0.50	0.41	0.33	0.30	0.59
Banff	0.58	1.08	0.88	0.66	0.48	0.31	0.31	0.29	0.73
Berwick	0.09	0.29	0.26	0.34	0.24	0.26	0.24	0.21	0.57
Bute	22.70	20.34	15.71	12.02	4.57	5.17	2.28	1.64	1.90
Caithness	9.48	11.96	9.16	5.62	3.76	2.59	1.25	0.90	1.55
Clackmannan	0.04	0.82	0.57	0.77	0.51	0.48	0.28	0.31	0.57
Dumfries	0.02	0.29	0.26	0.33	0.23	0.28	0.22	0.17	0.51
Dunbarton	2.02	4.13	2.96	2.46	1.44	1.34	0.89	0.77	1.04
East Lothian	0.83	1.50	1.29	1.19	0.59	0.45	0.38	0.33	0.52
Fife	0.08	0.42	0.42	0.55	0.33	0.29	0.21	0.23	0.56
Inverness	75.99	73.24	64.85	59.07	50.91	43.97	30.57	25.91	22.02
Kincardine	0.05	0.35	0.27	0.30	0.29	0.30	0.25	0.32	0.70

Kinross	0.16	0.96	0.85	0.61	0.85	0.76	0.61	0.46	0.73
Kirkcudbright	0.03	0.19	0.27	0.33	0.28	0.28	0.29	0.26	0.54
Lanark	1.28	2.40	2.19	1.86	1.29	1.19	0.90	0.22	0.57
Midlothian	0.60	1.57	1.28	1.05	0.70	0.63	0.45	0.21	0.53
Moray	2.63	5.64	4.48	2.98	2.08	1.38	0.59	0.53	0.88
Nairn	20.32	27.07	15.29	10.54	6.47	5.19	1.69	1.79	1.64
Orkney	0.12	0.31	0.26	0.31	0.27	0.27	0.21	0.25	0.55
Peebles	0.02	0.57	0.51	0.69	0.38	0.44	0.36	0.39	0.91
Perth	12.10	11.95	9.94	7.70	5.25	4.21	1.90	1.53	1.68
Renfrew	2.15	3.17	2.30	1.90	1.31	1.12	0.67	0.59	0.81
Ross and Cromarty	76.57	76.92	71.76	64.01	60.20	57.29	46.05	41.31	35.12
Roxburgh	0.05	0.35	0.29	0.32	0.24	0.22	0.21	0.21	0.39
Selkirk	0.05	0.29	0.26	0.30	0.20	0.24	0.24	0.27	0.72
Shetland	0.04	0.25	0.21	0.17	0.44	0.15	0.11	0.10	0.42
Stirling	0.49	1.60	1.55	1.17	0.82	0.67	0.41	0.38	0.71
Sutherland	80.40	77.10	71.75	61.75	52.25	44.05	25.26	18.83	14.51
West Lothian	0.12	1.02	0.97	0.74	0.23	0.23	0.17	0.22	0.55
Wigtown	0.08	0.20	0.29	0.31	0.35	0.36	0.22	0.32	0.55

* Percentages based on the population aged three and over.

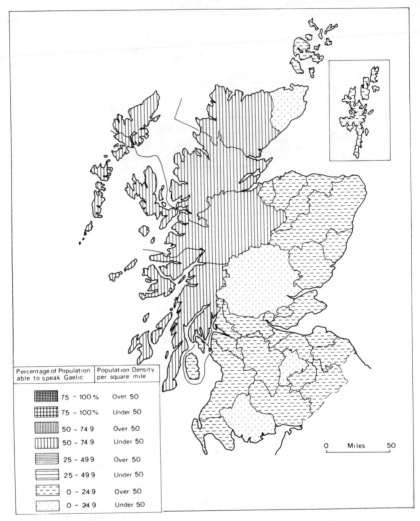

Percentage of Population able to speak Gaelic	Population Density per square mile
75 - 100 %	Over 50
75 - 100 %	Under 50
50 - 74 9	Over 50
50 - 74 9	Under 50
25 - 49 9	Over 50
25 - 49 9	Under 50
0 - 24 9	Over 50
0 - 24 9	Under 50

0   Miles   50

FIGURE 6.4   *Gaelic speaking in relation to population density, by county 1901*

1961 and 1971 (Table 6.1) — the result of Gaelic learners, chiefly in the urban Lowlands — represented one shift in the fortunes of the language: the presence of "non-Gaelic-speaking Gaelic literates" represents a further change in Gaelic's position (Withers, 1984: 239–40).

In review, the past geography of Gaelic has been marked by a shrinkage of the Gaidhealtachd toward the north and west and a decline

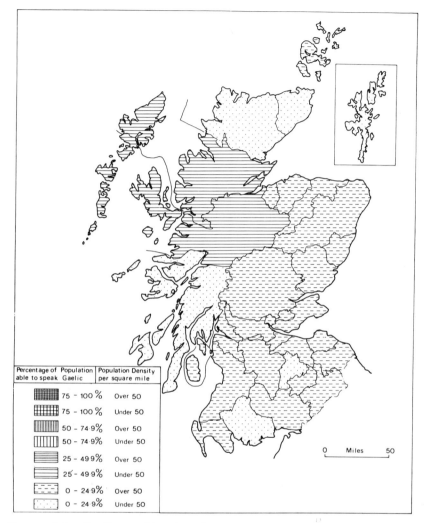

Percentage of Population able to speak Gaelic	Population Density per square mile
75 – 100 %	Over 50
75 – 100 %	Under 50
50 – 74·9%	Over 50
50 – 74·9%	Under 50
25 – 49·9%	Over 50
25′– 49·9%	Under 50
0 – 24·9%	Over 50
0 – 24·9%	Under 50

0   Miles   50

FIGURE 6.5   *Gaelic speaking in relation to population density, by county 1951*

in the use of the spoken language. This retreat has been marked by several variations in its pace and position. The declining intensity in the use of Gaelic has been more apparent in some domains than others and characterized by age and sex differences. Having thus sketched the "when" and "where" of Gaelic's geographical history, let us turn to the "why" and "how" of Gaelic's decline.

The processes of language change

The processes behind the geographical decline of the Gaidhealtachd may be divided into two broad types — those agencies and policies that sought the deliberate anglicization of the Highlander and those embraced within the gradual move toward "an English way of life". The first category includes, most importantly, the various educational and religious policies towards the Highlands, beginning in the early seventeenth century and continuing until the later 1800s, and embraces also the ideological mood for "Improvement", in the eighteenth century especially, which underlay the transformation of the Highlands as a culture region. The second category is more wide-ranging. It comprehends such things as the role of temporary migration to the Lowlands as an agent of language shift, the immigration of English speakers and emigration of Gaels, changes in the traditional social organization and agrarian economy of the Highlands, and the gradual, slow-moving incorporation, through trade, industry and culture, of Highland Scotland into a Greater Britain. Only some of these factors can be considered here. The final section of the paper considers the more recent effect upon processes of language maintenance and shift of Gaelic's place in contemporary Scotland.

As has been noted above, Gaelic became the focus of legislation at the same time as it declined in social status and prestige (see above). The use of Gaelic by the Highland populations was, in the minds of those in authority in the Lowlands, the cause of what contemporary sources term "the ignorance and incivilitie" of the Gael. This ignorance was the result of "the negligence of guid educatioun". The emphasis of education at this period was on religious instruction. To curb this negligence and bring the Highlands under the same social and political control as the remainder of Scotland, schools were established for "the better civilising and removing of the Irish language and barbaritie out of the heigh landes" (Withers, 1984: 29–31). The move to political and linguistic unity could only be meaningful, however, if the Gaelic populations were subject to the same religious jurisdiction as their Lowland counterparts. Administration of religion in the Gaidhealtachd necessarily involved the use of Gaelic, in the initial stages at least. At the same time as schools were set up in the Highlands to extend English, policies were begun to provide Gaelic clergy for the Highlands and ensure regular administration in the Gaelic language. This was not the paradox it seems. An education whose chief concern was religious instruction and whose end purpose was anglicization could never be effective if the tenets of religion were not, at first, propounded through the native language of the Highland population. Gaelic was used as a "missionary medium" upon which to base an education aimed at anglicization (Campbell, 1950: 54). Bearing in mind these close links between educational and religious policy, let us consider them separately.

An act of 1616 had made provision for a school to be maintained in every parish in Scotland, but was ineffective in the Highlands and even in the Lowlands the coverage was incomplete (Smout, 1969: 81; Donaldson, 1978: 262–69; Watt, 1981: 79–90). Some schools were established in Argyll by the mid-seventeenth century (Mackinnon, 1938), but the majority of Highland parishes remained without a school and their inhabitants without education. The 1696 Act for Settling of Schools (Act of the Parliament of Scotland, 1696: X, 63), intended to remedy the inadequacies of the 1616 act, suffered also from a lack of impact in the Gaidhealtachd, and not until the eighteenth century were schools established there in any number.

The principal educational agency involved in Highland affairs, certainly in the eighteenth century and first decade of the nineteenth century, was the Society in Scotland for Propagating Christian Knowledge (SSPCK), begun in Edinburgh in 1709 (Durkacz, 1978). Although this body modified its policy during the 1700s, its intended aim throughout was the extension of English. This is made clear in a statement of 7 June 1716:

"Nothing can be more effectual for reducing these countries to order, and making them useful to the Commonwealth than teaching them their duty to God, their King and Countrey and rooting out their Irish language, and this has been the case of the Society so far as they could, ffor all the Schollars are taught in English" (SSPCK, Minutes of General Meeting 7 June 1716: 163).

Shortage of schoolmasters, finance and Bibles (the main text used) hampered SSPCK plans in the first quarter of the 1700s, but by 1755 there were over 100 schools located in Highland parishes. Many Highlanders were introduced to English through SSPCK schools. Defoe, writing in 1742, noted "There appears a great Disposition in the Rising Generation to be instructed; many have learned to read the Scriptures, and attend Divine Service in English, where formerly the Irish tongue was only understood" (Defoe, 1742: IV, 241). Of course, education was but one way in which the English language was furthered, but there is little doubt that SSPCK schools were of particular importance:

"None of the children, when they come to the parochial or charity schools, understand a word of English; yet in three years or in four at most, they learn both to read and speak it perfectly" (Walker, 1766 quoted in Withers, 1984: 128).

Boys attended in larger numbers than girls (McKay, 1980: 126), and the young more commonly than the old, which may account, in part, for the observed social differences in language shift at this time. Moreover, the location of SSPCK schools lent particular emphasis to the geographical patterns of decline. The great majority of SSPCK schools in the period 1709 to 1825 were located along what we have seen to be the language border — south-west and central Perthshire, in Argyllshire, and south and east Ross and Cromarty and Inverness-shire.

The SSPCK continued to maintain schools in the Highlands until the Education (Scotland) Act of 1872, but by the second decade of the nineteenth century, Gaelic Society schools were more important in directing educational policy. The Edinburgh Society for the Support of Gaelic Schools was begun in 1811. A Glasgow society was begun in 1812, and one in Inverness in 1818. The sole object of Gaelic Society schools was to teach Gaelic speakers to read the scriptures in their native language. Their schools were circulatory, usually moving to another parish or elsewhere in the same parish after a period of eight months. Despite the efforts of the SSPCK, there were many Highlanders without education and unable to read Gaelic in the early 1800s. Gaelic Society schools were, in turn, an important agent of language shift. Their effect was two-fold. Firstly, since reading the scriptures in Gaelic was the only teaching method, these schools strengthened the Highlanders' feeling for Gaelic as a spiritual medium, as the preferred language of salvation and worship. Secondly, Gaelic schools furthered the English language through Gaelic because the inhabitants in parishes where a Gaelic school had been located would, upon that school's relocation, pay a schoolmaster to teach them English. Teaching Gaelic reading only was strictly adhered to: but it was also an incitement to further learning, learning that could only be achieved through English (Withers, 1984: 147). The spread of English through such instruction went hand in hand with the extension of literacy in Gaelic and the reinforcement of that language as a religious language.

Gaelic schools were located chiefly in the northern and western Gaidhealtachd (Withers, 1984: 148–50). As in the case of the SSPCK, it is too much to claim that the location of Gaelic schools alone determined the later retreat of Gaelic in those parts — both bodies should be regarded as accelerants of existing trends — but there is little doubt that both institutions were crucial influences behind the decline of Gaelic.

Other bodies, such as the General Assembly of the Church of Scotland and several benevolent institutions, operated schools in the Highlands, but SSPCK and Gaelic Society schools were the most important educational agencies of language change. The 1872 Education (Scotland) Act which formalized education under a central system, ignored Gaelic completely (Macleod, 1966). Gaelic was slowly incorporated into Highland educational schemes in the last years of the nineteenth century and first years of the twentieth, but not until the Education (Scotland) Bill of 1818 was Gaelic made a compulsory part of education in the Gaelic areas. Even today, schools still have 'anglicising roles' (MacKinnon, 1977: 87–92). Gaelic's place in education has been at best secondary, usually unimportant and mostly non-existent in any meaningful way since the seventeenth century. The language has been only slightly better served by the Church.

The Highlands had always been without a sufficient complement of Gaelic-speaking clergy and even in those parishes where ministers did officiate, the large parishes and dispersed population made administration difficult. Sources of the seventeenth and early eighteenth centuries abound with references to Gaels being "without benefit of the Word" and "being in damnable atheisme" (for example, Cramond, 1906: 122–23). Neither irreligion in the Highlands nor a shortage of Gaelic ministers could be permitted if the Gaelic populations were to be brought to recognize the word of one God and one King and, in time, to speak English. The Scottish Parliament and the General Assembly of the Church of Scotland planned to meet these difficulties by awarding bursaries to suitable Gaelic-speaking young men to train for the ministry and then serve in the Highlands. But their policy had as its end in view the promotion of English, not the fostering of Gaelic as the language of religious ordinance. The General Assembly cautioned its bursars "that every student that shall be trained for the ministry in the Highlands . . . shall, when he comes to be settled as a minister, preach every Lord's Day in English, as well as in the Irish Language" (Acts of the General Assembly of the Church of Scotland: 1756; VII, 727).

It is important to examine the impact of these policies. Argyll seems to have been better served than the north and west, but in general, the policies for recruitment of a Gaelic ministry were unsuccessful, owing to a shortage of suitable candidates, financial difficulties and the sheer scale of the problems involved in administering to the Highland populations. These problems were shared also by Catholic, Episcopalian and Free Church of Scotland clergy. In those parishes and for those people regularly administered to in Gaelic in the past, Gaelic was reinforced as a spoken language, specifically in church and generally because of its continued use in this one area. But what the problems of Gaelic clergy and infrequent Gaelic services meant for the majority of the Gaidhealtachd is that Gaelic was not bolstered as it might have been because the language could not rest on a firm base provided by regular use in church and chapel. This lack of support in one social situation would probably not have affected the day-to-day use of Gaelic had the Highlands remained untouched by other anglicizing influences. But the fact that religious administration in Gaelic was, for many people, infrequent and often accompanied by an English language service meant that using Gaelic in church services did not provide a bulwark against the spread of English through schooling, temporary migration or in other ways. It did, however, lead to two things: firstly to a separation between Gaelic as a church language, and, to an extent, in the home, and the increasing use of English in education and in daily conversation, and secondly, to the commonly-occurring situation in which Gaelic's decline as a religious language marked the final stages in its retreat.

These changes through school and church occurred alongside the general "improvement" of Highland life in other ways, stemming from the growing involvement, in economy, manners, and politics, with England and the anglicized Lowlands (Cregeen, 1968: 165). Space precludes a detailed assessment of this general incorporation, but several agencies of language shift may be discussed briefly: temporary migration; population decline and the related elements of emigration and immigration. The break-up of traditional economic and social systems in the Gaidhealtachd has been well-documented elsewhere (Gray, 1957; Carter, 1971; Hunter, 1976).

Temporary migration of Highlanders from the Gaidhealtachd to work at the harvest in the Lowlands, at the fishing on the north-east coast, as labourers in the textile industry or as domestic servants, was commonplace in the eighteenth and nineteenth centuries (MacDonald, 1937; Howatson, 1982). Even today the patterns persist (Mewett, 1977). Just as returning migrants brought back cash crucial to the support of a largely subsistence economy, so they also brought back a knowledge of English. Young men in particular introduced English words into their Gaelic or spoke English in place of Gaelic, many from a feeling that English, not Gaelic, was the language of social status and prestige. A report on Gairloch parish in 1836 epitomises a pattern common throughout the Highlands by that period:

> "Some young men . . . consider they are doing great service to
> the Gaelic by interspersing their conversation with English

words ... These corrupters of both languages ... introduce words of bad English or bad Scotch which they have learned from the Newhaven or Buckie fishermen, whom they meet with on the coast of Caithness during the fishing season" (*N.S.A.*, 1836: 14, 95–96).

Assessment in detail of the timing and regional variation in the rise and fall in population of the Highlands is difficult (Flinn, 1977: 221). In general terms, the pressure of too many people on too few resources, exacerbated by the continual sub-division of holdings, the dependence on the potato and the failure to develop a market-oriented economy, was everywhere apparent by about 1800. The effect was twofold: depopulation, as arable land gave way to incoming Lowland sheep, and overcrowding along the coastal fringes. The long-term result was a decline in population and the emigration of Highlanders to North America, Australia or New Zealand. Periodic crises, such as the destitution of the 1840s or early 1850s, or the wholesale and abrupt clearance of people from traditionally-held lands, have tended to colour our opinion of this population loss (Richards, 1982). The decline of Gaelic resulting from the out-movement of native speakers was more drawn out than is usually supposed, but the effect of draining the Gaidhealtachd of its language and people was real enough. And as Gaelic speakers emigrated under the influence of a new economic and social order, so English speakers — farmers, tenants, landowners, industrialists, sportsmen — moved into the Highlands. These changes were noted by Murray in 1873:

"... the Gaelic people are gradually going to the provincial towns in their neighbourhood, while Lowlanders who have been successful in business in the towns, or farmers from the south, go to occupy farms or residences within the Gaelic area" (Murray, 1873: 232–33).

These and other changes in the Highland way of life that determined, directly or indirectly, a change in the past fortunes of Gaelic, should not be considered in isolation in understanding the mechanics of language shift. The decline was never a simple retreat from south-east to north-west and never involved the dropping of Gaelic for English for all social purposes at one instant. Emphasis was given to the geographical shift through such things as the location of schools, the presence or not of Gaelic clergy, and proximity to the Lowlands, and Gaelic continued longer in certain social situations than others, but these patterns varied from parish to parish and even within families. Considerable variation existed in the past in the use and strength of Gaelic, just as it does today.

The present and future geography of Gaelic

Gaelic's present geographical strength — in the Western Isles Region
and in Skye and Lochaber District of Highland Region (Figure 6.6) —
represents the relics of past geographies. But in several ways, Gaelic is

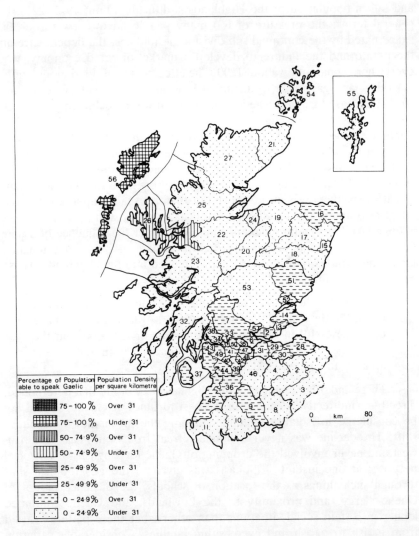

FIGURE 6.6   *Gaelic speaking in relation to population density, by region
and district 1981*

Scottish regions and districts in 1981

Borders Region

1 Berwickshire
2 Ettrick and Lauderdale
3 Roxburgh
4 Tweeddale

Central Region

5 Clackmannan
6 Falkirk
7 Stirling

Dumfries and Galloway

8   Annandale and Eskdale
9   Nithsdale
10 Stewartry
11 Wigtown

Fife Region
12 Dunfermline
13 Kirkcaldy
14 North-East Fife

Grampian Region

15 Aberdeen City District
16 Banff and Buchan
17 Gordon
18 Kincardine and Deeside
19 Moray

Highland Region
20 Badenoch and Strathspey
21 Caithness
22 Inverness
23 Lochaber
24 Nairn
25 Ross and Cromarty
26 Skye and Lochalsh
27 Sutherland

Lothian Region
28 East Lothian
29 Edinburgh
30 Midlothian
31 West Lothian

Strathclyde Region

32 Argyll and Bute
33 Bearsden and Milngavie
34 Clydebank
35 Cumbernauld and Kilsyth
36 Cumnock and Doon Valley
37 Cunninghame
38 Dumbarton
39 East Kilbride
40 Eastwood
41 Glasgow City
42 Hamilton
43 Inverclyde
44 Kilmarnock and Loudoun
45 Kyle and Carrick
46 Lanark
47 Monklands
48 Motherwell
49 Renfrew
50 Strathkelvin

Tayside Region

51 Angus
52 Dundee City
53 Perth and Kinross
54 Orkney Islands
55 Shetland Islands
56 Western Isles

much more vital and important a part of Scotland's cultural life in the later twentieth century than when it was spoken by more people and over a wider area.

Since 1975 a Bilingual Education Project, founded by the Western Isles Council (*Comhairle nan Eilean*) and the Scottish Education Department, has been using Gaelic as a medium for all general education in many schools in the Western Isles and has been working alongside community projects to introduce a curriculum which will enable children to learn all subjects in Gaelic as well as English. Even in the eastern parts of Ross and Cromarty and Sutherland — areas much less strongly Gaelic today than in the past and certainly less Gaelic than the Outer

Isles — many parents are today in favour of some Gaelic education for their children (Dorian, 1978; 1981). This increased sympathy for the language is a recent phenomenon; much still remains to be done to secure future educational needs (M. Macleod in Thomson, 1976).

Gaelic has persisted longer as a church language in the twentieth century than in most other domains (MacKinnon, 1975: 52). In several ways, the fate of the language today is much bound up with its continued strength in religion, especially in the Free Church and especially in the Western Isles (Thomson, 1971: 136–37). The decline of Gaelic as a church language has, to some extent, marked the later stages of the retreat of the language in the modern period, but more common today is the replacement of one Gaelic service by one in English rather than the wholesale displacement of Gaelic from the pulpit. In most Highland parishes where the language is widely spoken in other situations, Gaelic's place as a church language is strong. As has been noted for Catholic Barra and Free Church Harris alike, Gaelic is much valued as the language of religion, and, through religion, as "the language of social solidarity and affection" (Vallee, 1954; MacKinnon, 1975: 53).

Although modern Gaelic is everywhere characterized by these domain differences and by the "borrowing" and "switching" of English words and idiom (MacAulay, 1979), there is considerable loyalty to the language from persons who might have adopted English had not local economic opportunities been available (Prattis, 1981). Gaelic's increased exposure on television, radio and in the press since the 1950s has helped strengthen the language. Gaelic was first introduced in radio programmes in 1926, but not until 1935 when a Gaelic Department was formed in the B.B.C. were there regular broadcasts (Thomson, 1971: 142). By the late 1960s Gaelic radio services averaged three and a half hours per week: a total reduced in the 1970s. In the 1980s, Gaelic learner and topical television programmes such as *Can Seo, Cearcall, About Gaelic* and *Crann Tara* have reflected and stimulated interest in the language, but Gaelic's relationship with the media is still a subordinate one.

Gaelic is still only modestly represented in the press, although the foundation in 1951 of *Gairm*, an all-Gaelic magazine containing poetry and prose and commentaries on local and national affairs, has been a major success. Gaelic authors have several publishing outlets: *Acair* in Stornoway, *Gairm* in Glasgow, Club Leabhar in Portree being perhaps the most important, and the foundation in 1968 of the Gaelic Books Council has done much to stimulate Gaelic publishing. Over 100 Gaelic language books of one sort or another have been published in every

decade since 1939 (Thomson, 1976: 82). These events have been mirrored
in the rise of Gaelic music and theatre, and the foundation of a Gaelic
College on Skye in 1973. Several branches of Scotland's banks provide
Gaelic cheque-books and display Gaelic signs (Thomson, 1981: 12). The

FIGURE 6.7   *Scottish counties before 1974*

registered increase in Gaelic speakers between 1961 and 1971 (Gaelic-and-English learners) signified renewed interest in the language and the culture it represents.

What is lacking for Gaelic today despite all these things is a co-ordinated strategy for community education, the dispersal of Gaelic speakers in administrative positions, a greater recognition of its contribution, past, present and future, to Scotland's culture, and of course, the political goodwill (D. Macleod in Thomson, 1980: 24–27). To some extent, this goodwill does exist. The Western Isles Council has been pursuing a bilingual policy since its foundation in 1975. But the language has no place in national government, and only the Scottish National Party has considered any role for it (S.N.P. Policy Statement on Gaelic 1981). Neither Highland Region — an area embracing 17,098 Gaelic users in 1981 nor Argyll District (6,408 Gaelic users in 1981) have much to do with the language for official purposes. The same is true of the Highlands and Islands Development Board. There is still much to be done to provide a contemporary relevance and sound future for Gaelic.

Gaelic's geographical history has been marked by several crucial events: the appearance of the Gaidhealtachd as a distinct linguistic area by the mid-fourteenth century; decline as a language of status; deliberate attempts at anglicization through education; and overtly oppressive attitudes toward the language and its speakers. But Gaelic's decline has also stemmed from the more gradual move toward "an English way of life", in the late eleventh century or the late twentieth century. Only the broad outlines have been sketched here. Recent events and policies must await examination for their contemporary impact and future influence on Gaelic. In this sense, the geographical history of Gaelic in Scotland is a continuing narrative.

Bibliography

ARMSTRONG, R.B. (ed.) 1884, *Archaeological Collections relating to the counties of Ayr and Wigton*. Dumfries: Clark.
ARNOT, H., 1779, *History of Edinburgh*. Edinburgh: Walker.
BANNERMAN, J., 1974, *Studies in the History of Dalriada*. Edinburgh: University Press.
BARROW, G.W.S., 1973, *The Kingdom of Scots*. London: RKP.
BURT, E., 1726, Report on Argyll in 1726. In D.C. MACTAVISH (ed.), *Minutes of the Synod of Argyll*. Edinburgh: Scottish History Society.

—— 1754, *Letters from a Gentleman in the North of Scotland*. 2 vols., London: Murray.

CAMPBELL, J., 1950, *Gaelic in Scottish Education and Life*. Edinburgh: Johnston.

CARTER, I., 1971, Economic models and the recent history of the Highlands, *Scottish Studies*, 15 (2), 99–120.

CENSUS OF SCOTLAND, 1881–1981, Gaelic Reports.

CRAMOND, W., 1906, *Extracts from the Records of the Synod of Moray*. Elgin: Murray.

CREGEEN, E., 1968, The Changing Role of the House of Argyll in the Scottish Highlands. In I.M. LEWIS (ed.), *History and Social Anthropology*. London: RKP.

DAICHES, D., 1977, *Scotland and the Union*. London: Murray.

DELGADO DE CARVALHO, C.M., 1962, The geography of languages. In P.L. WAGNER & M. MIKESELL, *Readings in cultural geography*. New York: Wiley.

DEFOE, D., 1742, *A Tour through the Whole Island of Great Britain*. London: Smith.

DONALDSON, G., 1978, *Scotland: James V to James VII*. Edinburgh: Oliver and Boyd.

DONALDSON, J., 1936, *Caithness in the Eighteenth Century*. Wick: Sinclair.

DORIAN, N.C., 1978, *East Sutherland Gaelic*. Dublin: Institute for Advanced Studies.

—— 1981, The evaluation of Gaelic by different mother-tongue groups resident in the Highlands, *Scottish Gaelic Studies*, XIII (II), 169–82.

DUNCAN, A.A.M., 1975, *Scotland: The Making of the Kingdom*. Edinburgh: Oliver and Boyd.

DURKACZ, V.E., 1978, The source of the language problem in Scottish education 1688–1709, *Scottish Historical Review*, LVII, 28–39.

—— 1983, *The Decline of the Celtic Languages*. Edinburgh: Donald.

FLINN, M.W. (ed.) 1977, *Scottish Population History*. Edinburgh: University Press.

FLOM, G.T., 1952, The transition from Norse to Lowland Scotch in Shetland, 1600–1850, *Saga Book of the Viking Society*, X, 145–64.

FRASER-MACKINTOSH, C.M., 1881, The Gaelic Census of the Counties of Inverness, Ross and Sutherland, *Celtic Magazine*, VI (71), 438–41.

GRAY, M., 1957, *The Highland Economy 1750–1850*. Edinburgh: University Press.

GRANT MICHIE, J., 1908, *Deeside Tales*. Aberdeen: Wright.

HOME, J., 1802, *The History of the Rebellion in the Year 1745*. London: Murray.

HOWATSON, W., 1982, The Scottish Hairst and Seasonal Labour 1600–1870, *Scottish Studies*, 26, 13–36.

HUNTER, J., 1976, *The Making of the Crofting Community*. Edinburgh: Donald.

IORDAN, I. & ORR, J., 1970, *An Introduction to Romance Linguistics*. Oxford: Clarendon.

JACKSON, K.H., 1953, *Language and History in Early Britain*. Edinburgh: University Press.

JAKOBSEN, J., 1928, *An Etymological Dictionary of the Norn Language in Shetland*. Copenhagen: Olsen.

JOANNIS DE FORDUN, 1759, *Scotochronicon (cum Supplementis et continuatione Walter Bowrie)* 2 vols. Edinburgh.

LETTICE, J., 1794, *Letters on a Tour through Various Parts of Scotland in 1792*. London: Murray.

MACAULAY, D.S., 1979, The state of Gaelic language studies. In A.J. AITKEN & T. MACARTHUR (eds), *Languages of Scotland*. Edinburgh: Literary Studies.

MACDONALD, D., 1937, *Scotland's Shifting Population*. Glasgow: Sinclair.

MCKAY, M. (ed.) 1980, *The Rev. Dr. John Walker's Report on the Hebrides of 1764 and 1771*. Edinburgh: Donald.

MCKERRAL, A., 1948, *Kintyre in the Seventeenth Century*. Edinburgh: Oliver and Boyd.

MACKINNON, D., 1938, Education in Argyll and the Isles, 1638–1709, *Records of the Scottish Church History Society*, 6, 46–54.

MACKINNON, K.M., 1974, *The Lion's Tongue*. Inverness: Club Leabhar.

—— 1975, *Gaelic in Scotland 1971: some sociological and demographic considerations of the census report for Gaelic*. Hatfield: Hatfield Polytechnic.

—— 1977, *Language, Education and Social Processes in a Gaelic Community*. London: RKP.

MACLEOD, D., 1976, Gaelic in Public Life. In D.S. THOMSON (ed.), *Gaelic in Scotland*. Glasgow: Gairm.

MACLEOD, M., 1966, Gaelic in Highland Education, *Transactions of the Gaelic Society of Inverness*, XLIII, 305–34.

—— 1976, Gaelic in Secondary Schools. In D.S. THOMSON (ed.), *Gaelic in Scotland*. Glasgow: Gairm.

MARSHALL, W., 1794, *General View of the Agriculture of the Central Highlands of Scotland*. London: Murray.

MARTIN, M., 1703, *A Description of the Western Isles of Scotland*. London: Wright.

MEWETT, P., 1977, Occupational pluralism in crofting, *Scottish Journal of Sociology*, 2 (7), 31–49.

MITCHELL, D., 1900, *History of the Highlands and Gaelic Scotland.* Paisley: Sinclair.

MITCHELL, A., 1906, *Alexander Macfarlane's Geographical Collections Relating to Scotland.* Edinburgh: Scottish History Society.

MOWAT, I.R.M., 1981, *Easter Ross, 1750–1850.* Edinburgh: Donald.

MURISON, D., 1974, Linguistic relationships in medieval Scotland. In G.W.S. BARROW (ed.), *The Scottish Tradition: Essays in Honour of R.G. Cant.* Edinburgh: Academic Press.

MURRAY, J.A.H., 1873, *The Dialect of the Southern Counties of Scotland.* London: Murray.

NICOLAISEN, W.E.H., 1964, Celts and Anglo-Saxons in the Scottish Border Counties: the Place-Name Evidence, *Scottish Studies*, 8, 141–71.

—— 1970, Gaelic Place-Names in Southern Scotland, *Studia Celtica*, 15–35.

—— 1976, *Scottish Place-Names*, London: Batsford.

NICHOLSON, R., 1978, *Scotland in the Later Middle Ages*. Edinburgh: Oliver and Boyd.

PRATTIS, J.I., 1981, Industrialization and minority language loyalty. In E. HAUGEN, J.D. MCCLURE & D.S. THOMSON (eds), *Minority Languages Today*. Edinburgh: University Press.

PRICE, G., 1976–1978, Gaelic in Scotland at the end of the eighteenth century (Part I), *Bulletin, Board of Gaelic Studies*, 27, 561–68.

—— 1979, Gaelic in Scotland at the end of the eighteenth century (Part II), *Bulletin, Board of Gaelic Studies*, 28, 234–47.

RAIT, R., 1914, Traces of the Celts in the Lowlands: A plea for investigation, *Scottish Review*, XXXVII, 258–65.

RAVENSTEIN, E.G., 1879, On the Celtic Languages in the British Isles: a Statistical Survey, *Journal of the Royal Statistical Society*, 579–643.

RICHARDS, E., 1982, *A History of the Highland Clearances.* London: Croom Helm.

SELKIRK, EARL OF, 1806, *Observations on the Present State of the Highlands of Scotland with a view of the Causes and Probable Consequences of Emigration.* Edinburgh: Nelson.

SHARP, L.W., 1928, The Expansion of the English language into Scotland. Unpublished Ph.D. Thesis, University of Cambridge.

SMOUT, T.C., 1969, *A History of the Scottish People 1560–1830.* Glasgow: Collins.

THOMSON, D.S., 1971, Gaelic Scotland. In D. GLEN (ed.), *Whither Scotland.* London: Gollancz.

—— 1976, *Gaelic in Scotland.* Glasgow: Gairm.

—— 1981, Gaelic in Scotland: Assessment and Prognosis. In E. HAUGEN, J.D. MCCLURE & D.S. THOMSON (eds), *Minority Languages Today*.

Edinburgh: University Press.

—— 1983, *A Companion to Gaelic Scotland*. Oxford: Blackwell.

VALLEE, F.G., 1954, Social Structure and Organisation in a Hebridean Community: A study of social change. Unpublished Ph.D. Thesis, University of London.

WALKER, J., 1808, *An Economical History of the Highlands and Hebrides*. 2 vols., Edinburgh: Wright.

WATSON, W.J., 1914–1916, The position of Gaelic in Scotland, *Celtic Review*, X, 69–84.

WATT, D.E.R., 1981, Education in the Highlands in the Middle Ages. In L. MACLEAN (ed.), *The Middle Ages in the Highlands*. Inverness: Inverness Field Club.

WEINRICH, U., 1953, *Languages in Contact*. New York: Bloom.

WILLIAMS, C.H., 1980, Language contact and language change in Wales, 1901–1971: A study in historical geolinguistics, *Welsh History Review*, 10, 207–38.

WITHERS, C.W.J., 1980, The Highland Parishes in 1698: An examination of sources for the definition of the Gaidhealtachd, *Scottish Studies*, 24, 63–88.

—— 1982, Gaelic-speaking in a Highland parish: Port of Mentieth 1724–1725, *Scottish Geographical Magazine*, 98 (1), 16–23.

—— 1983, A geography of language: Gaelic-speaking in Perthshire, 1698 to 1879, *Transactions of the Institute of British Geographers*, 8 (2), 25–42.

—— 1984, *Gaelic in Scotland 1698–1981: The Geographical History of a Language*. Edinburgh: Donald.

7 Sources and Methods in the Study of Language Areas: A Case Study of Wales

W.T.R. PRYCE
The Open University in Wales, Cardiff, U.K.
and
COLIN H. WILLIAMS
Department of Geography and Recreation Studies,
North Staffordshire Polytechnic, Stoke-on-Trent, U.K.

From the earliest times human geographers have been deeply interested in the relationships between language and territory. The numbers speaking one or more languages and the relative geographical strength of a specific language — especially "minority" tongues — continue to fascinate geographers, not least because these tend to endow a territory with a certain degree of uniqueness whilst, at the same time, raising the potentially conflicting questions of spatial interdependency and separateness. The territorial relationships subsisting in a "regional" context or within a nation state where a "world" language such as French or English continues its advance into areas previously the sole province of older indigenous "unofficial" languages such as Breton or Welsh are long-standing themes of continuing interest in human geography. Whilst experts in "linguistic geography" focus their specialist interests on spatial variations in word usage, idioms or, for example, the linguistic forms and structures in a community speaking a common language, human geographers have tended to concentrate on identifying and then explaining the *processes* relating to the territorial dominance of particular languages. In such studies it is the "macro" or aggregate issues that receive emphasis because, along with other indicators such as religion, language is often taken as a convenient practical surrogate measure of cultural distinctiveness. And in human geography, as in anthropology, studies of the culture region have a long tradition, especially amongst French and American scholars (see, for example, Pryce, 1982; Kofman, 1981).

Geographers, therefore, have interests in language primarily as a means of unlocking other, more intangible human characteristics, but their analytical techniques yield quite useful explanations in the study of linguistic distributions for their own intrinsic interest. All these contributions stem from the basic concern of geographers with territorial, regional or *spatial* differences as the fundamental variable. At the most elementary level of analysis, geographers are interested in the question "where?": geographers are expert at the production of maps showing the dominant areas where language X as opposed to language Y is spoken and they can call on a range of statistical and cartographic techniques for the identification of the "zones of transition" between the two. Not all distributions exist as a continuous variable with slight but progressive changes of intensity as, for example, in maps showing the rainfall received over a wide area of the countryside. In language mapping, sudden breaks can, and do occur as, indeed, may happen at a political boundary or, as we shall see later, when a newer language is being diffused via the urban hierarchy into the territories of a traditional long-established but declining speech community. Maps revealing such patterns are, in effect, statements as to changing linguistic ecologies.

Drawing on the body of theory which they have built up, human geographers are fully aware of and often make generalizations as to the processes which have operated over time to produce such spatial distinctions. Depending on the contextual assumptions, future trends can then be estimated from these observations. Moreover, using similar methods, past linguistic geographies can be reconstructed and further light may then be thrown on the nature of long-term trends. In this way the analysis of process can be pursued, back as well as forward in time.

Several problems may arise from too-rigid an adoption of these approaches. There is the very real danger that spatial processes may themselves be accepted as the sole basis of change when, in reality, they constitute a part of a whole complexity of explanations. Today, in their study of social change, geographers have come to place considerable emphasis on underlying causes which, in themselves, may not be inherently spatial in nature. Whilst the end result of ongoing changes gives rise to spatial differences, the processes bringing about these changes may have *aspatial* origins. Thus, for example, in explaining the decline of a traditional language such as Welsh, it is necessary to look at the distribution of speakers amongst the various age groups in the population, linking these structural changes to changes in, say, educational policies and opportunities in Welsh-medium schools over several generations. In addition, there is the need to recognize social attitudes towards, for example, the retention of a second language or its abandonment in favour of a "world" language such as English. Behavioural considerations such as these may have been engendered as much by social class or lifecycle as, indeed, by the geographical location of that individual (*where* he/she lives) and the linguistic status of the community around him/her. Questions of the "ecological fallacy" pose further problems: in aggregate studies there is a strong temptation for geographers to formulate generalizations on the widely-accepted assumption that all parts of a community share the same linguistic affiliation. Small-area statistics are essential if these latter problems are to receive the recognition they deserve. Unfortunately, as we shall see, small-scale census data are not available consistently over time. Even if they are, then there is the very real temptation of falling into yet another trap of a similar kind and assume that all individuals will necessarily "fit in" with the overall linguistic status of the areas in which they are enumerated.

All these problems have been stated here more or less as objections to the adoption of the spatial approach. Yet, as other specialists from time-to-time remind us, the geographer has much to contribute in the study of language areas. In this chapter we shall draw upon studies of the changing relationship of Welsh and English in Wales in order to attempt a more searching assessment of what is possible. We begin by looking at the primary source material, namely the censuses of language, and how the data provided in these official sources can be exploited to reveal overall trends.

The census returns of 1981

In 1981 the census was taken on the night of Sunday April 5 and the first overall results appeared soon afterwards in the *County Monitors*, a new series of publications issued by the Office of Population, Census and Surveys (OPCS) aimed at the rapid dissemination of the new information. The *County monitor for South Glamorgan*, for example, became available on 24 November, 1981. This included a short statement of the numbers of Welsh speakers in 1981 and 1971 so that by consulting each of the County monitors broad trends can be worked out for the whole of Wales. These early publications were to be followed by a series of more substantive volumes on each country, the first being entitled *County Reports: Part 1*, which, depending on the county, appeared at various dates during 1982.

The householder's schedule had been redesigned for the 1971 census so that not only would it collect information from individuals as to their ability to *speak* Welsh but also whether the inhabitants of each dwelling were able to *read* and *write* in the Welsh language. These same questions were used again in 1981. The final tabulations using information derived from these returns appeared in two of the official publications. First, Table 42 of the 1981 census *Country Reports: Part 1* provides an age breakdown of *residents* speaking, reading and/or writing Welsh within Administrative Counties and Districts together with an additional column by which it is possible to calculate the numbers of *visitors* in each of these broad categories. Secondly, there is the full report itself, entitled *Census 1981: Welsh language in Wales* which appeared late in 1983. This runs to some 50 pages of detailed tables with basic maps and brief explanatory notes.

Except for the changes which had occurred in the administrative units, the tabulations in this full report are comparable to those used at previous censuses. The single exception is to be found in Table 3 (pp. 48–49) which, in showing linguistic abilities in *age groups* according to *birthplace*, is a new tabulation of considerable interest. This information is presented for Wales as one territorial unit and, moreover, only in terms of three broad birth-place categories: (1) born in Wales, (2) born in the rest of the United Kingdom, and (3) born outside the United Kingdom. Therefore, its information is of strictly limited value to human geographers with their primary interests in the study of the detailed variations over territorial space. Nevertheless, this new table does show that of the 503,549 Welsh speakers in 1981, 32,554 (6.5%) had been born outside Wales somewhere or other in the rest of the UK whilst 3,137 (0.6%) recorded birthplaces overseas. In themselves these are somewhat surprising figures and demonstrate the mobility of the Welsh-speaking population.

The 1981 census recorded 21,283 persons as Welsh monoglots. Even more surprising is the fact that 1,098 (5%) recorded birth places outside Wales in the rest of the UK whilst 126 persons (0.6% of all Welsh monoglots) stated that they had been born *outside* the UK. Further interesting differences stand out when the age structures within these major birthplace categories are examined. Thus, whilst it is widely understood that numbers of Welsh monoglots are more numerous in the older age groups (45 years and over), larger numbers were returned in the younger cohorts (5–14 and 25–44 years) born elsewhere in the UK. Similar trends are evident amongst Welsh speakers born overseas.

Because these new data offer useful insights as to how people themselves perceive their own national identity, it is clear, even from this preliminary analysis, that Table 3 of the main report needs further exploration.

Following the last re-organization of local government in 1974, the 1981 census tabulates details of the Welsh language for the new larger county areas together with the administrative districts within each county and wards. In the published tables the latter are listed solely in terms of anonymous wards but with numerical identification. In consequence, this makes recognition virtually impossible without access to the unpublished detailed boundary maps kept by local authorities. Although retrospective language trends are published back to 1921 for the new counties or, as in the case of age structures, only for the whole of Wales, the adoption of these new administrative units means that comparisons with previous censuses are quite impossible using the published tabulations. These data problems can be overcome by resorting to the use of Small Area Statistics (SAS's). These can be purchased directly from OPCS at the cost of production.

By combining the data collated for individual enumeration districts local comparisons with previous returns can be made. This form of reconstitution has been carried out by geographers at the University College of Wales, Aberystwyth with impressive results which we shall examine later (see Aitchison & Carter, 1985).

The first language census in Wales in 1891

The first population census was conducted in 1801. Nevertheless, despite the General Registry Act of 1836 and the adoption of new administrative arrangements for the civil registration of births, marriages and deaths, it was not until 1841 that census taking in Britain was established on a sound basis. Previously, the enumeration amounted to a mere head count, household by household, by local Overseers of the Poor. In 1841 resident registrars and their assistants acted as enumerators. The system was further improved in 1851 when, presumably due to poor responses to official enquiries, the householder's schedule was issued in the Welsh language as well as in English. Unfortunately, no records seem to have been kept as to the extent to which this first Welsh version was used, nor are there any details of the localities concerned (Pryce, 1976: 114–43). In the second half of the nineteenth century isolated surveys on the relative importance of Welsh and English at specific locations were made (see, for example, *Reports, Commissioners of Inquiry into the State of Education in Wales,* 1847), but it was not until 1891 that the British census, as it was administered in Wales, began to collect information on the languages spoken in Wales — a decade after census officials were required to estimate the numbers "in the habit of making colloquial use of the Gaelic language" in Scotland (Census, 1881; Interdepartmental Committee on Social & Economic Research, 1951; Withers, 1984). In 1879 the Royal Statistical Society published Ravenstein's "statistical survey" of the four Celtic languages in Britain. This seems to have paved the way for the introduction of a question on language in both Scotland and Wales by 1891. Ravenstein (1879: 579–636) highlighted the fact that, despite all the "advances" of the Victorian era ". . . the reign' of one universal language appears to be more remote than ever before". His surveys consisted of information received from large numbers of local informants and he relied on their evidence as a basis for making estimates of speakers. This pioneering work on the geography of language, together with the plea of Ellis (1882: 173–208) to the London Honourable Society of Cymmrodorion in 1882 for a full survey for educational purposes appears to have convinced the census authorities of the appropriateness of including the question on language in the next census. This, it seems, is how the first official language census came to be taken in Wales on Sunday April 5, 1891. To collect the new information the census officers added a special column to the standard householder's schedule. The results of this first enumeration were later published as Table 24 in the special volume covering Wales. This shows the numbers of persons, two years of age or over, speaking (1) English, (2) Welsh, (3) both English and Welsh, (4) other languages, and (5) "those not making a return under any of these heads" (Census of England and Wales, 1894).

Numerous problems arose in the administration of this first census of languages in Wales. Southall (1895: 7) — author, printer and publisher of Newport — made a careful assessment of the 1891 census data and he concluded that the results completely failed to fulfil expectations, both in the ways in which the enumeration had been conducted as well as in the manner in which the results were finally published. In driving home his criticisms he suggested that the reluctance of the census authorities to make a proper enumeration was revealed by their overall attitudes in placing the published tabulations at the very end of their report together with all the other "unfortunates" — the numbers and ages of the blind, dumb and mentally deranged! And, he went on, this was the treatment afforded to one of the central, most distinctive historical indicators of Welsh national identity!

Serious mistakes were made in the actual administration of the census locally. In the growing Monmouthshire town of Newport, for example, the enumeration schedules designed specifically to collect the linguistic data were sent principally to Welsh-medium Sunday schools and not, as was intended, to every householder. Elsewhere in south Wales, fines were imposed on persons refusing to complete the standard form (intended for use solely in England) which did not incorporate the question on language (Southall, 1892: 356). Moreover, even more serious is the charge that, despite all these mistakes, the Registrar General does not state how these defective returns were aggregated. Did the Registrar General count all defaulting persons as speaking only English or were they included with others as having made "no statement"? (Southall, 1895: 7).

Another serious problem is that these returns are published for *registration* districts and counties. Even by this date these areal units had become redundant for statistical purposes, especially because they failed to coincide with counties, civil parishes and the new local administrative units. Indeed, the nonsense of these registration areas as the territorial framework for recording language data was highlighted in a number of quite absurd outcomes. For example, the Welsh-speaking communities of the Ceiriog valley in south Denbighshire as well as parts of both Radnorshire and Montgomeryshire were regarded as integral parts of registration districts in England. Therefore, no linguistic data were collected! Conversely, some areas classed as part of the Welsh registration division (for example, Forden, Knighton, Hay and Monmouth) actually included parishes situated in England! Within Wales itself several registration counties overlapped the boundaries of traditional counties still used as administrative units so that many of the published tabulations were virtually meaningless (Figure 7.1).

Language censuses, 1901–71

Problems of comparability are not limited just to the 1891 census for, over the decades, different territorial units have been adopted for the presentation of language statistics within Wales. One of the continuing problems in attempting to identify long-term trends for small areas is the fact that information is not presented on a systematic basis. No single territorial unit, large or small, has ever been adopted consistently from 1891 to the present time. The sole exception is Wales as a whole but, as we have seen, even in 1891 the Registration Division of Wales did not equate to the widely recognized political boundaries of the country as defined in the Act of Union of 1536 (see Rees, 1967). Below the national

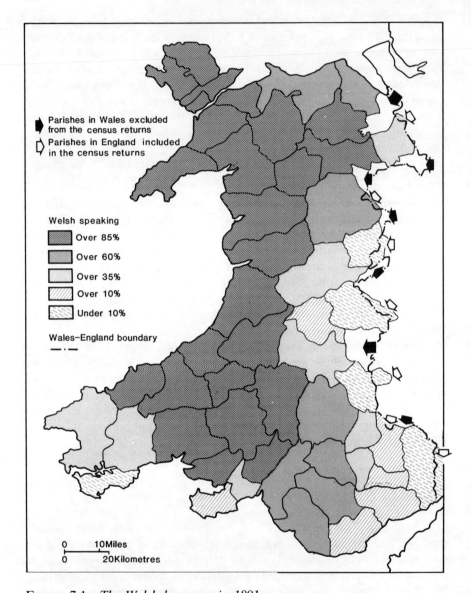

FIGURE 7.1   *The Welsh language in 1891*
Source: Based on the original map by J.E. Southall (1895) but with additional material relating to the overlap of registration districts in Wales and England.

level the returns relating to the 13 traditional counties provide the largest continuous series starting in 1901 (when the registration counties and districts were finally dropped) and ending with the 1971 figures which were collected before the re-organization of local government in 1974.[1]

The actual territorial units used reflect, of course, the specific internal administrative needs of central and local government. This has meant that the same territorial frameworks have usually been adopted for whole ranges of data: demographic information, housing provision, age structures, socio-economic characteristics, birthplace and migration information, residential and cultural variables. Since each census collected data primarily for official purposes priorities were decided according to the requirements as perceived by the various departments of state. It was not until 1964, when the first Secretary of State had been appointed and the Welsh Office had been set up in Cardiff, that Wales was officially recognized as a coherent unit for administrative purposes. Now demands could be made on the census office for information relating to the specific needs of Wales. Before this important development special *ad hoc* arrangements had evolved to meet the data needs of Education (1907), National Insurance (1911), Health (1919) and, also in 1919, Agriculture and Fisheries. All these earlier forms of "devolution" were, in reality, small units that functioned primarily as agents for the appropriate central departments of state. Thus, hitherto, specific Welsh administrative needs had had to compete with the many other conflicting demands for statistical information from within the parent administration (Randall, 1972: 353–72).

Looking back through the published census volumes we find that, as a result of these circumstances, language data are available on a consistent basis only for the larger units of local administration between 1971 and 1901: that is, for counties, county and municipal boroughs, for urban and rural districts (Table 7.1). Statistics are totally absent for the civil parish, that smallest and most locationally specific of all the territorial units in the administrative hierarchy, until 1921. We have to wait until 1961 before data are available for enumeration districts and similar small areas. In 1921, too, separate tabulations were first made available for the larger urban populations (towns with 50,000 or more). Smaller urban communities (20,000 people) had to wait another decade before appearing in the 1931 tables together with the figures for the remaining areas aggregated and presented as a somewhat unhelpful residual statistic within each county. Modern geographers are surprised to find that there are no language data for wards within each urban community before 1961 when, for the first time, they are treated as the equivalent in statistical terms of civil parishes in rural areas. Local government reorganization meant that whilst a completely new territorial framework was adopted for the tabulation of the 1981 census results, the old terms *county*, *district* and *ward* were retained but in quite a different administrative context. To avoid confusion with earlier units, these are referred to as New Counties, New Districts or New Wards in Table 7.1. In general, therefore, longterm trends in the layout of the census data are towards increasingly finer territorial detail. The most important innovations arrived in 1921; and again, in 1961 when significant detail at the local scale becomes available for the first time.

Categories of information, 1891–1981

Insufficient thought had been devoted to the actual wording of the question on the language or languages spoken by individuals when it was first included in the 1891 census. In particular, the question was asked of everyone, including infants who could not be expected to have acquired the ability to speak in any tongue! Therefore, in an attempt to bring a basic measure of validity to all the returns, children under the age of two years were excluded from the published returns (Census, 1891: 82). Subsequently, in 1901, this lower age limit was raised to three years. This continues to be the minimum age to which all the published language statistics still relate.

Six different categories of information on the Welsh language have appeared in the published tabulations at one time or another since 1891:

1. Sex groupings;
2. Numbers of speakers;
3. Writers and readers of Welsh;
4. Age groupings;
5. Retrospective statistics;
6. Birthplace and language.

Table 7.2 records details of the published information that is available. It is strange to discover that the first language census of 1891 failed to distinguish speakers by their sex in the published tables. No doubt this resulted from an oversight in the preparation of the final tabulations, for we know from other tabulations that the sex of individuals was recorded in the census enumerators' books. We shall have to wait until 1991 before these original documents can be properly consulted when they will become available for public scrutiny under the "hundred

TABLE 7.1 *Territorial units used in published census reports on the Welsh language 1891–1981*

(1) Territorial units	(2) 1891	(3) 1901	(4) 1911	(5) 1921	(6) 1931 (Census years)	(7) 1941 (Census years)	(8) 1951	(9) 1961	(10) 1971	(11) 1981
WALES[1]	X	X	X	X	X		X	X	X	X
Registration Counties	X									
Registration Districts	X									
Administrative Counties		X	X	X	X		X	X	X	
County Boroughs		X	X	X	X		X	X	X	
Municipal Boroughs		X	X	X	X		X	X	X	
Urban Districts		X	X	X	X		X	X	X	
Urban areas with populations of 20,000 or more				X	X		X	X	X	
Urban areas with populations of 50,000 or more					X		X	X	X	
'County remainders'					X			X	X	
New Towns								X	X	
Wards			X					X	X	
Rural Districts		X		X	X		X	X	X	
Civil Parishes				X	X		X	X	X	
Enumeration Districts/Small Area Statistics[2]								X	X	X
New Counties[3]										X
New Districts[3]										X
New Wards[3]										X

Note: column (7) 1941 — NO CENSUS TAKEN.

1. Registration Division of Monmouthshire and Wales 1891; aggregates of the thirteen administrative counties 1901–71; aggregates of the eight new administrative counties 1981.
2. These unpublished tabulations are available from the Office of Population, Censuses and Surveys, Titchfield, Fareham, Hants, PO15 5RR.
3. New areas produced by local government reorganization with effect from April 1 1974.

years' confidentiality rule" that has been maintained for all British census records. Until 1971 all census data relate solely to the ability of individuals to *speak* in Welsh and/or in English. Since the tables are based directly on the returns as filled in by householders, these published statistics do not imply anything concerning the linguistic proficiencies of individuals. It is most important to keep in mind this very point as to the nature of these language data, particularly when public policies are to be based on research using this information. Despite the availability of these census data, local education authorities have found it necessary to conduct their own more detailed surveys as to the "home" language of children and their linguistic proficiency before adopting appropriate policies in schools.

The problem of what the returns actually mean in reality was raised and discussed on many occasions in the official census reports. Thus, in 1921 it was stated that "standards of proficiency" were not necessarily reflected in the returns because they were based on "self assessment" and this meant that "the replies may have varied, for example, according to the attitude taken with regard to the object of enquiry ..." (Census, 1921: 184). Earlier censuses reported that bilinguals may have returned themselves as "Welsh monoglots" on the assumption that officials required information on the language spoken "habitually or preferentially" (Census, 1891: 28).

Official concern about apparent overstatements as to the numbers of monoglots, English as well as Welsh, is echoed on successive occasions. In 1911 the various dilemmas facing the census takers were neatly highlighted as follows:

"It is at least probable that some ability to speak both languages is in many cases not acknowledged in the census return when one language is in common use, but it is not obvious from the figures whether the consequent exaggeration of the monoglot population is greater among persons returned as able to speak 'English only' or among those returned as able to speak 'Welsh only'." (Census, 1911: iv).

Another problem with which all censuses up to and including that taken in 1921 have had to contend is the failure of many individuals to record any linguistic data concerning themselves despite the provision of full details on all other topics of enquiry! In 1901 no language returns were received from 2,757 people. By 1911 the numbers of incomplete schedules had jumped considerably to 58,517. In commenting on these defaults, the 1911 official census report suggested that a decade earlier the apparent deficiencies were small because local enumerators had "adjusted" their returns, putting down everyone in a household as speaking the same language or languages as the head of that household. Therefore, in 1911 the enumeration procedures were tightened up and clarified. In consequence, the published tabulations have one set of columns for linguistic status as actually returned on the schedules with another set headed "no statement" where, in the absence of a return, individuals are classified according to the language or languages used by the head of their household. On this basis, in 1911 34,248 persons in Wales were assigned a linguistic affiliation — either as English monoglots (19,647), Welsh monoglots (2,803) or as bilinguals (11,798 persons). The remainder, some 24,269 persons, are listed as having made no statement whatsoever because the household head had failed to record details of the language he himself spoke in the appropriate column of the enumeration schedule (Census, 1911).

In 1921 similar approaches were adopted for the handling of deficient returns. Industrial and transport disputes led to further complications when the actual day of enumeration, set originally for April 24 1921, had to be postponed to June 19. This, the authorities stated, was one of the main reasons why over 36,000 people failed to return details of the languages they used. On this occasion, in compiling their tabulations the census office assigned children aged 3–15 years to the household head's linguistic category. At the time of enumeration the holiday season was already in full swing and it was thought that many of the incompleted schedules had been filled in by visitors who, as temporary residents, would not have been present if the census had been taken at the "originally appointed date in April". So, to enable comparisons to be drawn with earlier returns, correction tables were issued. These were intended to help users by applying "inflation factors" to take account of the unusual circumstances under which the enumeration had been made (Census, 1921: 198–201). Nevertheless, despite the foresight of the census office, when applied to the small-area statistics needed by geographers, these correction factors produce results of doubtful validity. The "no statement" columns, intended to cater for all those who could not be assigned a linguistic status by reference to that of the head of household, disappear from all the language tabulations published after 1921.

As far as we are aware, hitherto it has not been generally recognized that up to and including the 1911 enumeration, the census, as administered in Wales, was in reality a genuine language census in the fullest sense: not only were details collected concerning those speaking Welsh or English, but also, as tabulated in the published returns, the numbers of speakers of "other languages". Individual languages are not recognized

TABLE 7.2 *Categories of information and the smallest territorial units used in the published census reports on the Welsh Language 1891–1981*

(1) Tabulated data	(2) 1891	(3) 1901	(4) 1911	(5) 1921	(6) 1931	(7) 1941	(8) 1951	(9) 1961	(10) 1971	(11) 1981
	Smallest territorial unit for which data are available. See below for details of these numerical codes.									
					census years					
Sex	·	2	2	1	1		1	1	1	1
Speakers										
Welsh monoglots	5	2	2	1	1	NO	1	1	1	1
Welsh–English bilinguals	5	2	2	1	1	CENSUS	1	1	1	1
English monoglots	5	2	2	1	·	TAKEN	·	·	·	·
Other languages (unspecified)	5	2	2	·						
No statement	5	2	2	1						
Readers of Welsh	·	·	·	·	·		·	·	1	1
Writers of Welsh	·	·	·	·	·		·	·	1	1
Age structure in five groups[a]	·	2	·	·	·		·	·	·	·
Age structure in seven groups[b]	·	·	2	2	2/3		2/3	2/3	2/3	·
Age structure in nine groups[c]	·	·	·	·	·		·	·	·	6

Retrospective figures – one decade	·	·	·	2	2	·	2	·
Retrospective figures – several decades(d)								
Birthplaces – generalized(e)	·	4/7	·	4/7	4/7	·	8	9

(a) 3–14, 15–24, 25–44, 45–64, 65+ years.
(b) 3–4, 5–9, 10–14, 15–24, 25–44, 45–64, 65+ years.
(c) 3–4, 5–9, 10–14, 15–24, 25–34, 35–44, 45–54, 55–64, 65+ years.
(d) 1911–61 in 1961; 1911–71 in 1971; 1921–81 in 1981.
(e) Usually resident population aged 3 years and over born in (a) Wales, (b) rest of UK, (c) outside UK.

TERRITORIAL UNITS (COLS. 2–11 ABOVE)

Codes
1. Civil Parishes 1921–71; New Wards 1981.
2. Rural Districts; Urban Districts; Municipal Boroughs; County Boroughs; New Towns.
3. Urban areas with populations of 20,000 or more; 'County remainders'.
4. Urban areas with populations of 50,000 or more; 'County remainders'.
5. Registration Districts (1891 only).
6. New Districts (1981).
7. Administrative Counties (1901–71).
8. New Counties (1981).
9. Wales.

locally but, no doubt, all the actual details were recorded on the actual enumeration schedules. Unfortunately, under present legislation these are not available for detailed study. From the published tables we do know, however, that in 1891 3,076 persons in the Welsh Registration Division (virtually the whole of Wales — see Figure 7.1), spoke languages *other than* Welsh or English and these accounted for 1.7 per thousand of the population. The numbers varied, as we would expect, from relatively high concentrations in port towns (Cardiff 9.2, Newport 2.5, and Swansea 4.3 per thousand) to very low proportions elsewhere (Holywell 1.8, Conwy 1.4, Ffestiniog 0.9, and Aberystwyth 0.3 per thousand). At the 1901 census Wales (including Monmouthshire) recorded 1.9 per thousand of the population speaking "other languages" and the proportion reached 3.6 per thousand in Glamorganshire. The census ascribes this high concentration as due to "the presence of Foreign Seamen on vessels in Port etc. on census night" (Census, 1901: 294). In 1911, whilst Wales overall still recorded 1.6 persons per thousand speaking "other languages", the ratios varied from 2.6 per thousand in Glamorganshire to 8.8 per thousand of the residents in the Ystradgynlais Rural District! As is to be expected in industrial and maritime communities, overwhelmingly, the speakers of these other languages were recorded as men.

Changes in the instructions printed on the enumeration schedules meant that information on "other languages" did not appear in 1921. The scope of the question on language was further narrowed when the Order in Council for the 1931 enumeration omitted any reference for the need to collect data on English monoglots living in Wales. This change was deliberate and was recognized as such in the following explanation which appeared in the General Report on the 1931 census:

"... it [the question on English monoglots] having been included at previous Censuses ... with a view to making the question as to ability to speak Welsh or not exhaustive and obtaining *some* reply in the case of every individual". (Census, 1931: 182)

By 1931, therefore, it was officially recognized that the census should be reduced in scope to focus primarily on the use of Welsh as a popular medium of speech and that it had never been intended to be a general survey of all the languages used in Wales. Thus, as Table 7.2 shows, since 1921 the questions put in successive censuses related specifically to Welsh monoglots and Welsh-English bilinguals. The actual numbers of Anglophones are worked out later in the tabulation stages, by extracting these totals from enumerated population. In this way not only did the census come to sharply focus the nature of its enquiry concerning specific issues but, at the same time, valuable printing space was saved by excluding the "English-only" column from the tabulation.

Forty years were to elapse before the basic "speaking question" was to be supplemented by the request in 1971 for information as to whether Welsh speakers were able to read and/or write the language. Again, as in all previous censuses, no minimum standards of proficiency were laid down: individuals were left to make their own assessments as to their own proficiencies in these different modes of communication. Despite declining numbers, the defenders of Welsh earned an enhanced status for the language in the decades leading up to 1971. Eventually, this has come to be recognized, somewhat grudgingly, by officials in central and local government, especially in the fields of education and social planning. We are not surprised, therefore, to find that the original request to extend the 1971 census enquiries to include these new questions on readers and writers of Welsh emanated from that growing nexus of central government administration in Wales, the Welsh Office itself.[2] The same questions were repeated in 1981. The information which resulted from these additional topics was tabulated in the published reports in close detail, parish by parish. As we shall see, its analysis has produced a whole range of new, important findings concerning Wales as a distinctive culture area, particularly concerning the processes, social as well as spatial, which continue to bring about significant changes (Carter & Carter 1974a,b; Bowen & Carter, 1974, 1975; Carter & Aitchison, 1986).

Age structures within the Welsh-speaking population constitute the fourth major category of data collected in the census. These aspects first appeared in 1901 and they have been tabulated consistently ever since — the only changes being an expansion in detail from five age groups to seven in 1911, followed by still further detail in nine categories by 1981. These improvements seem to have been designed to identify the different cohorts of school pupils (1911 census) and, more recently, as Table 7.2 shows, with the growth of Welsh in adult education and in the social services, distinctive client groups over the age of 25 years.

Retrospective figures, covering several decades, usually expressed as ratios of Welsh speakers per thousand of the enumerated population, made their first appearances for local/administrative units in 1931. Previous to this date, as the table shows, actual numbers were printed for the current and the one previous census.

Birthplaces and the numbers speaking Welsh in each of six broad age groups constitute the last and most recent innovation in the data now available concerning the Welsh language. These interesting tabulations first appeared in 1981 and their scope has been described earlier.

Table 7.2 also indicates the various territorial administrative units used in the published census reports for the presentation of data on all six of the major categories of information which have been outlined in this section. Spatial data in finest detail is reserved for the actual numbers speaking, reading and/or writing Welsh. In contrast, information on age structures is available only for the larger units of local government — boroughs, urban and rural districts; new towns from 1901 to 1971 inclusive; and for the new district council areas in 1981. Researchers needing more local details will be able to find them in the unpublished Small Area Statistics available in 1961 and subsequently. Nevertheless, a word of warning to the unwary! Because of changes in boundaries and the different ways in which enumeration districts were defined at each successive census, these sources do pose a number of serious interpretative problems for comparisons over time.[3]

Problems of cartographic interpretation

Welsh geographers can claim a long record of map making concerning the linguistic distributions within their own country. Although, as we have seen, maps were published in the late nineteenth century, it was not until 1926 that the first work by a "professional" geographer, Mr Trevor Lewis (1926: 413–18) appeared, written — perhaps significantly — in the French language, in that world-famous journal, the *Annales de Géographie*. In many respects, probably, this was *the* first piece of scientific writing on the geography of the Welsh language even if, as D. Trevor Williams (1937: 146–51) pointed out a decade later, the mapped distributions related solely to the monoglot Welsh rather than, as later users of Lewis's map assumed, the total numbers *able to speak* the language, bilinguals as well as Welsh monoglots. This pioneer study was followed by a series of important papers by D. Trevor Williams (1935: 239–66; 1936: 194–229) himself which mapped the percentages of Welsh speakers, parish by parish, within each county. Despite the detail of his work, Williams was careful to point out that, even at this scale of analysis, many local features were obscured. Therefore, after identifying the "border-zone of language change" from county maps, he went on to conduct

> "personal enquiries to the schools, churches and chapels, and in the villages and towns ... to delineate a more accurate language *divide* ... than is posisble from parish data only."

These divides were then superimposed on the parish distributions within each county. "It was found", Williams wrote, "that certain parishes, county boroughs, and urban districts . . . provided too large a territorial unit for accurate representation merely from statistics." Once they had been identified, Williams claimed that his language divides marked "the limits of anglicization, the area in which Welsh is no longer the medium of cultural interpretation or of ordinary conversation to the majority of the population".

Since those early papers, a whole series of maps and interpretative comments have appeared after each census in the leading journals for the publication of geographical research.[4] Long before the development of geography as the "spatial" science — when increased emphasis was to be placed on the recognition of social areas and the limits of specific cultural domains — Williams' concept of the language divide was, in itself, a most imaginative and original concept. Cultural area and language divide are complementary ideas. No doubt, Williams imported these from social anthropology or, perhaps, from the terminology of physical geography to mobilize his own studies into the changing language geography of Wales. And these were proved to be fertile concepts and capable of further development in the work of William Rees, who completed an important Doctoral thesis in 1940. Nevertheless, until the publication of the studies on the 1971 census by Carter and Bowen the main emphasis has been on the interpretation of percentage *relative* statistics in each area rather than on *absolute* numbers. Taken in isolation, these "intensity" maps can easily turn out to be quite misleading. Thus, for example, the County of Mid Glamorgan recorded only 8.3% of its population as Welsh-speaking — a low ratio or "intensity". Yet, in absolute terms this meant 42,691 individuals — more than twice as many as were recorded in the whole of Merionydd District (20,944) where 71.2% of the population spoke Welsh. Whilst the percentage figures indicate something as to intensities of Welshness, actual figures provide a quantitative measure of the utmost significance when it comes to planning a consumer service such as local education facilities or, for example, the circulation of magazines published in the Welsh language.

These aspects of the census figures had not gone unrecognized in the earlier writings of Southall (1855–1928). Southall was a vociferous advocate of bilingual education in day schools throughout Wales. After submitting evidence to the Royal Commission on Education, 1886–87, as we have seen, eventually he published his arguments in full together with surveys of the historical background in his authoritative book *Wales and her Language* (1891). The work for this had been completed much earlier and in advance of the first language census in that same year. In consequence, his first map, published in colour as the fold-out frontispiece to this volume showed, in a very generalized way, areas where Welsh was estimated to be understood by (a) over 60% of the adult population; (b) less than 60%, and (c) those districts mainly in south Pembrokeshire, the Gower and in the English borderlands where "no native Welsh [is] understood or spoken". The information used for the preparation of this map had been obtained from local informants, and from Southall's own personal knowledge and field surveys. His methods of collecting data were not in themselves original for, as we have seen, Ravenstein (1879) and Ellis (1882) had been forced to rely on similar sources and techniques.

Despite his English nationality and educational background, Southall learned Welsh and became a great enthusiast for the language. To keep his arguments alive and in high profile he published, at his own expense, an important sequel to *Wales and her Language*. This was based on the first enumeration of Welsh speakers taken in 1891 and the pamphlet included the first map based on census statistics to be published for Wales (see Figure 7.1) (Southall, 1895).

From his writings it is abundantly clear that Southall was disgusted by the failure of the Registrar General to provide a meaningful interpretation of the new language data — hence the need for his own analysis and commentaries. As we have seen, this first census was unacceptable on numerous grounds but especially because of the overlap into England of its statistical areas. To rescue what information he could from the published tabulations, Southall embarked on a series of *ad hoc* analyses and interpretations of the linguistic situation then prevailing in each of the 13 ancient counties of Wales. To do this he was obliged to make statistical adjustments and estimates to accommodate differences between the areas covered by registration districts and administrative counties. His efforts are commendable. But, although his results do offer a much clearer picture of reality than the official census report, underlying statistical inadequacies and evidence, here and there, of defective enumeration do mean that not too much reliability should be placed on the more detailed aspects of his revisions.

Nevertheless, Southall's 1891 language map census still remains a work of considerable interest. In the "preface" to his 1895 pamphlet, Southall took care to point out a number of methodological issues still of relevance to map making today. Thus, for example, he emphasized that the map "affords no means of discrimination between the native and the non-native Welsh, nor any linguistic boundaries at all, save those of the Poor Law Unions or Registration Districts" (p. 3). Then, in a significant warning against the failure to recognize that some generalizations may be based on what today we refer to as the *ecological fallacy*, Southall went on to point out that the shadings in each administrative area represented "average" conditions: in reality, within any single registration area, some communities and groups would have been much more Welsh or much more English than others. Therefore, in having to rely on such extensive territorial units, significant local differences remain hidden and, in consequence, a misleading linguistic affiliation and status are attributed to these communities.

Finally, in a short pungent statement which, as it has turned out, can only be regarded as remarkable for its foresightedness, he wrote:

"Pamphlets are usually temporary in their use. I hope, however, this one will be found to be a repertory to historical facts of a kind very apt to be overlooked by the generation in whose time they occur, and as such will prove of some service in the future." (1895: 4).

Southall was to go on to write and publish a further analysis and detailed map of the 1901 census. By this date registration areas had ceased to be used by the census authorities in favour of the administrative county, urban and rural districts. For the first time the census had managed to escape from the use of anachronistic statistical areas and this meant that Southall could now concentrate on the interpretation of processes — the roles played by migration, urban and industrial development and the resultant effects on language changes within each county (Southall, 1904).

In showing percentages of adult Welsh speakers Southall's 1891 map reveals the *relative* significance of the language in the various regions of the country. This approach stands in marked contrast to more recent studies where the *actual* as well as relative numbers are used. In *Wales and her Language* (1891) Southall adopted 60% and over for the identification of those areas still dominantly Welsh in speech. No doubt this critical measure was selected because, in a relative context, it represented a clear majority. This same idea seems to have been applied in the choice of class intervals for his later map based on the published results of the 1891 census (Figure 7.1). But from the percentage data he is now able to identify intermediate areas with decreasing densities of, as he puts it, "over 35 and under 60 per cent" followed by those with "over 10 and under 35 per cent Welsh speaking". In these ways Southall's analysis was beginning to move towards a much more meaningful interpretation of regional differences. Nevertheless, the large statistical units (which, in the absence of more local details, he was obliged to use)

meant that he was denied the possibility of identifying the long-established
linguistic transition of bilingualism between Welsh-speaking and English-
speaking areas. This very feature has always been of importance in the
cultural life of the Welsh nation and of considerable practical significance
in so far as government and public policies are concerned. Yet, the
inadequacies of both the 1891 and 1901 censuses meant that this interesting
feature could not be pinpointed accurately on the ground!

The statistical shortcomings of the early twentieth century censuses
were reflected, very clearly, in the long-running, often acrimonious public
debate concerning the role of the Anglican Church in Wales. Up to the
mid-nineteenth century there are clear signs that, as administered in
Wales, the Established Church used the language or a combination of
the two languages most appropriate to local needs in public worship.
However, after this date the spiritual needs of the overwhelming majority
of Welshmen were increasingly catered for in their own language by the
chapels of the nonconformist denominations and there is much evidence
that parish church services became progressively more and more anglicized
in the later decades of the nineteenth century (Pryce, 1978a: 2–6, 19).
Together with a whole range of other serious matters, this was to
become an issue of widespread public concern that led eventually to
disestablishment and the setting up of the Church in Wales in 1914.
Linguistic considerations figured prominently in the evidence collected
by the Royal Commission on Religious Bodies in Wales, whose report
appeared in 1910.

The most contentious matters revolved around the appropriateness
or otherwise of holding services completely in Welsh or completely in
English. Whilst the use of the two languages was actively encouraged
where this met the needs of local churches in the Diocese of St. Asaph,
in the larger Dioceses of both Bangor and St. David's, the bishops
preferred separate Welsh and English services, thus catering for different
congregations within the same communities. In marked contrast, within
the ancient Diocese of Llandaff, which accommodated rapidly-growing
communities in the colliery valleys of south Wales and their large numbers
of very recent migrants from rural Wales, the emphasis was on the
provision of services solely in the English language. The Bishop of
Llandaf, in his evidence to the Royal Commissioners, argued that he was
quite prepared to organize services in the Welsh language for monoglot
Welshmen but otherwise services in his churches were to be held in
English because "... a large number of people who understood Welsh
naturally prefer an English service" (Royal Commission on the Church
of England and other religious bodies in Wales and Monmouthshire,

1911). It is clear that different policies were being pursued in different dioceses and these policies were sometimes quite unrelated to local conditions and actual needs.

It is not surprising to find, therefore, that some of the more influential members of the Royal Commission (1910: 235, 297) felt that Welsh had not been given due recognition in the services of the Anglican Church. And, having obtained details of the languages used in individual churches throughout Wales, they examined actual practice for its appropriateness in the light of the 1901 census figures. To aid them in their work a new type of language map was compiled and this was published as part of the evidence they had received.[5] This presented a synoptic view of linguistic relationships throughout the country, showing those local government areas (urban and rural districts) where (a) the monoglot Welsh, or (b) the monoglot English formed the majority, as well as (c) the dominance of one or other of these groups where neither formed a clear majority in the population. No specific details are offered by the Commissioners as to how this interesting new map was prepared but from the table included in the Appendices to their *Report* it does seem that the linguistic status of each area was decided individually by comparing the *actual* numbers of speakers in each category. Therefore, the final result is a *qualitative*, "status" map derived from actual numbers rather than percentages (Figure 7.2). These approaches were original and, at the time, quite innovatory; and the results so achieved are a first-class example of a map prepared to illustrate the inappropriateness of church policies — at least in the industrial south. Yet, at the same time, in identifying the monoglot Welsh as a distinctive category — a group which was to diminish progressively in numbers in the following decades — this was very much a map of its own time. The continuous expanse of the Welsh-speaking core areas survived almost into our own times, although today the numbers of Welsh monoglots are insignificant. The broken cross-hatched areas of the borderland, Gower and south Pembrokeshire, constitute the main Englishries as they had developed up to 1901, whilst the adjacent areas with continuous diagonal shading are those neighbouring districts where English was continuing to advance into the Welsh Heartland through contact diffusion. Similarly, the small "in-liers" within the Heartland itself record the impact and roles of small country towns in the diffusion process. Urban centres were functioning as incipient centres of anglicization. This applies especially to the seaside resorts between Rhyl and Conwy in the north; and equally to the smaller centres further west, such as Bangor, Holyhead, Barmouth and Aberystwyth, whose relative Englishness is explainable as the end result of diffusion downwards through the urban hierarchy.[6]

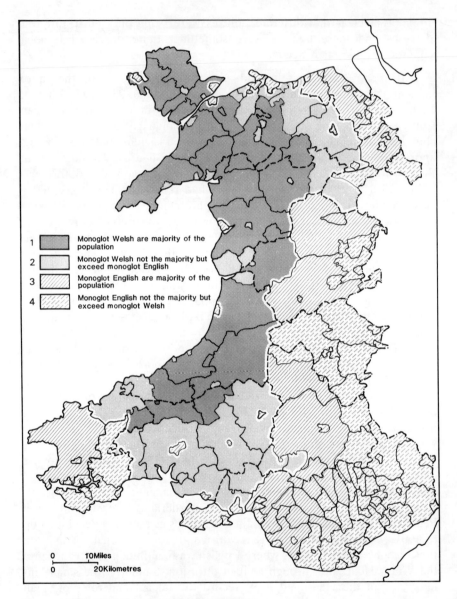

1 Monoglot Welsh are majority of the population

2 Monoglot Welsh not the majority but exceed monoglot English

3 Monoglot English are majority of the population

4 Monoglot English not the majority but exceed monoglot Welsh

0   10Miles

0   20Kilometres

FIGURE 7.2   *Language majorities, 1901*
Source: Based on *Report, Royal Commission on the Church and other religious bodies in Wales*, 1911 (vol. 1, pt. II, Appendices).

Mapping language change from census statistics

Cartographic analysis of regional change in a language and the changes over time raises a number of important issues. One of the easiest and most widely used approaches is to produce a sequence of maps recording the relevant distributions at specific dates. This was the method adopted by Humphreys (1979: 41–46, 89) in a recent important review of long-term changes in the language geography of Wales. As Figure 7.3 shows, this aspect of his analysis relates to the diminishing number of Welsh monoglots and his series of interesting maps effectively highlights the progressive fragmentation and decline of the very "core" of the Welsh culture area between 1921 and 1971. Because of successive changes in parish boundaries, the finer detail in these maps as to specific areas cannot be taken as definitive. Synoptic maps such as these offer us a series of regional changes capable of interpretation only in terms of broad outline trends. Moreover, because of the nature of these data, statistical comparisons in the form of areal percentage changes or correlation coefficients between one date and the next are not possible. Instead, all the prevailing trends have to be analysed by visual comparison. This places heavy premiums on the mental imagery and background knowledge of individual observers. Some critics have argued that this form of analysis is too subjective an approach to gain widespread acceptance. Nevertheless, the nature of the source data often means that this is the only viable method that can be adopted for the study of territorial changes over time.

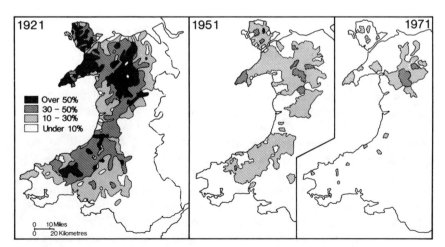

FIGURE 7.3   *Welsh monoglots 1921, 1951, and 1971*
Source: Based on H.L. Humphreys (1979: 89)

Maps drawn on this basis have value primarily as descriptive media: they record factual information of what is actually "there" at specific dates. But, in order to gain an understanding of the *spatial* processes underlying the observed patterns of language change, numbers and the regional distribution of Welsh monoglots need to be considered, as indeed they are in Humphreys' own work, in relation to bilinguals. This throws up a number of difficult problems concerning the availability of appropriate areal data.

Depending on the nature of the data and the scale of the research, different solutions can be sought. First and foremost, at *macro* levels of enquiry involving, for example, changes throughout the whole of Wales, there is the problem of lack of continuity in the areas to which the available data relate. In fact, as Table 7.1 has shown, between 1901 and 1971, the administrative county is the sole territorial unit appearing consistently in the published census reports. Although it is sometimes possible to conduct regional enquiries using the parish as the basic statistical unit (Ambrose, 1980; Ambrose & Williams, 1981a), there are no generally available language data for these local areas until 1921 and even after that date the study of long-term changes is bedevilled by successive boundary changes. Brief notes on such intercensal administrative modifications were published with the population figures for each parish but, even with this information, detailed first-hand knowledge is still a requirement if estimates of language changes are to be meaningful.

At the simplest level of analysis long-term trends in the numbers of Welsh monoglots and the numbers of bilinguals can be presented as small bar graphs superimposed on each county area. For comparative reasons all the figures are standardized as percentages. The declining slopes of the bar graphs in Figure 7.4 indicate quite clearly that all counties recorded progressive falls in the numbers of Welsh speakers (that is, all persons aged three years and over able to speak the language, monoglots and bilinguals) between 1901 and 1971. Moreover, closer examination of the relative differences between the two distributions reveals that after 1911 Welsh monoglots declined at a faster rate than the Welsh-speaking population as a whole. Some commentators have argued that this very feature is central to the processes of decline within any language community. At first the declining numbers of bilinguals were offset in every county by the addition of those who had recently acquired fluency in English. Once this source of Welsh speakers was depleted, then, without adequate institutions to support the language, rapid declines in the remaining bilingual population have ensued. Preliminary work on the 1981 census indicates that in those districts where Welsh schools have

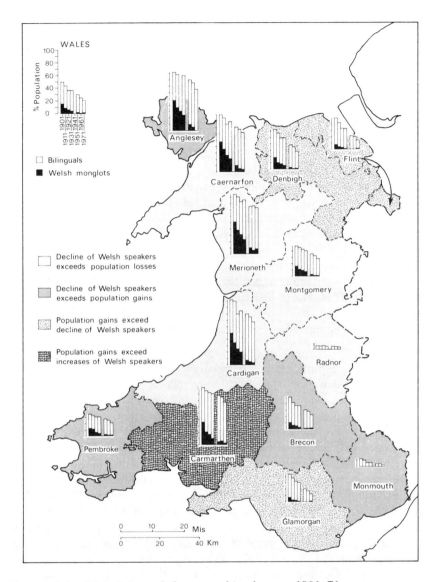

FIGURE 7.4   *Linguistic and demographic changes 1901–71*
The status of each county (the shaded area) is based on the summation of intercensal
percentage changes of population and Welsh speakers
Source: Based on W.T.R. Pryce (1978b: 231).

been established and where new, more positive attitudes to the nourishment of Welsh culture are evident, this decline has showed signs of a small but significant reversal that has attracted much attention (Aitchison & Carter, 1985; Williams, 1986a).

Intercensal changes can easily be calculated in percentage terms and this provides an acceptable measure of relative change between successive censuses. This method has been widely used to reveal changes over longer periods of time spanning several decades, e.g. 1901–31, 1901–71. One disadvantage of this approach is that, for periods spanning more than one decade, differences are measured only between the two terminal years cited. In reality, considerable decadal variation may have occurred between these dates and these changes will not be reflected in the apparent differences. Therefore, there is a statistical need to adopt an approach which is more representative of actual events. This involves the calculation of percentage changes in each of the decades under review. For example, in an examination of the trends between 1901 and 1971, intercensal percentage changes for 1901–11, 1911–21, 1921–31, 1931–51, 1951–61 and 1961–71 are first calculated. Taking account of the direction (negative or positive) of change, these are then summed in each county area to give aggregated indices of long-term movements 1901–71.

Long-term changes in (a) the percentage of Welsh speakers, and for comparative purposes (b) population trends 1901–1971 within each county have been calculated in this way (Pryce, 1978b: 233). Then, by plotting these measurements on a Cartesian co-ordinate graph whose field is divided on the basis of two dichotomous (gains, losses) variables, four categories of relationship between concurrent movements can be recognized (for details of the method, see Webb, 1963: 103–48). In this way, each county is allocated a status classification as shown by the different types of shading used in Figure 7.4. The trends revealed from our examination of the super-imposed graphs can now be interpreted by reference to overall changes in the population of each area. Thus, we find that the decline in the use of Welsh was greater in relative terms in the northwest and in the rural counties of central Wales than the long-standing decline of the population generally. Contrary trends are evident in the majority of areas, particularly within the industrial northeast and in southeast Wales where the percentage *decline* of Welsh exceeded the percentage *growth* of population. Only in the old county of Carmarthen, straddling as it does both industrial and rural communities, did the usage of Welsh increase in step with the overall increases of population recorded between 1901 and 1971.

The Location Quotient is another descriptive measure that has been used to record changes in the distribution of Welsh speakers. This index has a long history of usage in geographical research and in industrial economics, particularly in studies of plant location as measured by employment statistics. The value of this approach is that the location quotient shows the linguistic status of a particular locality in relation to that prevailing within the wider regional setting. Thus, in their analysis of the 1971 census, Emery & White (1975: 26–30) divided the Principality into two major culture areas based on the relative strength of Welsh. "Welsh Wales", in their terminology, comprises all those local government areas where 50% and over of the population (aged 3 years and more) is recorded as able to speak the language; all the remaining areas are classed by them as "Anglicized Wales". Location quotients were then calculated for local authority districts within each of these major language areas. The quotient is obtained simply, by dividing the *proportion (%)* of the population in a specific locality by the *proportion (%)* in the overall language region (that is, either "Welsh Wales" or "Anglicized Wales") in which that area is set. A locality with the same proportion as its region will score 1.0: that is, Welsh speakers there are represented in the same proportion as their occurrence throughout the wider area. A location quotient of more than 1.0 indicates "over representation" of Welsh speakers; a value of less than 1.0 shows "under representation".[7] Clearly, it is important to define carefully the limits of the wider regional setting and calculate the overall numbers of persons speaking Welsh before proceeding to deal with each area.

Location quotients of Welsh speakers signify their relative concentrations locally. Moreover, this useful exploratory index can be prepared for a whole succession of different census returns over time. Once these data have been prepared, changes between one census and the next can be further measured just as easily by taking each area in turn and dividing the location quotient for the later date (for example, 1971) by that for the earlier date (for example, 1961). The final scores can then be presented in cartographic form (Figure 7.5). Unity (a location quotient of 1.0) indicates that the proportional *change* in Welsh speakers in a specific area mirrors overall change within "Welsh Wales" or "Anglicized Wales" as the case may be. A score 1.1 or above informs us that, in relative terms, Welsh has increased in strength in that area; conversely, scores of 0.9 or less show a weakening of the language between these two dates. Once prepared in this way, such a map needs further careful analysis and interpretation to pinpoint underlying causes.

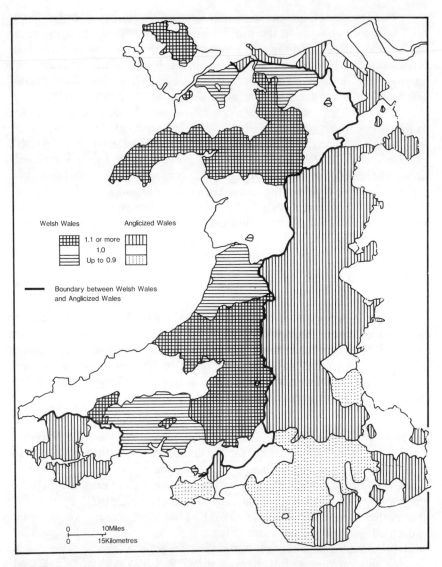

FIGURE 7.5   *Location quotient changes for Welsh speakers 1961–71*
The Location Quotient has been calculated separately for (a) "Welsh
Wales" and (b) "Anglicized Wales". See text.
Source: Based on Emery & White (1975: 29).

Thus, the location quotient offers the researcher a series of *relative* comparisons that neatly complement the more orthodox analytical techniques based on the straightforward percentage changes described earlier. The particular value of this measure is that it constitutes an index relating changes in specific localities to the regional statistical context in which they occur. Although used in urban social studies, hitherto this measure has not been widely applied as an analytical device for recording distributions in cultural and linguistic geography. It is a technique that needs further exploration.

Intercensal changes and their underlying processes can be more easily examined, perhaps, at the local regional level rather than for Wales as a whole. In other words, the geographic scale of analysis has an important bearing on the research strategy and approach. This has been demonstrated by Clive James in his two interesting studies of the fortunes of the Welsh language within the counties of Clwyd and Gwynedd between 1921 and 1971. Although, as we saw earlier (Table 7.1), the language figures have been available for urban and rural administrative districts since 1901, they were not published for parishes until 1921. Subsequently, a whole series of returns appeared for these, the smallest of the local authority areas, until local government reorganization in 1974 when parishes were swept away and community councils took their place. These data constraints determined the terminal dates chosen by James (1974: 3–15; 1975: 25–35) for examining the long-term changes within these two particularly interesting counties.

James's analysis is based on the proportion of Welsh speakers recorded in the 1921 census. The linguistic situation recorded in that census was closely scrutinized by him and "communities" (that is, civil parishes) were placed in one of six "situation" categories. These range from Situation A, where over 90% of the local population were returned as being able to speak Welsh, and Situation B with 76–90%, down to minority statuses such as Situation E (25–50%) or Situation F (less than 25% Welsh speakers).

Changing linguistic trends were next interpreted, not as straightforward percentage changes, but in terms of the numbers of communities falling into each of these "situations" at successive dates. In 1921 23 of Clwyd's 117 parishes were recorded in Situation A (over 90% Welsh speakers): by 1971 this had declined to just two communities. At the other end of the linguistic spectrum Situation F parishes (less than 25% Welsh speakers) amounted to some 24 in 1921 but these had nearly doubled in number to 41 by 1971 (Table 7.3). The table indicates the

TABLE 7.3   *Communities in Clwyd and intensity of Welsh 1921–1981*

Year	Sitn. A >90%	Sitn. B 76–90%	Sitn. C 67–75%	Sitn. D 51–66%	Sitn. E 25–50%	Sitn. F <25%
			numbers of communities			
1921	23	26	14	17	13	24
1931	18	26	14	21	12	26
1951	5	27	9	24	21	31
1961	4	35	12	19	22	35
1971	2	16	12	11	35	41

Source: Based on C. James (1975: 27).

progressive changes of status that occurred during the intervening years. More recently, this same sort of analysis, involving the changing linguistic status of specific localities, has received attention at a Welsh national level in the work of Aitchison & Carter (1985) whose "interpretative atlas" of the Welsh language covers the years 1961–81 which we shall discuss below.

James's earlier studies include very effective cartographic treatment of these status data in addition to his tabular information. These methods focus attention on the continuing contraction of the core of the Welsh culture area (parishes in Situations A, B and C). All these long-term trends were, in the view of James, closely linked to movements in local demographic structures (particularly changing age groupings) and education policies. His study concludes with the division of each of the counties into a number of language regions for which the criteria seem to have been of an intuitive kind. Rather than place the emphasis on percentage change or, indeed, *changes in percentages*, in these approaches the focus is related explicitly to the linguistic status of individual communities over time. It is clear that this sort of analysis is fully appropriate to the context of policy formulation in local administration, particularly in relation to settlement planning and the language or languages of instruction in schools.

Changes related to external structural considerations

Once the basic spatial parameters have been established, if meaningful interpretations are to be made there is the clear need to relate linguistic changes to movements in society generally. In Figure 7.4, for example, long-term changes in the proportions of Welsh speakers are linked to population trends. A preliminary but, nevertheless, significant paper by S.W. Williams in 1981 set out to explore relationships between urbanism and the diffusion of the English language into Wales between 1901 and 1971.[8] Using a range of standard statistical and graphical techniques, Williams found that, throughout these decades, the Welsh language was increasingly concentrated in those towns which occupied the lowest ranges of the urban hierarchy. This, he concluded, resulted from the fact that as the hierarchy of centres became stabilized, anglicization was engendered from the constant flow of messages along established channels of communications and by the discharge of central place functions within the urban system. In particular, this, he postulated, occurred "as commercial and other links are made between the more anglicized and the traditionally 'Welsh' centres". Adopting Carter's urban status classification (which recognizes nine different functional categories of town) Williams went on to examine the dates when specific towns returned less than 50% of their population as able to speak Welsh. Places ranking high in urban status, such as Merthyr Tydfil (Urban Rank No. 2a), fell below the 50% Welsh threshold early (in 1911); in contrast, lower ranking centres, such as Abergele (Urban Rank No. 6), Llanfyllin (Rank 9) or Llanwrtyd Wells (also Urban Rank 9), recorded less than half of their population as Welsh speaking much later. As Williams, himself, was careful to point out, this analysis fails to take into consideration the linguistic nature of the region in which a specific town is set so that the "neighbourhood effect", a consideration of some importance in diffusion studies, does not receive the attention it merits. Thus, despite their low ranking in the urban hierarchy, centres such as Prestatyn (Urban Rank 8), Llanidloes (also Rank 8), Bedwas (Rank 6) and Margam (also Rank 6), all recorded less than 50 per cent Welsh speaking populations before 1921 (Figure 7.6).

Despite problems concerning the nature of the source data and, consequently, the somewhat tentative nature of his conclusions, the approaches explored by Williams are of the utmost interest and relevance: his techniques relate the specific patterns of language change to evolutionary aspects of the urban system as it has developed in Wales. In this way his work begins to take us into a much fuller and long-overdue exploration of the operant social and economic processes.

Finally, in this section we need to mention some interesting new research developments in investigations concerning spatial patterns of language change and the underlying processes. These make exclusive use of the data collected at a single census: that is, data that relate specifically

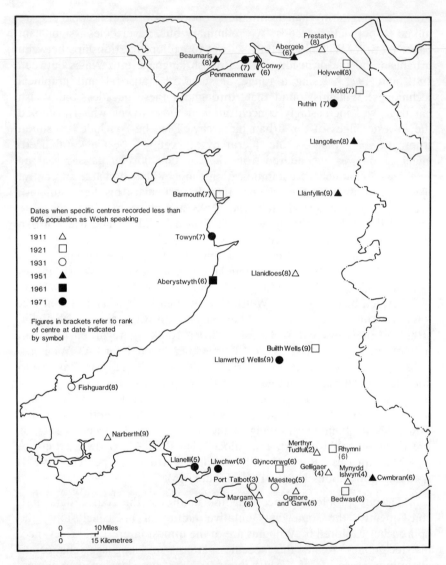

FIGURE 7.6   *Relationships between urban status and the Welsh language 1901–71*
Based on S.W. Williams (1981: 46).

to a single year. Careful analysis now enables researchers to begin to identify likely causes of a behavioural nature and in so doing make generalizations as to the nature of long-term trends. Earlier work in this genre has been concerned with the analysis of Welsh speakers in the various age cohorts in the population generally. This is an approach with a long tradition in social and population geography, particularly insofar as the findings relate to the stability or otherwise of local populations. As we have seen (Table 7.2), in 1971 the census began to collect information on the ability of Welsh speakers to read and write their own language. The information was obtained by self-assessment and, for this very reason, it cannot be regarded as fully reliable in every respect. Since the data on speaking Welsh continue to be collected in exactly the same manner, we would not expect it to be any less reliable. Yet, since reading and writing are skills acquired after the ability to speak, it is clear that the published returns include substantial numbers of very young children of pre-school age: although infants are excluded, the main census questions are still geared to the basic criterion that only persons aged three years and over are counted.

In 1981 the census recorded 542,425 persons in Wales as able to speak Welsh. Of these, 72% (1971: 73%) stated that they could read as well as write the language; a further 8% (1971: 10%) were able to read but not write in Welsh. Some 20% (17% in 1971) stated that whilst they spoke Welsh they were not able to read or write the language. As can be seen from the proportions in brackets, these figures are roughly of the same order as those recorded in 1971.

These clear aggregate differences have been evaluated carefully by Bowen & Carter in their important paper of 1975. They draw our attention to two particular aspects of this seemingly unusual situation — unusual, that is, from the perspectives of persons speaking a major world language such as English. Bowen & Carter pose two key questions that need proper consideration: (1) Why was it that only 73% of Welsh speakers are literate in their own language? And, (2) why do distinctive regional variations occur in the proportions of readers and writers?

In response to the first of these questions Bowen & Carter remind us that these differences can be related, in part, to the historical background. Welsh has evolved primarily as the everyday language of the ordinary people whilst, until comparatively recently, English has been the sole language used by officialdom. In short, the political and social climate in which Welsh has managed to survive over the generations into our own time is a context not very dissimilar from "colonial situations" elsewhere. Outside the main religious denominations which grew to majority strength in the nineteenth century, until recently the Welsh language enjoyed no official status whatsoever. Therefore, Welsh has not had the opportunity to become ". . . a means of bureaucratic communication in an urbanized society". Today a much more sympathetic educational policy ensures that larger numbers of the young are taught to write in Welsh compared with previous generations. This, Bowen & Carter point out, is reflected in age-specific differences amongst speakers, readers and writers generally.

While this appears to be an underlying cause, the age structure differences are not all that relevant as explanations concerning the regional differences amongst readers and writers. Bowen & Carter's initial hypothesis was that these differences relate expressly to specific stages reached in the process of language decline: the differences reflect the general feelings of confidence or lack of confidence that communities have in the language as a medium of communication, now and in the future; they are indicators as to how individuals perceive Welsh as a medium of personal and social communication to be preserved and passed on to the next generation:

> "Where the Welsh cultural tradition is becoming attenuated, where doubts are felt as to the 'value' of the language in commercial terms, where, in summary, a variety of other ends are deemed more important than facility in Welsh, then it can be argued that the spoken language might well be acquired on the hearth but there will be no motivation towards attaining a high standard in the written form. The effort and discipline required to write Welsh will be judged out of proportion to the rewards to be gained. Each Welsh-speaking family will in effect carry out its own cost-benefit study." (Bowen & Carter, 1975: 9–10)

Thus, in reality, if this is the situation then the observed differences are conceived as having been "locationally controlled", and relate to where Welsh is, on other criteria, under challenge. These differences, therefore, are directly associated with areas of decline.[9]

To test this hypothesis Bowen & Carter identified parishes with the greatest differences between the proportions speaking and writing Welsh in 1971. These areas were then superimposed on an outline map together with the 70% isopleth which marks the outer limits of the dominantly Welsh speaking areas. As Figure 7.7 shows, areas with the greatest anomalies are located around the margins of the core areas for the language in the northern and western parts of the country. All these localities are regionally located within the "intermediary zone" where, in 1971, between 40 and 70% of the population was recorded as speaking the language. Moreover, these particular locations coincide with those very districts recording more than twice the national rate (that is −5.2%) of decline 1961–71. On this basis, Bowen & Carter's initial hypothesis concerning the underlying reasons for decline gains considerable acceptance. However, as they themselves were careful to point out, the changing linguistic situation is complex and further detailed local studies are needed if all the processes are to be explored in meaningful and relevant ways. Nevertheless, this research demonstrates convincingly the sorts of approaches that are needed if underlying spatial processes as well as the attendant social considerations are to be identified and then carefully evaluated.

This rich tradition of detailed inter-censal language investigation was maintained by Aitchison, Carter and Williams for the 1981 Welsh language census results. Their research confirmed many of the earlier geolinguistic distribution patterns and revealed newer trends in the location of Welsh speakers (Aitchison & Carter, 1985; Aitchison, Carter & Williams, 1985; Williams, 1985; Carter & Aitchison, 1986). Of particular interest are their maps of the absolute changes in the geography of language 1971–81 which reveal substantial losses of Welsh speakers in the industrial south-west, throughout much of heartland Wales and in several key market towns and service centres of the north (Figure 7.7). By contrast the gains in the absolute numbers of Welsh speakers are limited primarily to four regions, viz. Cardiff and its hinterland, South Pembroke, industrial Clwyd and Anglesey — all areas of relative economic growth in the decade (Figure 7.8).

Whilst both proportionate and absolute figures are crucial in geolinguistic mapping, a more innovative aspect of this recent work is the attempt to relate linguistic change to population migration. Aitchison & Carter present an eightfold categorization of the 993 census communities based on the direction of absolute change (positive and negative) for the period 1971–81. The advantage of this method of data presentation is that it allows for a more dynamic interpretation of language change whilst still allowing for a very precise interpretation of specific local areas. Thus with reference to Figure 7.9 we may highlight three contrasting categories. Within groups 1–4, communities where the total population has increased during the decade, one may identify communities where increases in the Welsh-speaking population have surpassed those of the non-Welsh speaking population (groups 1 and 2) along the borderland, and the

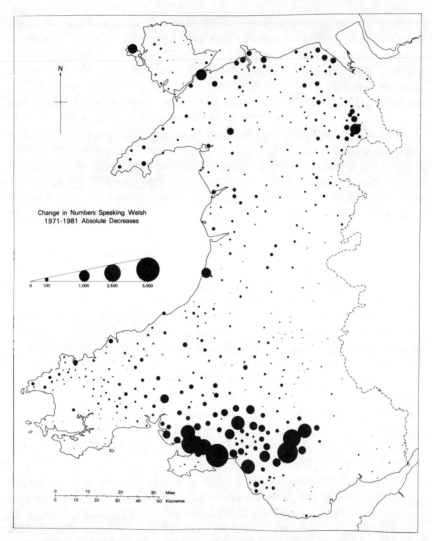

FIGURE 7.7   *Change in numbers speaking Welsh, 1971–1981: absolute decreases*
Reproduced with permission from Aitchison & Carter (1985: 20).

coastal fringes of West Wales. A second category, groups 5–7, incorporates communities with decreasing populations overall. Particular attention is paid to group 5 by Aitchison & Carter, in which the "fall in the number of Welsh speakers has not been compensated by a sufficient increase in the non-Welsh speaking population" (1985: 32). The majority of these

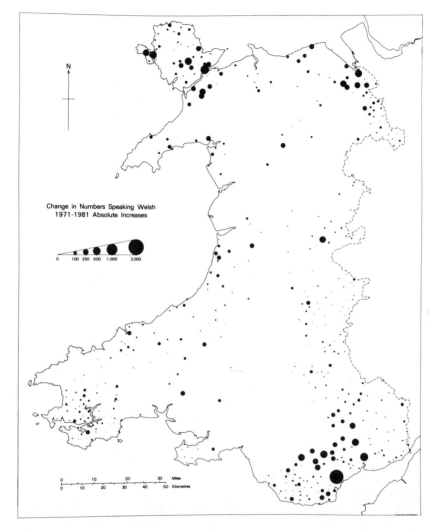

FIGURE 7.8   *Change in numbers speaking Welsh, 1971–1981: absolute increases*
Reproduced with permission from Aitchison & Carter (1985: 21).

communities are to be found in "Y Fro Gymraeg", particularly the traditional core areas of Llŷn and Meirionydd, but they are also located in urban-industrial areas such as Swansea, Aberdare and Merthyr (Figure 7.9). A final category offers some hope for the future of Welsh in the most economically active areas. This final group (8) includes 91 communities in which the numbers of Welsh speakers increased, whilst those of non-Welsh speakers decreased significantly. As is evident on Figure 7.9 these contexts are concentrated in the Cardiff hinterland and western Gwent and may be related to a number of social developments, such as the in-migration of Welsh speakers, the education of a new generation of Welsh youth in formally designated bilingual schools and the attraction of adult Welsh evening classes for some of the local population in these anglicized regions.

The detailed evidence now available from the interpretation of the recent census provides a generalized, but adequate data base for a whole gamut of public decisions concerning such issues as language planning, bilingual education, public administration, the law and economic development. We would argue that research by human geographers in Wales has been essential in providing a localized dimension to social change, not least, of course, in the field of language policy where place and context are vital determinants of language choice in particular situations.

Pre-census sources

The first official state population census in Britain was taken in 1801 but, as we have seen earlier, no language data were collected until 1891. Therefore, researchers have been forced to explore other sources for the historical geography of language for all earlier periods. The data in these sources were compiled originally for a whole range of quite different purposes and, moreover, by a diversity of methods. In the absence of even the slightest scrap of information on language in the early-nineteenth century census reports, all these alternative sources have to be regarded as surrogate measures of Welshness. Ultimately, none is entirely satisfactory. Nevertheless, in the circumstances, a considerable amount of work has been done on the territorial extent of the Welsh language for a range of different dates and periods before 1891.

General surveys

The earliest of these studies, which appeared during the later-nineteenth century, took the form of very generalized surveys. These include, for example, a wide-ranging review by Ivor James (the first registrar of University College, Cardiff) published in 1887. This is a scholarly work which, though tending to be weak on overall territorial distributions, carefully marshalled evidence concerning the continuing

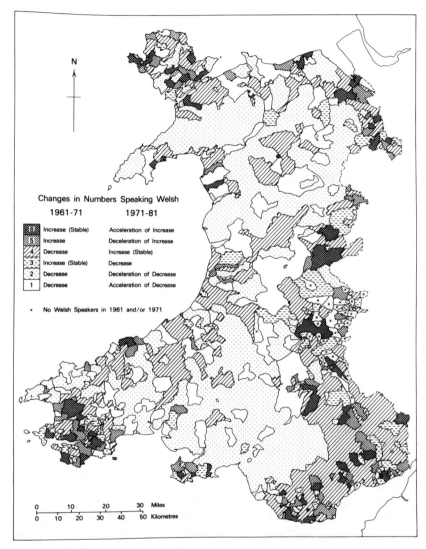

FIGURE 7.9   *Changes in numbers speaking Welsh, 1961–71, 1971–81*
Reproduced with permission from Aitchison & Carter (1985: 25).

buoyancy of the Welsh language during the sixteenth and seventeenth
centuries. James made extensive use of literary sources, including details
such as the numbers of books published in Welsh during this period, the
incidence of Welsh surnames in parish registers from selected churches
in Pembrokeshire, and the occurrence of foreign loan words in Salesbury's
dictionary of the Welsh language of 1547. This is an invaluable general

208 LANGUAGE IN GEOGRAPHIC CONTEXT

survey that provides an appropriate contextual framework in which more detailed empirical studies can be set.

Information on particular localities

Occasionally, more detailed surveys appeared for specific places. Often, these were the by-product of Victorian enthusiasm for the collection of all sorts of factual information relating to concerns of social reform. Such studies include, for example, detailed statistical surveys of the growing industrial townships of Trevethin (Trefddyn) and Blaenavon in what is now Gwent. The data had been compiled at first hand from field surveys and included information on a range of linked topics. Amongst these the details included statistics on the origins of migrants, demographic structures, contemporary standards and ways of life, social relationships amongst the Welsh, the Irish and the English together with details of age groups, national origins and statements that some 106 persons in Trevethin were recorded as "not speaking English". Blaenavon had another 21 Welsh monoglots. A somewhat surprising statistic relates to the fact that these two industrial settlements included 2,362 "drunkards" over the age of twelve years, accounting for 17% (Trevethin) and 8% (Blaenavon) of the local population! Whilst providing aggregate statistics for each of these townships, unfortunately there are no detailed breakdowns of information for individual areas within each of these communities (Kenrick, 1841: 366–75).

The appendices to the famous Education Report of 1847 also contain much information on the languages spoken in specific localities. Amongst these there is the so-called "Memorial" from nonconformists in the Montgomeryshire parishes of Llanfair Caereinion, Castell Caereinion and Manafon. Fearing the purposes to which their information might be put, these religious dissenters refused to fill in the official questionnaires issued by the Parliamentary Commissioners. Instead, and fortunately for us today, they carried out their own surveys as to the literacy and educational attainments of the people. Details, together with the actual numbers of Welsh monoglots, English monoglots and bilinguals, and, significantly, the Welsh or English national affiliation of individuals, were collected and published for each of the various townships within these parishes. This constitutes a remarkable body of statistical information which, so far, has not been fully analysed using modern techniques (*Reports, Commissioners of Inquiry into the State of Education in Wales*, 1847: 337–58).

Historical data of this nature have survived only somewhat spasmodically, both in temporal as well as in spatial terms. Where such information does exist, its prime usefulness is to illuminate, in remarkable detail, the linguistic situation at one or two particular locations and perhaps throw, incidentally, further light on aspects of the prevailing regional situation. Wider range studies are needed if the changing linguistic geography of the pre-census years is to be explored from a regional point of view.

Studies based on information from local informants

From the number of studies that appeared it is clear that there was very considerable interest in the linguistic geography of Wales during the later nineteenth century. Lack of easily available data meant that investigators were driven to carry out their own surveys. These used a variety of methods and objectives. Thus, as mentioned earlier, Ravenstein — probably one of the earliest pioneers in writing the population and cultural geographies of Britain — relied on a large number of local informants. They included village schoolmasters, the clergy, members of the gentry (occasionally) and local affiliates to the Royal Statistical Society of London. When these correspondents failed to produce the required information, as a last resort Ravenstein contacted, successfully it seems, a number of "leading innkeepers" in each locality. In commenting that "no official notice has ever been taken of the existence of persons in Wales and the Highlands of Scotland able to speak Welsh or Gaelic", Ravenstein, as mentioned earlier, had begun the campaign for the census to collect such data. The replies to his 1,200 circulars (we are not told how many of these refer specifically to Wales) were augmented by information obtained as a result of Ravenstein's "voluminous correspondence" with persons who had shown a "special interest" in his enquiries. His published findings included a series of maps. That devoted to Wales showed areas where, it was estimated, Welsh was spoken by (a) the majority, (b) between 25 and 50%, and (c) 10–15% of the population. Detailed treatment was given to each of the counties where aggregates of Welsh speakers and proportions were calculated for 1871, based on the linguistic status of the localities in which the population had been enumerated in that census. Despite several printing errors in the statistical estimates, there is no doubt that, in every respect, Ravenstein's "statistical survey" constitutes a remarkable and pioneering piece of research. Even today it retains much interest. It is important to remember, however, that Ravenstein was concerned primarily to chart the linguistic situation as it existed in the early 1870s. He made no serious attempt to deal with its historical geography up to that date (Ravenstein, 1879: 579–636).

The two other important studies of this period are those by the dialectologist Ellis (1882: 173–208) and the publisher Southall (1894), mentioned earlier. Both collected information in much the same ways as did Ravenstein. Ellis was interested in educational considerations and sought to establish, in territorial terms, the western limit of the English language, noting the differences between colloquial English and acquired or, as he referred to it, "book-English". His study was of a preliminary nature and sought to demonstrate methods to convince the Honourable Society of Cymmrodorion that a much fuller and more exhaustive survey be undertaken under their auspices. His pleas for their involvement seem to have met with no overt response. Southall, as we have stated, was also interested primarily in education but with quite different objectives. In 1892 he emerged as a strong advocate for a genuinely bilingual policy in the schools of Wales in his famous book *Wales and her Language*. Southall was writing before the results of the first language census in Wales had become available. His arguments were supported by a coloured map, based on his own personal knowledge and that of informants. This showed areas where (a) no native Welsh was understood or spoken (mainly in the borderland, Gower and south Pembrokeshire), (b) where 60% and over of the *adult* population understood or spoke Welsh (the greater part of the whole country), and showing (c) the narrow, transitional zone where less than 60% understood or spoke the language.

Although recognizing the latter, intermediate, transitional zone the prime aims of all these early geographical studies were to establish, as unambiguously as possible, the dividing line on the ground between Welsh and English speech. In these respects, and in the total absence of any meaningful census statistics, the methods and results of Ravenstein, Ellis and Southall compare favourably with those used today by continental scholars in their studies concerning the former territorial limits of the French language (see, for example, the Appendix in Brunot, 1967).

More recent studies using historical data

In our own times better equipped scholars have re-examined a whole range of different types of historical source material. With the use of appropriate techniques, these can be made to throw considerable new light on the territorial distribution of the Welsh and English languages in the past, particularly their relationships in pre-industrial times. Several studies have been completed using place-name evidence. That by Charles (1963: 85–110) concerning those parts of Herefordshire and Shropshire which, until the Act of Union in 1536, were an integral part of Wales, is of particular interest. In a similar way, Sir Joseph Bradney, who appeared as a witness before an important government committee enquiring into the place of the Welsh language in education, used place-name as well as literary evidence to chart the decline in the use of Welsh by the ordinary people in eastern Gwent (Bradney, 1926, see also Board of Education Departmental Committee, 1927). Yet, since the early nineteenth century increasing anglicization has meant that many place-names have been corrupted and mutilated into forms that are virtually unrecognizable in their origins, even for Welsh speakers; or, indeed names have been changed altogether into full English versions. In consequence, researchers have attempted to seek out historical sources that recorded place names in forms reflective of their origins. Field names as preserved in estate records often provide reliable, even if not always fully accurate, data for these purposes.

The maps and schedules of the tithe surveys of the 1840s are major sources and these have been explored in a large number of local studies. Using field and place-names evidence from these sources, Dr Michael Williams (1972: 61–69) has been able to reconstruct the medieval linguistic geography of Gower in west Glamorgan, producing, on the basis of the proportions of English/Welsh place-names within each parish, a series of new maps charting the division of this ancient Lordship into *Gower Anglicana* and *Gower Wallicana*. Williams carefully assesssed the validity of his sources:

> "... Field names have a greater stability than language but not as great a stability as place names ... If ... the farm changes hands there is no guarantee that the field names will survive, being less durable than farm names which have a legal entity. Therefore, there is a considerable time-lag of possibly many generations between changing language and changing field names."

Moreover, he concludes, urban development often means that fields become buried beneath built-up areas. But, since there is a tendency to adopt field and farm names for new streets and urban communities, the cultural differences of the past are not usually fully obliterated.

Nevertheless, whilst useful for examining the long-term and traditional "personality" of a region (or, in Welsh, *bro*), place-name evidence is of limited value if the researcher is interested primarily in questions relating to linguistic change. In these circumstances other sources, specific in time and to place, need to be consulted. Amongst these can be counted surveys such as that conducted by Ivor James (mentioned earlier) concerning the incidence of distinctively Welsh or distinctively English surnames in parish registers. A few researchers have followed the pioneering work of Thomas (1962) and have examined the occurrence of Welsh and English names in local records such as jury, freemen or burgher lists in medieval or late-medieval times. Since names on such lists may not be representative of the wider community — especially in districts where it is known or suspected that there existed a deliberate anti-Welsh selection policy — this sort of evidence has to be used with considerable care.

This need for caution led Lewis (1979: 131–44) to draw on sources more directly linked to the ordinary people. These include, for example, data concerning the locations of the Welsh circulating charity schools of the eighteenth century together with other information on the language of worship as recorded in ecclesiastical visitation papers. Because their data relate closely to the language or languages as used in everyday life, considerable confidence can be placed in these sources.

As stated earlier, many more records relating to local linguistic conditions were compiled from the mid-nineteenth century onwards than ever before. Although not as specific in its information as the census material that began to appear in 1891, from now on the detail is much more statistical in nature: it tends to be arranged in a standard format and, moreover, offers full coverage of communities throughout Wales. The detailed information collected in 1846 for the famous Education Report published in 1847 is, perhaps, the most important of these sources. This has been explored by several researchers. The data relating to Sunday schools and the language of instruction therein are particularly valuable for, when analysed systematically, these returns yield clear evidence of the transitional bilingual zone between Welsh-speaking Wales and English-speaking areas. In north-east Wales, for example, in 1846 the bilingual zone coincided with the exposed coalfield and encompassed all the then expanding industrial communities of Clwyd (Pryce, 1975). The language data from the Education Report have also been used by Lewis (1979) in a somewhat different manner to chart the progressive decline eastwards of Welsh in the central borderland. Moreover, together with day-school information, this important source has been used selectively to support literary evidence in James's (1972) important study of language changes within the Vale of Glamorgan.

The language of worship in churches and chapels

All the studies mentioned so far use historical sources to reconstruct the language geography of selected regions and localities within Wales. The published researches of Bowen (1976, 1986), particularly his key paper on "the geography of Wales as a background to its history" together with the important interpretative work of Carter and Thomas (1969) (using data relating to the 1960s) and subsequent further studies by Carter (1976) himself (using data for the 1970s), have stimulated new insights into the changing linguistic situation. Bowen inferred the existence of distinctive regional structures within Wales which he wrote of as the "Welsh Heartland" — that is, the dominantly Welsh-speaking areas. Later, however these were to be reformulated as "Inner Wales" (Welsh speaking areas) and "Outer Wales" (Anglicized districts). In applying Meinig's concept of the culture region to Wales, Carter effectively revised and redefined these concepts. From now on Welsh-speaking Wales was to be identified, in Meinig's terminology, as the "core" area of the Welsh culture region with the complementary "sphere" and "domain" areas equating to anglicized Wales and the bilingual zone respectively. This spatial model has now placed *Cymru Gymraeg* (Welsh speaking Wales) and *Cymru ddi-Gymraeg* (anglicized Wales) into a much more meaningful theoretical context.

All these ideas were applied initially to the distribution of Welsh speakers as recorded in the 1951 census and subsequent enumerations. These stimulating interpretations and re-interpretations implied a dynamic relationship between the various regional components and, moreover, that changes in the structure of the Welsh culture area could be traced back in time. Bowen had pointed out that industrialization and the growth of large urban communities in north-east Wales and in the valleys of the Glamorgan coalfield had themselves been processes which reinforced regional contrasts.[10]

In order to test these ideas, particularly with reference to the latter consideration concerning the impact of industrialization, information is needed that relates to localities throughout Wales for a succession of dates. In the absence of any linguistic data in the censuses before 1891, the only known data that go a long way to meet these requirements are to be found amongst the centralized records of the Anglican church and these returns record details of the language or combinations of Welsh and English used in public services in parish churches. These are preserved amongst the Church in Wales archives at the National Library of Wales. They include returns from some 646 (out of a total of 1,022) parish churches dated c.1750, 673 (from a total of 1,038) parishes c.1800, 913 (out of 1,086) c.1850, and 773 (from a total of 1,173) parishes c.1900. In addition, the survey carried out in 1906 and published in the *Report of the Royal Commission on the Church of England in Wales, 1910* provides verification in its returns from 1,143 (from a total of 1,200) parishes throughout Wales (for details see Pryce, 1978a: 1–36).

Until recently it was widely assumed that these church records were, in reality, not very representative of actual local conditions. Recent work has shown that in all probability this criticism is valid for the later nineteenth century. By this time, in Wales the established Church had been overtaken by the nonconformist denominations with their very large membership. Previous to that period, however, there are good grounds for accepting that the church returns are valid as indicators of actual local conditions. There were legal requirements that public worship, as conducted in parish churches throughout the dioceses of Wales, should be in the language or combinations of Welsh and English that were appropriate to the needs of parishioners. Bishops and rural deans made regular checks, parish by parish, that these obligations were being respected — even if they themselves were of English nationality (as many, indeed, were) or otherwise showed no overt sympathy towards the Welsh language. The documentary records produced by these surveys comprise a vast body of data on linguistic conditions throughout Wales.

The actual returns take the form of either (1) short but detailed reports made by rural deans after visiting specific parishes, or (2) answers sent in by local clergy to specific questions, such as the following:

"How often on the Lord's Day is Divine Service performed in your Church or Chapel, and in what language?"[11]

It is significant that this is the first of a large number of questions concerning public worship and the maintenance of the church fabric in each parish. In Bangor Diocese, for example, these amounted to a total of between twelve and twenty different topics of enquiry.

Once extracted from the hundreds of source documents, verbatim and in their exact original form, the specific statements need careful scrutiny before allocating each parish a linguistic status using the criteria summarized in Table 7.4.

Next, the information is transferred to a master base map where the name of every parish within Wales and the exact location of the parish church is recorded. This provides the fundamental locational information on which the language map for a specific period date is to

TABLE 7.4 *Language classification of parish churches*

Language status	Statements as to the language or languages used in parish churches
1. Welsh	1a. All services in Welsh 1b. Welsh but not more than one English service in three months 1c. Welsh but some English in summer months for visitors
2. Mainly Welsh	2a. Welsh but one English service each month 2b. Welsh always in the evenings but morning services alternately Welsh or bilingual 2c. Welsh always in the evenings but two morning services, one in Welsh and one in English 2d. Bilingual services but more Welsh than English
3. Bilingual	3a. Two services every Sunday, one in each language 3b. Alternating Welsh/English services
4. Mainly English	4a. English always in the evenings but morning services alternately English/Welsh 4b. Bilingual services but more English than Welsh 4c. Main services in English but afternoon services alternately English/Welsh 4d. English but one or two services in Welsh each month
5. English	5a. English with rare use of Welsh (at most four times in the year) 5b. All services in English
? Uncertain	*statement is illegible or no return*

be built up. First, point symbols, representative of each of the six language statuses shown in Table 7.4, are placed over the site of each parish church. These constitute the "hard" evidence from which the areas shown in Figure 7.10 are interpolated to give the three principal language zones: (1) overwhelmingly Welsh areas, (2) the bilingual zone, and (3) dominantly English-speaking areas. When the investigation is conducted at a lower regional scale of analysis, the boundaries between these three language zones can be plotted conventionally to follow parish or township limits (for an example, see Pryce, 1972: 343–63). Before 1900 Wales was divided

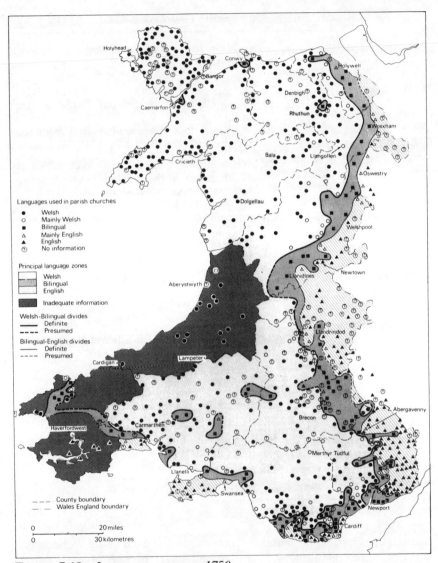

FIGURE 7.10   *Language zones, c.1750*
Source: Based on W.T.R. Pryce (1978a: 11).

into four Anglican dioceses and visitations took place on different dates
in each of these. Therefore, it is necessary to draw on returns that occur
close together in time. The data on which Figure 7.10 is based thus refer
to the specific years of 1749 (in Bangor, and in St. Asaph Dioceses),
1755 (St. David's Diocese) and, because it offers the earliest available
set of extant returns, 1771 for the Diocese of Llandaf.

Maps can be prepared for any specific date for which data can be found. Moreover, long-term changes can be worked out for specific parishes by scanning the language stadials for a succession of dates and allocating each locality a trend classification (Table 7.5). This information can then be transferred to the base map. In Figure 7.11 the point symbols refer to long-term trends at specific locations whilst the shaded areas represent the language zones as they had evolved by 1900. Depending on the needs of the specific research hypothesis under investigation, the bank of data can be extended by, for example, adding population numbers from the 1801 and later censuses. Although actual numbers of Welsh speakers cannot be stated, nevertheless, by this means statements can be made concerning the numbers or proportions of the population enumerated within the various language zones. Moreover, these approaches allow changes in population numbers and/or migration characteristics to be related to language trends at specific locations and within particular regions over time. Thus, through a variety of techniques, data which were collected originally for quite different purposes can be made to yield insights not otherwise available and objective material for testing a range of research hypotheses concerning the evolution of Wales as a distinctive culture region in its own right.

In 1952 Professor Emrys Jones published his pioneering study of language (and, thereby, cultural) changes in the Welsh community of Utica in New York State. Jones (1952: 15–39) used data obtained by content analysis from *Y Drych* (the newspaper serving Welsh settlements in the USA) as well as yearbooks of the Welsh Presbyterian Church to chart the decline in the use of Welsh in these communities. His findings were interpreted and discussed in the wider context of social and cultural change generally. Much more recently, Dr P.N. Jones (1976: 347–60) drew on similar sources and methods to verify the linguistic areas as indicated by the language of worship in Anglican parish churches. The Baptist Diary and Hand Books published between 1861 and 1914 constituted the main sources for this research. From these records, dates when individual chapels had been opened were extracted together with details as to the language of worship in the chapels. As P.N. Jones himself pointed out, the Baptists constitute one of the older dissenting groups and, unlike the "newer" dissenters, such as the Calvinistic Methodists, were never orientated primarily towards any one cultural group. They demonstrated "a pragmatic attitude to the linguistic transition, giving priority to the religious demands of the population through whatever medium was felt necessary, Welsh or English". Their chapels were numerous and at many different locations throughout the valleys of the coalfield. Jones's analysis concentrates on the language of worship at the

LANGUAGE IN GEOGRAPHIC CONTEXT

TABLE 7.5 *Classification of long-term language trends, c.1750–1906*

Ecclesiastical parish	Ancient county	Language stadials[1]					Trend classification*
		c.1750	c.1800	c.1850	c.1900	1906	
Aberffraw	Anglesey	1	?	1	1	1	W
Garthbeibio	Montgomery	1	1	1	1	1	W
Llanfihangel-ar-arth	Carmarthen	1	1	1	1	2	W
Abergwili	Carmarthen	3	3	2	2	2	aW
Betws-yn-Rhos	Denbigh	1	1	1	2	2	aW
Llanasa	Flint	2	2	3	2	2	aW
Llanerfyl	Montgomery	2	1	1	2	2	aW
Morfil	Pembroke	?	1	2	1	1	aW
Beddgelert	Caernarfon	1	1	2	2	3	WB
Cadoxton-juxta-Neath	Glamorgan	1	?	3	?	3	WB
Llanerchaeron	Cardigan	1	2	3	3	3	WB
Treuddyn	Flint	1	1	1	3	3	WB
Halkyn	Flint	3	3	3	3	3	B
Kidwelly	Carmarthen	3	?	3	3	3	B
Llandeloy	Pembroke	?	3	2	3	3	B
Llandybie	Carmarthen	3	3	2	3	2	B
Meifod	Montgomery	3	3	3	2	2	B
Aberystwyth	Cardigan	?	3	3	3	4	BE
Castell Caereinion	Montgomery	3	4	3	5	5	BE
Chirk	Denbigh	3	5	5	5	5	BE

Conwy	Caernarfon	3	3	3	4	*BE*
Llanfoist	Monmouth	3	5	5	?	*BE*
Llangorse	Brecknock	?	3	1	5	*BE*
Beaumaris	Anglesey	4	3	4	?	*bE*
Cregina	Radnor	4	5	5	5	*bE*
Llangibby	Monmouth	4	5	?	?	*bE*
Cardiff	Glamorgan	5	?	5	?	*E*
Erbistock	Denbigh	5	5	5	5	*E*
Hay	Brecknock	?	5	5	?	*E*
Laugharne	Carmarthen	5	?	5	5	*E*
Aberysgir	Brecknock	?	1	1	5	*WBE*
Bonvilston	Glamorgan	1	4	5	?	*WBE*
Colwyn Bay	Denbigh	1	1	4	4	*WBE*
Cwm-iou	Monmouth	1	3	5	?	*WBE*
Denio	Caernarfon	1	1	3	4	*WBE*
Ferryside	Carmarthen	1	?	5	5	*WBE*
Llanfair Caereinion	Montgomery	2	3	5	4	*WBE*
St. Dogwells	Pembroke	?	2	3	4	*WBE*
St. Harmon	Radnor	1	2	3	5	*WBE*

W: consistently Welsh;

aW: dominantly Welsh but introduction of some English; or bilingual, reverting to dominantly Welsh;

WB: dominantly Welsh, becoming bilingual;

B: consistently bilingual;

BE: bilingual, becoming English or dominantly English;

bE: mainly English, becoming completely English;

E: consistently English;

WBE: originally Welsh, then bilingual before becoming English or dominantly English.

1. See Table 7.4.

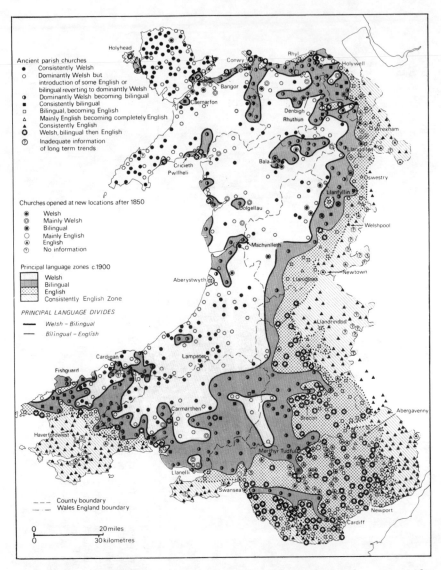

FIGURE 7.11 *Language zones c.1900 and overall trends at specific locations, c.1750–1900*
Source: Based on W.T.R. Pryce (1978a: 20).

specific dates when individual chapels were actually set up. His findings are presented in map form and they confirm the same gradual, progressive "rolling back", as he puts it, of the Welsh language from east to west that is evident from the results based on the language of worship in parish churches. It is clear that, until recently, "bilingualism" was, in effect, the agent of anglicization. As P.N. Jones concluded, bilingualism was, in every respect, a transient "resting place" in the rapid changes that swept through the coalfield of south Wales.

Language divides

Throughout the various commentaries that researchers have offered on the territorial relationships between the Welsh and English languages within Wales, a constant theme emerges. This concerns the recognition of the "line" or "language divide" between the two languages, separating the principal language areas. As we have seen, D.T. Williams was one of the first to write specifically on this notion in the 1930s. Even then, however, he recognized that, in reality, the language divide was of a transitional nature. Later scholars have sought to identify critical dividing lines in their searches for changing locations and orientations. This particular theme is well developed in the works of Bowen and Carter; and, more recently, in the published studies of Aitchison and Carter. Studies relating to the impact of industrialization on the cultural geography of Wales have recognized these transitional areas as the "bilingual zone". This, it has been shown, is strongly dynamic in nature and, in the nineteenth century, was related particularly to differential in-migration. Its inexorable westward retreat in north-east Wales demonstrates its role as a key agent of anglicization, diffusing English ways of life, organizations and values from the "outside world" into Welsh Wales (see Pryce, 1975b: 79–107).

Stimulated by some of the methods used to pin-point linguistic differences in France, Humphreys (1979) recently developed a fresh approach to the problem of identifying this transitional zone using census data. His techniques involved comparisons in the language geography of Wales in 1931 and 1971 — dates chosen because they were effectively a generation apart, as well as representing pre- and post-World War II conditions. Neighbouring parishes showing the greatest percentage differences in the proportions able to speak the Welsh language were then identified. Their contiguous boundaries were traced and then superimposed on a new base map. This approach reveals that throughout the country the greatest contrasts (or more pronounced "breaks") in the distribution of Welsh speakers occur in three broad categories represented by (1) the third and fourth; (2) the fifth and sixth; or (3) the seventh and over deciles. As Figure 7.12 shows, Humphreys's technique effectively charts changing language "fronts". Not only do these results show the

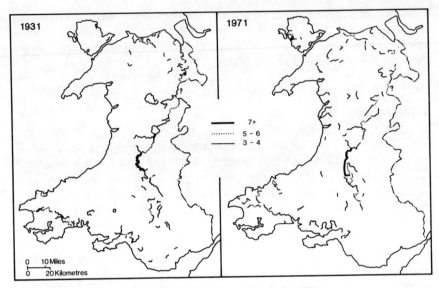

FIGURE 7.12 *Major language divides, 1931 and 1971*
The individual short lines indicate maximum decile differences between contiguous
parishes in the proportions of the population able to speak Welsh.
Source: Based on Humphreys (1979: 83).

progressive westward contraction of *Cymru Gymraeg* between 1931 and
1971, but this approach also reveals signs of the removal, by 1971, of all
local linguistic contrasts within industrialized south-east Wales and, by
the same date, incipient anglicization at many different locations within
the core Welsh-speaking areas, especially in Gwynedd. These maps
delineate what has become known today as the "crisis areas" for the
Welsh language. The spatial distributions yielded by this technique should
be compared with those identified by Bowen & Carter in 1975.

Multivariate analyses

The development of sophisticated multi-variate techniques in the
1960s enabled geolinguistics to go beyond the analysis of univariate
distribution patterns of Welsh. This newer, ecological approach sought
to relate patterns of language change to their socioeconomic contexts;
thus providing a holistic view of language in its social setting. Two
recent doctoral theses indicate the advantages of adopting multi-variate
regionalization procedures in identifying distinct sociocultural regions
(C.H. Williams, 1978a; S.W. Williams, 1980). Stephen Wyn Williams

selected 29 variables from the 1971 census for the 51 rural and urban administrative districts of Wales and subjected them to a Principal Component Analysis (PCA). This, together with a secondary factor analysis, confirmed the rural nature of the Welsh heartland and identified suburbanization and tourism as twin processes conducive to language decline (Carter & Williams, 1978). In an earlier study Colin Williams selected 48 variables for the 168 Local Authority units that existed in Wales prior to local government re-organization in 1974. The variables, taken from census and non-census sources for 1961 and 1971, related to age structures, social class, residential mobiity, linguistic characteristics, socio-economic attributes, household tenure and amenities, variations in the level of educational experience, voting behaviour and religious affiliations.

These variables summarized both the variety and complexity of distinct culture areas in Wales (C.H. Williams, 1978a, 1979, 1982a). These data sets, in turn, were then subjected to a principal component analysis and the eight components of the primary solution were rotated using the varimax procedure to yield interesting results (Table 7.6). The first component was interpreted as a Welsh cultural dimension, comprised of Welsh-speaking, religious non-conformity features and radical political support for the once firmly-established Liberal Party and its more modern competitor, Plaid Cymru. At the negative end of the scale was the Conservative Party, historically identified as an agent of anglicization and of the centralizing state apparatus. When the component loadings are mapped we find that the scores for each Local Authority indicate distinctive spatial variations (Figure 7.13). Districts with a high ethnicity score ($>+0.5$ Standard Deviation) (S.D.) are concentrated in a single culture region running north to south from Anglesey to Carmarthenshire. The rates are highest around Bala and Dolgellau, in the Llŷn Peninsula and at a number of rural market centres such as Llangefni, Tywyn, Newcastle Emlyn. Just below the $+0.5$ S.D. occur the outlying areas of the core complex. These are characteristic of the industrial and urban parts of *Y Fro Gymraeg* and include such locations as Carmarthen, Burry Port, Llanelli and Cwmaman in the south; Aberystwyth and New Quay in the west; and Llanidloes, the Machynlleth area, and Llanrwst further north. All these are market and service centres, occupying part of the middle rank of the Welsh urban hierarchy, the towns most subject to the influences which dominate the domain and thus most likely to be removed from the culture core if the anglicization processes continue unabated.

The local authority units which cluster either side of the mean fall into two distinct regions. The first is a girdle stretching inland from the

north Caernarfonshire coast, skirting the core area as far as Builth in
mid-Wales. The second is a region corresponding to the Glamorganshire
and Monmouthshire coalfield with outliers along the coast from Gower
to Cowbridge. It is akin to Meinig's domain concept discussed earlier. It
is an area which, until recently, was still dominated by the indigenous
culture, but with less intensity and homogeneity than the core. When
local field work is carried out to supplement this aggregate level analysis
we find that extensive tracts of the northern sector, e.g. Dyffryn Conwy,
Mynydd Hiraethog, Aled, Nant Ffrancon, Amlwch and Beaumaris,
though included in this statistical category, are more able to withstand
cultural encroachment in this period than the southern sector. This
indicates clearly the limitations of P C A at a macro-level analysis, but
nevertheless this consideration does not detract from its utility as a
classification technique.

The cultural periphery (i.e. below −0.5 S.D.), where Welsh culture
traits are weakest in proportional terms comprises four areas: 1) the
coastline of north Wales where tourism and retirement functions have
increased dramatically since 1945; 2) the border counties of Brecon and
Radnor, which have long been anglicized since Tudor times; 3) south
Pembrokeshire, "Little England Beyond Wales", an English-style enclave
since the sixteenth century; and 4) the Severn coastal plain comprising
the urban-industrial corridor of Newport, Cardiff, Penarth and Barry
(Figure 7.13). These are the areas where, proportionally, language and
radical voting scores are weakest and where the Anglican Church is the
dominant religious system, followed by English based nonconformity and
Catholicism. Despite their position at the other extreme from the core,
these latter areas are the very locales wherein attempts have been made
to institutionalize Welsh within the educational system with some creditable
success (C.H. Williams, 1986a: 111–30).

The other seven components for both 1961 and 1971 display national
variations for the whole of Wales in elements such as housing quality,
employment, population structure, electoral behaviour and social class.
Taken together they provide an excellent summary of the wider social
context within which language changes may be interpreted. At this level
the value of multivariate regional analysis is evident: these techniques
yield ecological patterns of culture regions which are of interest in their
own right. Of course, and here we argue the applied merit of the
geographical approach, such regions may also be accepted as sociocultural
milieux, within which more detailed behavioural analyses may be
undertaken.[12] Additionally, they may be used as a preliminary framework
for the implementation of functionally-related language planning zones,

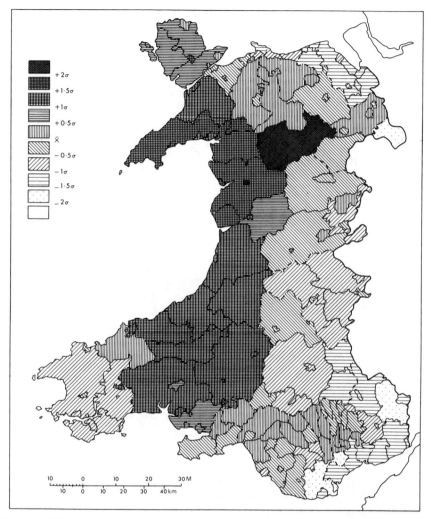

FIGURE 7.13 *Principal component analysis, 1961, component one*
Source: Based on C.H. Williams (1982: 300).

an increasingly-pressing issue as the Welsh language is recognized as a
social good capable of being planned for, along with more traditional
aspects of life such as housing, roads and education.[13]

 In this chapter we have reviewed a variety of sources and their
interpretation derived from official institutional surveys, government
census and sectoral interest groups in order to identify language areas.
One final source remains to be described and evaluated.

TABLE 7.6 *1961 Principal components analysis with varimax rotation of 8 components*

No. variable	1	2	3	4	5	6	7	8
1. Soc Class 1+2	−	+	+	+	−0.3794	−	−0.4020	−
2. Soc Class 4+5	−	−	−	−	+	−	0.7249	−
3. Soc Class 5	−	0.3686	+		+	−	0.5953	−
4. Pers Under 4	−	+	−	−0.6765	+	+	+	+
5. Pers 5–14	−	−	+	−0.3882	−	−	+	−
6. Pers 15–24	−	+	+	−0.3156	+	+	−	0.3574
7. Pers 25–44	+	−	−	−0.3358	+	+	+	+
8. Pers 45–64	+	−	−	0.7041	−	+	−0.4001	+
9. Pers 65+	−	−	−	0.6099	+	+	−	+
10. Owner Occupied	+	−	+	0.5265	+	0.3530	+	−
11. Priv. rent. unfur	+	−	+	0.4399	+	−	+	+
12. Priv. rent. furn	+	+	−	0.4148	+	−	−0.4119	+
13. Counc House	−	0.6780	+	−0.5165	−	−	+	−
14. Basic amenities	−	0.8707	+	−0.6845	+	+	−	−
15. Water closet	−	0.8692	−	+	−	+	+	−
16. No bath	−	−0.8623	+	+	+	+	+	−
17. % employed	+	−	0.9129	−	−	−	+	+
18. % unemployed	−	+	−0.9153	+	+	−	+	+
19. Females employed	−	0.5464	+	+	−	−	−	+
20. Females unemployed	+	−	−	+	−	+	+	−0.5267
21. Males unemployed	−	+	−0.9192	+	−	−	+	+
22. Pers per room	−	−	−0.4473	−	−	+	0.3246	+
23. Pers per H:H	−	−	+	−	−	−	+	+
24. Males agriculture	+	−0.7909	−	−	0.3300	+	+ −	+ −

25. % H:H shared	–	–	+	+	0.5171	+	+	0.4029
26. Outmigration	–	+	+	–	–	-0.5954	-0.5708	+
27. Int. Cens. Change	–	0.3878	+	–	+	0.3200	+	–
28. Immigration	–	+	+	+	+	0.5586	-0.5329	–
29. School 15	+	–	+	–	+	+	0.7235	+
30. Educate 18+	+	+	+	+	+	+	-0.5714	–
31. Educate 20+	+	+	+	+	–	–	-0.5703	+
32. Welsh only	0.5763	-0.4166	–	–	–	–	–	–
33. English + Welsh	0.7772	–	–	–	–	+	–	–
34. Migration balance	–	–	+	+	–	0.9250	+	–
35. Plaid 1959	0.7574	+	+	+	–	+	–	–
36. Liberals 1959	0.5431	–	–	+	-0.6250	+	–	0.3125
37. Labour 1959	–	–	–	–	0.9186	–	–	+
38. Conservatives 1959	-0.8165	+	–	+	–	+	–	-0.3807
39. Plaid 1964	0.7740	–	–	–	–	–	–	–
40. Liberals 1964	0.4678	–	+	+	-0.6988	+	–	+
41. Labour 1964	–	+	–	–	0.9271	–	+	+
42. Conservatives 1964	-0.7339	+	–	+	-0.3995	+	–	-0.3231
43. Units of Plaid	0.5330	+	+	+	–	+	–	–
44. Nursery Schools	–	–	–	+	+	–	+	+
45. Anglicans	–	-0.4356	+	+	-0.4090	–	+	0.4854
46. Catholics	–	0.5954	–	+	+	–	+	–
47. Nonconformist	0.5040	–	+	+	–	–	+	+
48. W. Nonconformist	0.6384	–	+	+	–	–	–	–
Variance	10.913	10.748	6.973	7.833	9.334	4.472	8.513	3.891
Cum Variance	10.913	21.661	28.634	36.467	45.900	50.372	58.885	62.776
Eigen Values	5.238	5.159	3.347	3.759	4.528	2.146	4.086	1.867

Reproduced with permission from C.H. Williams (1982a: 294–95).

Perception studies

In recent years the behavioural and phenomenological approaches have added new dimensions to age-old questions of geographical enquiry.[14] One significant concern has been the attempt to measure spatial perception and its connotations (see Gould & White, 1973; Sack, 1980). Given the concern with sources and methods this chapter focuses on, it is evident that the perceived territorial extent of the Welsh-speaking areas would have obvious implications for the health of the language. In consequence, the identification and interpretation of Welsh culture space is postulated as being a significant element in cultural geographic research. This is because culture space suggests a definite territorial framework within which certain sets of meanings about place may be observed and recorded. In this context culture may be defined according to Bjorklund (1979) as the "ongoing outcome of organized experience" where, in her interpretation, "experience" stands for each individual's perception/cognition as shared with others; where "organized" stands for the ordered and repeated meanings assigned to things and their relationship by the group; where "outcome" represents the time-spatial expression of meanings in form, use or intention, and where "ongoing" stands for the dynamic continuity of the relevant past with the present and the future.

This definition of culture is couched in phenomenological terms to stress understandings about contemporary meanings as they are normally accepted in social intercourse. We do not argue that cognitive mapping should replace census-derived language mapping, but rather that it is supplementary to this objective source. However, we do wish to stress that objective analysis of language change does not necessarily correspond with the "perceived reality" as recognized by the general public. The perceived environment often influences behaviour and attitude formation, and therefore it is important that we recognize the relevance of subjectivity and phenomenological explanations in interpreting reactions to language decline and the shrinkage of "Y Fro Gymraeg".

Such concerns underpin Williams's (1981: 273–96) analysis of perceptual culture regions in Wales. The source evidence was derived from interviews of 816 sixth-form school pupils from some 22 schools in Wales. The population was selected from five different sociocultural environments and school types ranging from Welsh-medium high schools to English-medium Roman Catholic high schools located in predominantly English-speaking areas. Each participant was asked to identify which of the 30 stimulus towns were located within predominantly Welsh-speaking regions and aggregate maps were constructed that reflected each group's perception of the Welsh-speaking areas. The exact nature and extent of the area subsumed under the designation "Welsh-speaking Wales" varied and was dependent on the location and the linguistic affiliation of the informants. But a core area, common to all samples, was revealed, centred on the Gwynedd heartland (Figure 7.14). In the aggregate profile a second southern peak of Welshness was also identified on the Cardigan/ Carmarthen border region. It is remarkable that there was little overwhelming agreement that most of Gwynedd and Dyfed were indeed Welsh-speaking regions. However, several locations, such as Welshpool, Denbigh and Holyhead, were perceived with considerable uncertainty as to their linguistic composition, so reflecting the generally poor spatial appreciation of linguistic zones beyond the more readily recognized western core.

This study has suggested further lines for fruitful research and has argued that we should examine what effect a contracting culture region has on the predisposition of non-Welsh speakers to learn the language: especially when the range of speech situations in spatial terms was becoming increasingly attenuated. It also indicates that we need to investigate further the powerful emotional attachment of minority cultural groups to their ethnic homeland and examine to what degree this concern over loss of territorial dominance becomes translated into sociopolitical activity in its myriad forms.

Conclusion

This chapter has emphasized the sources and methods of analysis of Welsh linguistic geography. It has sought to highlight the numerous problems which arise in the interpretation of the census returns as well as in the use of surrogate sources for earlier times. In addition, problems of data reliabiilty and comparability have been discussed. Clearly our selection of techniques has had to be selective but nevertheless it demonstrates the development of geolinguistics from a predominantly descriptive tool of analysis to one which is capable of being incorporated into the planning process as an integral part of statistical and social forecasting in Wales. As yet, Gwynedd County Council is the only local authority which has devoted considerable energies to planning for specific linguistic communities and its Structure Plan and associated planning documents reveal the potential of geolinguistic analysis (Gwynedd County Council, 1985). It is evident that other local authorities will seek to emulate Gwynedd's lead as they become increasingly conscious of the merits of language planning in addressing social economic problems.

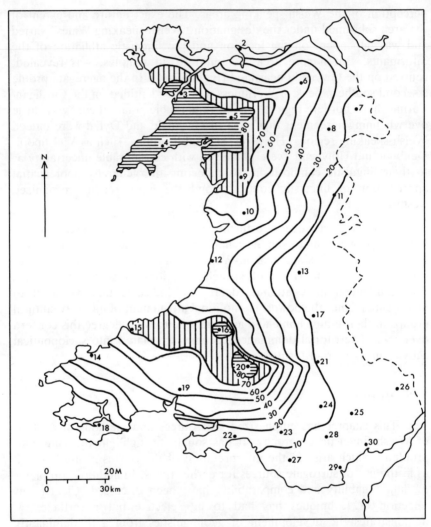

FIGURE 7.14 *Welsh culture regions: aggregate sample perception*
Source: Williams (1981: 248).

Three areas of further investigation deserve closer scrutiny by geographers and their fellow-travellers on the road to a more comprehensive understanding of language areas. The first is the evocative and richly veined source of landscape literature, including poetry and art, as exemplified in the novels of Kate Roberts, Emyr Humphries, Jack Jones and Saunders Lewis, or in the poetry of John Tripp and W.R. Evans.

The second source is detailed sociocultural surveys of the myriad cultural attitudes, artefacts and actions reflective of distinct Welsh places. By looking beyond the census to the reported behaviour of individuals in their communities we would surely gain a more precise and detailed picture of the pattern of social interaction, including linguistic behaviour, which characterizes various locales (Ambrose & Williams, 1981b; S.W. Williams, 1984).

Finally there is the abiding question as to how the national identity of the Welsh has been shaped, manipulated, invented or re-invented at various times. Historical sources provide an embarrassment of evidence on the theme of national culture being shaped in the image of various activists, protagonists and social groups, be they the organic intellectuals of the nineteenth century or the administrative bureaucrats and media pundits of the present (see Morgan, 1983). The degree to which various groups and regions correspond to the projected image of Wales is a fascinating topic for further study and one which will surely draw out the myriad nuances of this ongoing relationship between language, community and the land: J.R. Jones's "cydymdreiddiad" principle which is so characteristic of Wales through the ages (Williams, 1988).

Acknowledgement

The authors are indebted to John R. Hunt, Project Officer (Cartography) in the Social Sciences at the Open University and to Mrs Jane Williams, Cartographer at the North Staffordshire Polytechnic, for the final versions of the various maps appearing in this chapter.

Notes to Chapter 7

1. For the definitive maps of old and new counties, see Griffiths, 1980.
2. Letter to W.T.R. Pryce from Margaret Lane, Statistician, OPCS, St. Catherine's House, 10 Kingsway, London dated April 3, 1984.
3. See Table 7.1 for details of how small area statistics can be obtained.
4. Unpublished higher degree theses and published studies are listed in the Select Bibliography in Pryce, 1978a: 1–36.
5. *Royal Commission on the Church of England and other Religious Bodies in Wales and Monmouthshire*, no date, Language maps of Wales and Monmouthshire: North Wales; South Wales (scale 1: 253440 or one-inch=four miles). Fold-out sheets bound in at p. 176.
6. S.W. Williams (1981: 35–50). For an important study of urban growth and the role of towns as centres of diffusion see Robson (1973). The concept of the urban hierarchy is explained in Carter (1972).

7. A minor (editorial?) error in this paper invalidates the instructions Emery & White give for the calculation of Location Quotients.
8. There has been a stimulating debate on the impact of industrialization and the growth of towns on Welsh culture. For recent reviews see Pryce (1975a); and, more recently, Jones (1980).
9. For a detailed colour map of Welsh speaking/writing differences see Carter (1980), Map 3.2d.
10. The evolution of these ideas is traced in more detail in Pryce (1978b: 26–63).
11. NLW ms. Church in Wales Records B/QA/2 Question 1 (ii).
12. C.H. Williams (1978a: chapters 10 & 11, 1979: 35–56) provide elaboration of these behavioural techniques and results.
13. C.H. Williams (1978b, 1982b) and in a revised form with the same title C.H. Williams (1986).
14. Representative studies are Ley & Samuels (1978), Gale & Olsson (1979) and Pickles (1985).

References

AITCHISON, J. & CARTER, H., 1985, *The Welsh Language 1961–1981: An Interpretative Atlas*. Cardiff: University of Wales Press.

AITCHISON, J.W., CARTER, H. & WILLIAMS, C.H., 1985, The Welsh language at the 1981 census, *Area*, 17,1, 11–17.

AMBROSE, J., 1980, Micro-scale Language Mapping: An Experiment in Wales and Brittany. *North Staffordshire Polytechnic, Discussion Papers in Geolinguistics*, No. 2.

AMBROSE, J. & WILLIAMS, C.H., 1981a, Scale as an influence on the geolinguistic analysis of a minority language, *North Staffordshire Polytechnic Discussion Papers in Geolinguistics*, No. 4. 1–16.

—— 1981b, On the spatial definition of 'minority'. In E. HAUGEN *et al.* (eds), *Minority Languages Today*. Edinburgh: Edinburgh University Press. pp. 53–71.

BOARD OF EDUCATION DEPARTMENTAL COMMITTEE 1927, *Welsh in Education and Life*. London: HMSO. 210–11.

BJORKLUND, E., 1979, *Culture Space*. Department of Geography, The University of Western Ontario. mimeo.

BOWEN, E.G., 1976, *Daearyddiaith Cymru fel cefndir i'w hanes* London: BBC Publications 1964. English translations of this radio lecture appear in H. CARTER & W.K.D. DAVIES (eds), *Geography, Culture and Habitat: Selected Essays (1925–1975) of E.G. Bowen*. Llandysul: Gomer Press. 11–30. And also in I. HUME & W.T.R. PRYCE (eds), *The Welsh and their Country: Selected Readings in the Social Sciences*. Llandysul: Gomer Press. 64–87.

BOWEN, E.G. & CARTER, H., 1974, Preliminary observations on the distribution of the Welsh language at the 1971 census, *The Geographical Journal*, 140. 432–40.

—— 1975, The distribution of the Welsh language in 1971: An analysis, *Geography*, 60. 1–15.

BRADNEY, J., 1926, *A Memorandum, being an attempt to give a chronology of the Welsh language in the eastern part of the County of Monmouth*. Abergavenny: Minera Press.

BRUNOT, F., 1967, Appendix (Limite de la langue Française sous le Premier Empire) *Histoire de la Langue Française*. Paris: Librairie Armand Colin, Tome IX. 525–99.

CARTER, H., 1972, *The Study of Urban Geography*. London: Arnold.

—— 1976, Y Fro Gymraeg and the 1975 referendum on Sunday closing of public houses in Wales, *Cambria*, 3, 89–101.

—— 1980, The Welsh language in 1971. In H. CARTER & H.M. GRIFFITHS (eds), *The National Atlas of Wales*. Cardiff: University of Wales Press. Map 3.2d.

CARTER, H. & AITCHISON, J., 1986, Language areas and language change in Wales, 1961–1981. In I. HUME & W.T.R. PRYCE (eds), *The Welsh and their Country: Selected Readings in the Social Sciences*. Llandysul: Gomer Press. 1–25.

CARTER, H. & CARTER, M., 1974a, Cyfrifiaid 1971: adroddiad ar y iaith Gymraeg yng Nghymru, *Barn* 137, 206–10.

—— 1974b, Cyfrifiad yr iaith Gymraeg 1971: gwahaniaethau rhwng siarad ac ysgrifennu Gymraeg, *Barn*, 141, 398–402.

CARTER, H. & THOMAS, J.G., 1969, The referendum on the Sunday opening of licensed premises in Wales as a criterion of a culture region, *Regional Studies*, 3, 61–71.

CARTER, H. & WILLIAMS, S.W., 1978, Aggregate studies of language and culture change in Wales. In G. WILLIAMS (ed.), *Social and Cultural Change in Contemporary Wales*. London: R.K. Paul. 143–65.

CHARLES, B.G., 1963, The Welsh, their language and place names in Archenfield and Oswestry. In H. LEWIS (ed.), *Angles and Britons: The O'Donnell Lectures*. Cardiff: University of Wales Press. 85–110.

CENSUS, 1881, Scotland *Report*, vol. 1, London: HMSO (C3320).

CENSUS, 1891, *General Report*, IX Languages in Wales and Monmouth-shire. London: HMSO (C7222).

CENSUS, 1894, *Division XI Monmouthshire and Wales*. London: HMSO. 226–27.

CENSUS 1901, *Summary Tables*. LII Language spoken in Administrative Counties. London: HMSO (cd 1523).

CENSUS 1911, Vol. XII Language spoken in Wales and Monmouthshire. London: HMSO (Cd6911) 1913.

CENSUS 1921, *General Report with Appendices*. Part X. Welsh language. London: HMSO 1927.

CENSUS 1931, *General Report*. VII Welsh language. London: HMSO 1950.

DOWNS, R.M. & STEA, D. (eds), 1973, *Image and Environment*. Chicago: University of Chicago Press.

ELLIS, A.J., 1882, On the delimitation of the English and Welsh languages, *Y Cymmrodor*, 5, 173–208.

EMERY, F. & WHITE, P., 1975, Welsh speaking in Wales according to the 1971 census, *Area*, 7, 26–30.

GALE, S. & OLSSON, G. (eds), 1979, *Philosophy in Geography*. Dordrecht: D. Reidl.

GOULD, P.R. & WHITE, R., 1974, *Mental Maps*. Harmondsworth: Penguin.

GRIFFITHS, H.M., 1980, Administrative areas: 1284–1980. In H. CARTER & H.M. GRIFFITHS (eds), *The National Atlas of Wales*. Cardiff: University of Wales Press. Section 2.1.

GWYNEDD COUNTY COUNCIL, 1985, *Gwynedd Structure Plan*. Caernarfon: Gwynedd County Planning Department.

HUMPHREYS, H.L., 1979, *La langue Galloise: une présentation*. Faculté des Lettres de Brest, Université de Bretagne Occidentale: *Studi* No. 13, Vol. 1.

INTERDEPARTMENTAL COMMITTEE ON SOCIAL AND ECONOMIC RESEARCH 1951, *Guides to Official Sources – No. 2 Census Reports of Great Britain 1801–1931*. London: HMSO.

JAMES, B., 1972, The Welsh language in the Vale of Glamorgan, *Morgannwg* 16. 16–36.

JAMES, C., 1974, The state of the Heartland: Language and community in Gwynedd 1921–71, *Planet*, 23. 3–15.

—— 1975, The language in Clwyd, *Planet*, 28. 25–35.

JAMES, I., 1887, *The Welsh Language in the 16th and 17th Centuries*. Cardiff: Daniel Owen & Co Ltd (reprinted from the *Welsh Dragon*).

JONES, E., 1952, Some aspects of cultural change in an American Welsh community, *Transactions, Honourable Society of Cymmrodorion*, Session 1952. 15–39.

JONES, I.G., 1980, Language and community in nineteenth century Wales, in D. SMITH (ed.), *A People and a Proletariat: Essays in the History of Wales 1780–1980*. London: Pluto Press in association with Llafur. 47–71.

JONES, J.R., 1966, *Prydeindod*. Llandybie: Llyfrau'r Dryw.

JONES, P.N., 1976, Baptist chapels as an index of cultural transition in the south Wales coalfield before 1914, *Journal of Historical Geography*, 2. 347–60.

KENRICK, G.S., 1841, Statistics of the population in the parish of Trevethin (Pontypool) and at the neighbouring works of Blaenavon in Monmouthshire ..., *Journal, Royal Statistical Society*, Series A, 3, 366–75.

KOFMAN, E., 1981, The concept of the culture region in the social sciences in France, *L'Espace Géographique*, 4, 281–85.

LEWIS, G.J., 1979, The geography of cultural transition: The Welsh borderland 1750–1850, *Journal, National Library of Wales*, 21.

LEWIS, T., 1926, Sur la distribution du parler Gallois dans le Pays de Galles, d'après le recensement de 1921, *Annales de Géographie* 35.

LEY, D. & SAMUELS, M.S. (ed.), 1978, *Humanistic Geography: Prospects and Problems*. London: Croom Helm.

MORGAN, P., 1983, From a death to a view. In E. HOBSBAWM & T. RANGER (eds), *The Invention of Tradition*. Cambridge: Cambridge University Press.

PICKLES, J., 1985, *Phenomenology, Science and Geography*. Cambridge: Cambridge University Press.

PRYCE, W.T.R., 1972, Approaches to the linguistic geography of northeast Wales, 1750–1846, *National Library of Wales Journal*, 17, 343–63.

—— 1975a, Industrialism, urbanization and the maintenance of culture areas: north-east Wales in the mid-nineteenth century, *Welsh History Review*, 7, 307–40.

—— 1975b, Migration and the evolution of culture areas: Culture and linguistic frontiers in north-east Wales, 1750 and 1851, *Transactions, Institute of British Geographies*, 65.

—— 1976, The census as a major source for the study of Flintshire society in the nineteenth century, *Journal of the Flintshire Historical Society*, 26, 114–43.

—— 1978a, Welsh and English in Wales, 1750–1971: A spatial analysis based on the linguistic affiliation of parochial communities, *Bulletin of the Board of Celtic Studies*, 28. 1–36.

—— 1978b, Wales as a culture region: patterns of change 1750–1971, *Transactions of the Honourable Society of Cymmrodorion*, Session 1978. 229–61. Reprinted with corrections in I. HUME & W.T.R. PRYCE (eds) (1986), *The Welsh and their Country: Selected Readings in the Social Sciences*. Llandysul: Gomer Press. 26–63

—— 1982, The idea of culture in human geography. In E. GRANT & P. NEWBY (eds), *Landscape and Industry: Essays in Memory of Geoffrey Gullett*. London: Middlesex Polytechnic. 131–49.

RANDALL, P.J., 1972, Wales in the structure of central Government, *Public Administration*, Autumn 1972. 353–72.

RAVENSTEIN, E.G., 1879, On the Celtic languages in the British Isles: A statistical survey, *Journal, Royal Statistical Society*, 42.

REES, W., 1940, *The Vicissitudes of the Welsh Language in the Marches of Wales within Special Reference to its Territorial Distribution in Modern Times*. University of Wales unpublished PhD thesis.

—— 1967, *The Union of England and Wales*. Cardiff: University of Wales Press.

REPORTS, *Commissioners of Inquiry into the State of Education in Wales, Part III North Wales*. London 1847, 337–58.

ROBSON, B.T., 1973, *Urban Growth: An Approach*. London: Methuen.

Royal Commisison on the Church of England and other religous Bodies in Wales and Monmouthshire, 1910, *Report*. London: HMSO (Cd5432).

—— 1911, *Vol.IV Minutes of Evidence, Book III*. London: HMSO (Cd5435), Questions 45890–46613 (St. Davids), 47477–8 (St. Asaph), 48490 (Bangor), 48216–44 (Llandaf).

—— no date, *Appendices to the Report*, Vol. 1, Part III. Language maps of Wales and Monmouthshire: North Wales: South Wales.

SACK, R.D., 1980, *Conceptions of Space in Social Thought*. London: Macmillan.

SOUTHALL, J.E., 1892, *Wales and her Language* considered from a historical, educational and social viewpoint with remarks on modern Welsh literature and a linguistic map of the country. London: D. Nutt and Newport, Mon: J.E. Southall.

—— 1895, *The Welsh Language Census of 1891* with a coloured map of the 52 Registration Districts into which Wales is divided. Newport, Mon: John E. Southall.

—— 1904, *The Welsh Language Census of 1901* ... also a coloured linguistic map of Wales with a chapter on Welsh in the schools. Newport, Mon: J.E. Southall.

THOMAS, J.I., 1962, *The Anglo-Celtic Frontier in the Lowlands and Uplands of the Dee Basin of North-east Wales*. University of Liverpool, Unpublished MA thesis.

WEBB, J.W., 1963, The natural and migrational components of population changes in England and Wales, 1921–31, *Economic Geography*, 39, 130–48.

WILLIAMS, C.H., 1978a, *Language Decline and Nationalist Resurgence in Wales*. University of Wales, unpublished PhD thesis.

—— 1978b, Some spatial considerations in Welsh language planning *Cambria*, 5, 173–81.

—— 1979, An ecological and behavioural analysis of ethnolinguistic change in Wales. In H. GILES & B. SAINT-JACQUES (eds), *Language and Ethnic Relations*, Oxford: Pergamon Press. 27–56.

—— 1981, On cultural space: Perceptual culture regions in Wales, *Études Celtiques*, 18, 273–96.

—— 1982a, The spatial analysis of Welsh culture, *Études Celtiques*, 19 283–322.

—— 1982b, Language planning and minority group rights, *Cambria* 9, 61–74.

—— 1985, Public gain and private grief: The ambiguous nature of contemporary Welsh, *Transactions of the Honourable Society of Cymmrodorion*. Session 1985, 27–48.

—— 1986a, Bilingual education as an agent in cultural reproduction. In W.K.D. DAVIES (ed.), *Human Geography from Wales, Cambria* Vol. 13, 111–29.

—— 1986b, Language planning and minority group rights. In I. HUME & W.T.R. PRYCE (eds), *The Welsh and their Country*. Llandysul: Gomer Press. 253–72.

—— 1988, Minority nationalist historiography. In R. JOHNSTON *et al.* *Regionalism, Nationalism and Self-determination: Geographical Perspectives*. Beckenham: Croom Helm.

WILLIAMS, D.T., 1935, Linguistic divides in south Wales: A historico-geographical study, *Archaeologia Cambrensis*, 90. 239–66.

—— 1936, Linguistic divides in north Wales . . ., *Archaeologia Cambrensis*, 91, 194–209.

—— 1937, A linguistic map of Wales according to the 1931 census, with some observations on its historical and geographical settings, *Geographical Journal*, 89, 146–51.

WILLIAMS, M., 1972, The linguistic and cultural frontier in Gower, *Archaeologia Cambrensis*, 121, 61–69.

WILLIAMS, S.W., 1980, *Culture and Ethnicity in Wales: A Spatial Perspective*. University of Wales, Unpublished PhD thesis.

—— 1981, The urban hierarchy, diffusion and the Welsh language: A preliminary analysis 1901–71, *Cambria: A Welsh Geographical Review*, 8, 35–50.

—— 1984, Language maintenance, erosion and ethnic identity, *Discussion Papers in Geolinguistics*, No. 6.

WITHERS, C.W.J., 1984, *Gaelic in Scotland 1698–1981*. Edinburgh: John Donald Publications Ltd.

8 Language Policy and Internal Geopolitics: The Canadian Situation[1]

DON CARTWRIGHT
Department of Geography,
The University of Western Ontario, Canada

The development of policies of accommodation between French and English Canada has been a constant challenge; to the British Government before the British North America Act of 1867 and to the federal government of Canada since. Strategies have been directed toward the nation, selected provinces and even designated regions within provinces, and still a solution has not been achieved that is satisfactory to both groups.

In 1774, the British Parliament passed The Quebec Act. Intended as a means to nullify American influence in the colonies, it recognized the unique language, faith and many institutions of the province, and thereby provided cultural security to French Canada. When Confederation was achieved in 1867 these guarantees for Quebec were entrenched; a political action that won the support of the Church hierarchy in the province (Lower Canada) for the British North America Act. In spite of the rights obtained by the people of Quebec the fears of cultural erosion persisted throughout Canada's first century. The strong economic influence of the anglos in the province, their "we're-no-minority!" attitude, reinforced by location and situation, and a steadfast resistance to learn and use French entrenched the fears of the francophones. In the 1960s and 70s the government of Quebec promulgated several laws which were designed to promote and protect the French language. To this end the

238

laws have been successful but the cultural apprehension shifted to the anglos and many left the province. The national perception of Quebec's boundary is no longer one of merely a limit to jurisdiction but one that has become an impermeable cultural barrier.

While the culture of French Canada has been relatively safe within Quebec, francophones beyond the province have received setbacks, particularly in Ontario and Manitoba, against the use of French beyond the domain of the household. Since the 1960s several attempts have been made by the federal government to rectify this trend again at the national, provincial and regional scales. Through the Official Languages Act (1969) French and English were declared official languages of Canada in regard to all the functions of the Parliament and government of Canada and in all federal institutions. To ensure that the system of federal language services, as specified in the Act, would be applied throughout the nation, the concept of bilingual districts was adopted whereby regional concentrations of anglophones within Quebec and francophones beyond Quebec would be entitled to obtain full federal services in the language of their choice. These districts were intended to function as a model to provincial and municipal governments and in this way minority-language usage beyond the home was to be encouraged for those outside the respective English and French core areas. In spite of the recommendations of two Boards, bilingual districts were not created in Canada (Cartwright & Williams, 1982).

In the late 1960s, the *Report* of the Bilingual and Bicultural Commission recommended official-languages status for New Brunswick and Ontario. Such status was based upon the number of francophones who lived in the two provinces and on the "geographic contiguity" with Quebec which, at the time, was "already officially bilingual" (Canada Royal Commission, 1967: Book I, p. 96). While New Brunswick accommodated the recommendation, Ontario did not. More recently, Prime Minister Trudeau wrote to the premier of Ontario, shortly before leaving office, and is reported to have stressed the unique opportunity open to the provincial government to thwart the separatists in Quebec and provide a thrust for national unity by giving constitutional recognition and protection to the language rights of Franco Ontarians (*Globe and Mail*, June 15, 1984). Once again the government of Ontario resisted this request because it anticipated a negative reaction among non-francophones in the province. The situation appears at an impasse and we seem to face an unimpeded drift toward a linguistic division with French entrenched in Quebec and English in the rest of Canada; a situation that the Commissioner of Official Languages has described as "linguistic territorialization on the Belgian model". It is the intent of this chapter to suggest a policy that may thwart this territorial drift and incorporate a gesture toward national unity. The strategy will be focused upon a two-tier accommodation of the francophone minority within Ontario.

In his letter to the premier, Trudeau recognized the progress that has been made in Ontario for the provision of French-language services. Beginning in 1975, measures were introduced whereby Franco-Ontarians received the right to use French in all criminal cases. This was gradually extended into the civil courts in specified areas and culminated in official status for English and French in the Courts of Justice Act in 1983. Similar progress has been made in education, although the government has been criticized for needless delays between declarations of intent and actual performance. In June, 1984, the Ontario Court of Appeal ruled that French-speaking children in the province have the right to educational instruction in their mother tongue according to individual demand and not where numbers warrant. French-speaking citizens are also able to obtain services from ministry offices in designated areas across the province; areas selected to incorporate the significant concentrations of Franco-Ontarians. According to the Annual Report (1982) of the Government Co-ordinator of French Language Services, almost 83% of the minority population was serviced through these designated areas. Thus, the provincial government has opted for institutional bilingualism through a functional organization of territory based upon perceived needs rather than a formal organization of territory whereby the two languages would be declared official for the entire province. Even the concept of bilingual districts, a form of territorial organization embodied in the Official Languages Act, was rejected as politically impractical, partially because of the geographical patterns of Franco-Ontarian settlement and concomitant variation in minority-language usage (Minutes, Bilingual Districts Advisory Board, 1973. P.A.C., Ottawa[1]). Ontario, unlike other provinces, has a francophone settlement pattern that ranges from dispersed in Toronto, through small, rural enclaves in central and western Ontario, to strong and extensive concentrations close to the Ontario/Quebec border. It is the latter area, a cultural zone of transition, that has the potential for a type of formal recognition that may satisfy the "entrenchment" proponents.

The cultural zone of transition

Limits to political jurisdiction are identified by boundaries but the cultural features of societies that share a boundary seldom accord with these linear features of the landscape. People interact across these lines of jurisdiction so that characteristics of respective cultures become inter-mingled in a zone of transition; a frontier that contains social and cultural aspects of two different societies. Northern Ireland, for example, has been described as, "a sort of demographic half-way house between Great Britain — and the Irish Republic" (Compton, 1982: 75) where population characteristics of the British and Irish realms overlap. In this context Boal & Douglas (1982) developed the societal concept of integration/division as both attribute and process (the state of being integrated and the act of integrating respectively) that are applicable to cultural zones of transition. The analysis of economic, political and social features of the zone, therefore, will reveal which attribute/process is dominant, for integrative and divisive processes are essentially behavioural and may be depicted as opposite ends of a "seesaw". The behavioural processes that are dominant will tip the entire system toward integration or toward division or, if in balance, toward a delicate state of equilibrium.

The southern United States from Florida to California exhibit cultural features of the landscape that reflect the hispanic and anglo zone of contact and interaction. A recent resolution in the United States that proposes to amend the constitution to proclaim English as *the* official language of the country (Senate Joint Resolution #167, 9/12/83) may be interpreted as an attempt to re-establish control over this international boundary and to restore an integrative attribute to their portion of the zone of transition. Spanish is perceived by some as permeating the cultural zone of transition between Mexico and the United States at the expense of English. This is considered by the sponsors of the bill to be a divisive process; consequently policy must be brought forth to re-establish the dominance of English. In defence of the bill, Senator Walter Huddleston (D. Kentucky) cited Canada as evidence that bilingualism can generate divisiveness and threaten national unity (Congressional Record-Senate, March 7, 1983, p. 2413). To paraphrase House (1981), zones of transition between cultural realms are an aggravated microcosm of the general social, cultural, economic and political issues that dominate the relations between administrative systems.

Canada has a similar cultural zone of transition between French and English Canada where the two ethnic groups have interacted for generations (see Figure 8.3). It is the successes that have been realized zone, rather than the failures, that provide the basis for the mendations in this chapter and a rejection of Senator Huddleston's gy to justify his bill. The presence of the zone within Ontario may ｎ. contributed to the intransigence in Queen's Park but its existence can function as a positive feature for the province and for Canada.

Unlike New Brunswick and Quebec the minority population in Ontario (excluding allophones) is not as highly concentrated within the cultural zone of transition between French and English Canada; the area that Richard Joy (1972) identified as the "bilingual belt". According to the census of 1981, counties in Eastern and Northern New Brunswick (see Figure 8.3) contain 94% of the provincial French mother-tongue population and almost 97% of the census population who declared French as the language used most often in the home. That portion of the zone that is within Quebec (see Figure 8.3) contains almost 93% of the English, mother-tongue population of the province and 91% of the people who use English as home language. Beyond this zone in the two provinces, the minority population is dispersed or situated within a transient location, such as the military base in Bagotville, Quebec. In Ontario, 66% of the French mother-tongue population and 79% of the French home-language population live within the zone of transition in eastern and northern Ontario. The remainder are located within "language islands" such as Welland, Penetang and Essex County or dispersed within urban centres such as Toronto (Cartwright, 1980). Unlike New Brunswick and Quebec, language policy in Ontario must accommodate a minority that ranges from highly concentrated, with intensive usage of the mother tongue within and beyond the home, to a scattered urban group in Toronto with relatively weak language retention. The former are able to sustain numerous institutions that provide support for cultural continuity while the latter reportedly finds it difficult to sustain one elementary, French-language school. It is this requirement to provide for a diverse minority within a single language policy that may have contributed to the position taken by the government of Ontario to avoid a provincewide, formal language policy, whereby French and English are declared official languages, and to opt instead for a functional policy of services according to significant demand.

Selected characteristics of francophone communities, Ontario

According to the Census of Canada, 482,045 people were recorded as having French as mother tongue in Ontario in 1971. This constituted

6.3% of the provincial population. In 1981, the census registered 467,885 people with French as their mother tongue, forming 5.5% of the total population. An argument for a specific language policy that is based upon the numerical size of the minority alone must be considered weak. For example, one could argue in favour of the entrenchment of language rights because of the apparent erosion of the French mother-tongue population in Ontario. A symbolic move as well as the intensification of specific services could be tonic for the minority but this would scarcely convince the majority of the efficacy or necessity of such a policy. It is the contention of this writer that spatial and sociolinguistic analysis will provide a stronger foundation on which to place provincial language policy.

There are significant variations in language retention among the French mother-tongue population of Ontario, with distance from the core area of French Canada and with differences in the relative size of the minority settlements. Using the census data collected in 1981, it is possible to determine language retention rates by calculating the percentage of French mother-tongue respondents who continue to use French most often in the home by census divisions and subdivisions. In central and western Ontario the small size of the minority relative to total population and their dispersed settlement is reflected in a low retention of language (Table 8.1). This is particularly marked in metropolitan Toronto. In Essex County and in the city of Welland (Niagara Regional Municipality), a local concentration of the Franco-Ontarian population has helped some families to retain the language in the home (Cartwright & Taylor, 1979; Bennett, 1980). The existence of local social, cultural and educational institutions has played a significant role in this retention as well. Within the zone of transition, however, language retention rates are considerably higher, reflecting the geographical proximity to Quebec, the size of the population relative to the total, and a greater range of institutions that can be sustained (Table 8.1). The historical context of the Franco-Ontarian in this location is also significant for many can trace their heritage in the area over several generations to the original settlers in eastern and northern Ontario (Vallieres, 1982; Choquette, 1980; Savard, 1978; Gaffield, 1982).

The measurement of language retention is one way to demonstrate the range of a cultural attribute among Franco-Ontarians, since the calculation determines a relationship between the number who are now using the language in the home and the number who learned it as a child. Some social scientists are cautious in relying upon this as an indicator of linguistic assimilation because of the difficulty in comparing the two census populations for 1971 and 1981. This is particularly true for the

TABLE 8.1 *Language retention for Franco-Ontarians and index of language intensity for French and English, selected census divisions, Ontario, 1981*

Census division	French mother-tongue population	% of total pop. 1981	% of total pop. (1971)	language retention	index of language intensity French	index of language intensity English
Eastern Ontario						
Prescott	22,905	75	(81)	95%	0.39	0.70
Russell	16,175	72	(84)	95%	0.37	0.80
Ottawa/Carleton	104,120	19	(21)	75%	0.15	0.91
Glengarry	7,665	38	(44)	82%	0.21	0.82
Stormont	18,365	30	(34)	71%	0.15	0.86
Northern Ontario						
Cochrane	45,135	47	(49)	86%	0.26	1.03
Nipissing	22,830	28	(33)	77%	0.17	0.95
Sudbury District	9,685	36		75%	0.18	0.93
Sudbury Regional Municipality	46,940	29	(32)	74%	0.12	1.07
Timiskaming	10,850	26	(28)	77%	0.25	0.96
Central & Western Ontario						
Toronto (Metro)	31,260	1.5	(2.2)	35%	0.19	1.33
Simcoe	7,690	3.4	(4.6)	43%	0.15	1.04
Niagara	15,380	4.2	(4.9)	52%	0.15	1.17
Essex	19,625	6.3	(8.5)	40%	0.11	1.17

Source: Census of Canada, catalogues 93-942 (E576) and 95-942, vol. 3, Profile Series B, 1981.

mother-tongue population. Changes in definition, editing procedures and reduction algorithms for multiple responses have made decennial census comparisons problematic. To overcome reliance solely upon this measurement, and to determine the relative strengths of the two languages for a geostatistical unit, the index of language intensity may be applied. This index is calculated using the census populations of home language and official languages, unilingual (Cartwright, 1980). Responses to the official languages question of the census are less suspect than those to mother tongue, thus, by combining this census population (unilingual) with that of home language, errors can be reduced but not completely avoided. A brief explanation of the index of language intensity may help to clarify this.

A spatial feature that is significant in minority-language communities is the pervasiveness of one official language at the expense of the other, and the necessity for the minority to accommodate that dominant community-language in a daily routine of local contacts and interactions. In such a situation people frequently speak one language in the home and a second language outside the home. Geolinguistic analysis can provide a measure of this pervasiveness of one language over another and, thereby, provide an indication of the linguistic milieu that is encountered beyond the home.

If we can assume that people who encounter no pressure to learn a second language in their community will remain unilingual, we should anticipate a similarity in size between a home-language population and a unilingual population. Thus, to provide an indicator of the potential for language usage beyond the home, it was decided to use the unilingual population — those who replied "English only" or "French only" to the official languages question — in a cross-tabulation with responses to the home-language question. The former must be considered the least subjective of the language-related questions in the census, and while the latter can be confusing to respondents who were raised in a home where more than one language was used (Castonguay, 1976), it does provide a measure of those who are still able to speak their mother tongue. We are also comparing two census populations that have current time frames (Mackey & Cartwright, 1979). Thus, when the unilingual French/English population is cross-tabulated with the home-language (French/English) population we can establish an index that will range from 1.00 to 0.00.[2] By comparing these two census populations for any census division or subdivision the index may be expressed in the following form:

$$\frac{\text{official-language population } \frac{\text{French}}{\text{English}} \text{ only}}{\text{home-language population } \frac{\text{French}}{\text{English}}} = \text{index of language intensity}$$

Any community that has an index close to 1.00 may be considered one in which people can function well in their mother tongue during a daily pattern of contact and human interaction. When the index approaches 0.00 the opposite occurs; people must switch to the other official language for most services, to function at work, and for many (but not necessarily all) daily contacts and interactions. Hence, the index becomes a measure of the intensity with which a particular language permeates the area. For Franco-Ontarians, a low measure on this index should not suggest that they do not use French in specific places beyond the home, such as cultural centres or service clubs. A high proportion of French-home-language to French-mother-tongue for any community that has a low index of language intensity would indicate patronage of French-language institutions but English usage throughout the rest of the community. A high index for English in the same community would substantiate this pattern (Table 8.1). If both groups, however, have a low measure on the index it would indicate what Vallee & Dufour (1974) have called a balanced bilingual situation.

Further refinement in the application of the index of language intensity will reveal whether a measure obtained is truly representative for a population. By dividing the mother-tongue population into age cohorts and applying the index to each, it is possible to determine whether one or two of the groups are skewed, thereby affecting the overall measure. The graphs in Figures 8.1 and 8.2 provide a visual impression of the index by specified age cohorts, for French and English, in the census divisions within the zone of transition for Ontario. The graphs are derived from data obtained from Statistics Canada. For the two census years, data were assembled for each by mother tongue, by home language, by official languages, by sex and for specified age cohorts. These were run at the scale of the census subdivision with data then aggregated for the census division. To facilitate comparison, Statistics Canada was requested to make the 1971 data compatible with 1981 census boundaries, thereby overcoming changes in the limits of geo-statistical units between the two censuses. This is a very costly process, therefore it was done only for those units considered to be within the cultural zone of transition. The selected age cohorts did not include those below the age of five years because the range of interaction for these pre-school children is normally limited to the home. Furthermore, Statistics Canada classifies their ability with the official languages according to the declared home

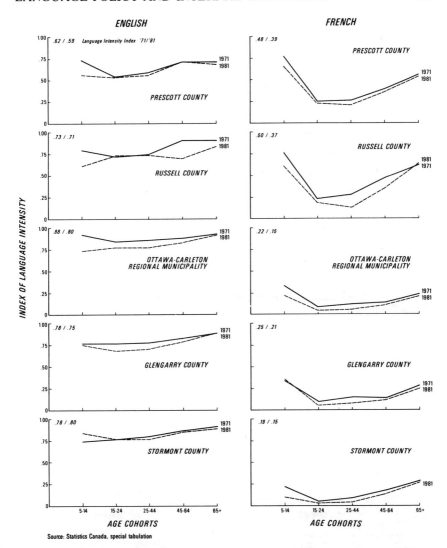

ENGLISH   FRENCH

Source: Statistics Canada, special tabulation

FIGURE 8.1 *Index of language intensity by age cohorts for French and English within the cultural zone of transition, eastern Ontario, 1971 and 1981*

language of the parents. Beyond this age, children begin to attend school and their range of interaction alters accordingly. The remaining age cohorts are intended to isolate groups entering the labour force, the youthful mobile element of the labour force, the entrenched and the retired.

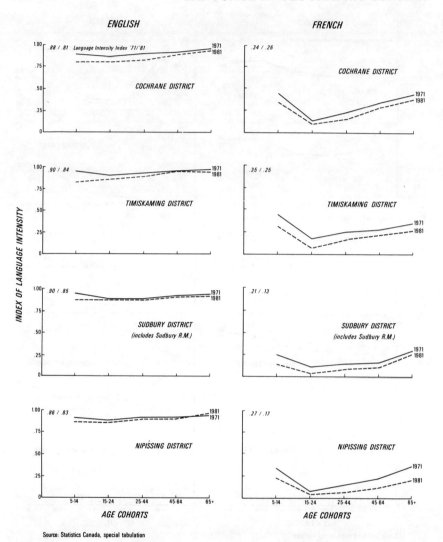

Source: Statistics Canada, special tabulation

FIGURE 8.2   *Index of language intensity by age cohorts for French and English within the cultural zone of transition, northern Ontario, 1971 and 1981*

The position of the two linguistic groups on the graphs reveals the pervasiveness of English throughout the zone of transition. Even in the counties in which the Franco-Ontarians are in the majority (Prescott and Russell) accommodation is unbalanced toward English. It must be remembered, however, that within these counties there are small communities in which francophones can function almost entirely in French (Vallee & Shulman, 1969; Lapierre, 1977). As one moves westward toward "unilingual" Ontario the index for French drops markedly. Overall the profiles for English have remained relatively unchanged between 1971 and 1981 except in Ottawa-Carleton and this may be attributed to the policy on language proficiency for federal employees (Lamy, 1976). The apparent anomaly in Russell County for English within the 45–64 age cohort may reflect an increase in the Ottawa labour force who have selected dormitory centres outside the capital. The most significant exception, however, resides in the youngest age cohorts and this will be discussed below.

There has been a slight drop in the index for French for most age cohorts between 1971 and 1981. Considering the position on the index for this linguistic group, even a small negative shift must be considered with concern, particularly since the other linguistic group has maintained a position closer to unity (1.00). Within each census division, there is a sharp drop in the index for the teenage francophones and the early labour-force cohort as their range of contact and interaction increases within the community. It becomes relatively high again for the older cohorts, indicating a reduced range of contact and interaction upon retirement, plus a residual population after the out-migration and/or assimilation of younger cohorts who have accommodated to English at an early age. These profiles for French also demonstrate the importance of providing public services in that language for the youngest and oldest members of the group; for example, in education and in health-care units.

Although the language retention rates (Table 8.1) for French within the transition zone are encouraging, the profiles of the index of language intensity indicate that, except for the very young and the oldest, Franco-Ontarians must function largely in English beyond the home.[3] The application of the index to the selected age cohorts provides a graphic illustration of what Lamy (1977) described as a rapid movement towards structural interdependence and cultural convergence in the Franco-Ontarian society.

"As in Quebec, the extended family declined as a social form, religious institutions declined in importance, and Ontario francophones became more and more inserted into an economic infrastructure and a social environment controlled and inhabited by the English" (Lamy, 1977: 3).

One outcome of this process is intensification of the sociocultural differences between the Franco-Ontarian communities; another is the high rate of exogamy and attendant linguistic assimilation (Maheu, 1970; Lachapelle & Henripin, 1982).

As one would expect when the index of language intensity is applied to the French-language minority in central and western Ontario the register is closer to zero, whereas that for English is greater than 1.00, demonstrating the economic and social significance of this language beyond the Quebec/Ontario frontier (Table 8.1). The majority of Franco-Ontarians who live outside the zone of transition must function in an English-dominant milieu beyond the home. They reflect the problems that arise in maintaining the mother tongue with increasing distance from the core area of French Canada and an irregular and unreliable in-migration of French speaking people. Language retention and cultural continuity must be realized mainly through reliance upon the family and a few local institutions rather than upon regular contact with the core area of French Canada.

Implications for provincial language policy

The provincial government has the option of continuing its present functional policy on minority language services, according to significant demand, or it can opt for an interim position between this and complete and provincewide, official-languages status for French and English; an option that seemed anathema to the premier and his cabinet. Indeed, with linguistic variations among the Franco-Ontarian communities, as discussed above, it is arguable that a single policy associated with official-language status is unsuited to the province of Ontario. On the other hand, it is possible that if the government retains its present policy, cultural erosion of the Franco-Ontarians in eastern and northern Ontario will proceed until only small, minority enclaves exist and the social and geographical characteristics of a cultural zone of transition will be lost. If this does occur, the process that Lachapelle (1980) refers to as "territorialization", whereby francophones are becoming more concentrated in Quebec and anglophones in the rest of Canada, may become unalterable. It may be possible to halt the "territorialization" process through a change in Ontario's language policy that will have both symbolic and practical attributes and, concurrently, will accord with variations in the sociolinguistic characteristics of the Franco-Ontarians.

During the administration of Mayor Pierre Benoit of Ottawa, municipal services in the two official languages were introduced gradually and without fanfare. Consequently, citizens were not required to make a sudden decision whether they were for or against a particular policy. The alteration in services became a part of their environment by degrees (Minutes, B.D.A.B., 1972). For the past decade, the provincial government of Ontario has been following a similar path, although in some instances the absence of fanfare has been notable. This has been classified as the *functional* organization of territory whereby accommodation is made to two official-language communities based upon a gradual introduction of services. This policy may be suited to the Franco-Ontarians of central and western Ontario but the provincial government is in a position to accommodate the cultural zone of transition and provide a gesture of national unity by adding a *formal* organization of territory to the functional policy now applied in eastern and northern Ontario. This portion of the province could be formally designated as the Official-Languages Zone of Ontario (Figure 8.3). It is possible that such a gesture by the provincial government will help to prevent cultural erosion in the zone by reinforcing what appears to be a positive development among young anglophones.

Ideally, realization of the potential for human contact and interaction within a cultural zone of transition requires *both* profiles on the index of language intensity to be more closely in balance at the lower end of the register (Figures 8.1 and 8.2). Success in this may be accomplished by focusing upon the younger members of the anglophone majority. Confirmation of the value of the minority language through formal designation of territory could reinforce the element of pride in maintaining the mother tongue among the minority and provide further incentive to obtain the language among the majority. There is evidence in Quebec that young anglophones, members of a group who traditionally considered themselves part of the English-Canadian majority, are benefiting from incentive to learn the second language. In their research among early graduates of French immersion in Quebec, Lambert & Tucker (1982) learned that those anglophones who entered the programme at an early age demonstrated a more positive attitude toward French-speaking Canadians, and were more inclined to make contact with and use the second language with French Canadian friends. One is tempted to view these findings as a harbinger for anglophones elsewhere in the zone, since their enrolment in French immersion and in second-language classes is increasing in Ontario and in New Brunswick, particularly at the elementary level (Edwards, 1984; Annual Report, Commissioner of Official Languages, 1982).

The profiles of the index of language intensity suggest that the younger age cohorts among the anglophones are beginning to accommodate

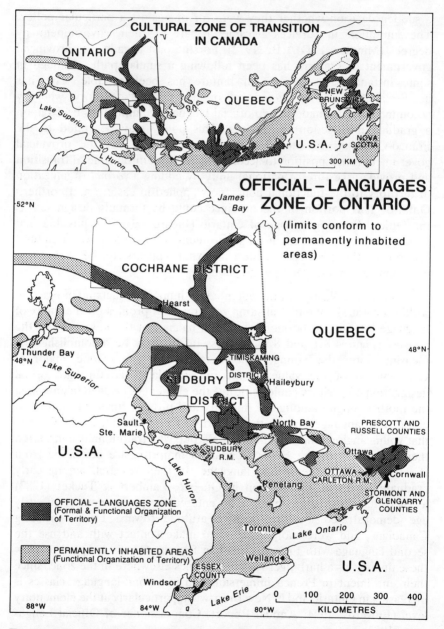

FIGURE 8.3   *Official-languages zone of Ontario*

to the French language in eastern and northern Ontario and this is perhaps the most significant feature revealed in Figures 8.1 and 8.2. Since census data and associated tabulations can provide only indications of trends toward integration/division within a plural society, it is desirable to seek corroborative evidence through field research. To this end such research has been conducted within a portion of the cultural zone of transition.[4]

Questionnaires were designed so that information could be obtained on early and current language usage by francophones and anglophones in various domains. Personal and parental attitudes toward second-language acquisition were also acquired. The format of this research design is illustrated in Figure 8.4. Responses have been selected from the survey conducted in Hawkesbury and Vankleek Hill (Prescott County) and in Alexandria (Glengarry County) in eastern Ontario. Within these urban centres, the population of English mother tongue constitute 12%, 51% and 35% of the total population respectively and represent a sample size of about 6% of this mother-tongue population. The respondents have been grouped into four cohorts to conform to those illustrated in the profiles of the index of language intensity. To determine whether field research will substantiate or refute the indicators obtained from these profiles, that the youngest anglophones have developed more positive attitudes and behaviour in the use of French, responses were tested through Chi-square analysis. The null hypothesis may be stated that there is no variation in attitudes toward, or behaviour in, second-language acquisition and usage among the four age cohorts.

The analysis of competence in the second official language is illustrated in Figure 8.5. For the francophone population there is no significant variation among the age cohorts in the ability to speak English. This concurs with the profiles illustrated in Figures 8.1 and 8.2. The Franco-Ontarians are in an English-dominant milieu in this province and this is reflected in their acquisition of the language. Variation in ability in French among the anglophone cohorts is significant, however. Among the youngest, no respondent replied that he/she was unable to speak French. There is a progressive increase in the percentage of anglophone respondents who stated that they are able to speak French "fairly well" or "very well" from the oldest to the youngest age group.

Parental attitudes toward second-language acquisition by the respondent (Figure 8.6) were not statistically different among the age cohorts for either group. This should not be surprising for the francophones. More than half for all age groups replied that their parents "strongly favoured" the acquisition of English by their son or daughter. The

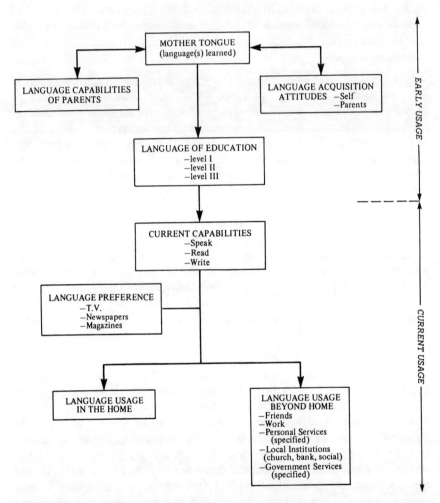

FIGURE 8.4   *Profile of field research*

interesting response among the anglophones is illustrated in the sharp increase among the youngest respondents whose parents "strongly favoured" the learning of French by their child.

A similar pattern is revealed in the respondents' attitude to the acquisition of the second language for both francophones and anglophones

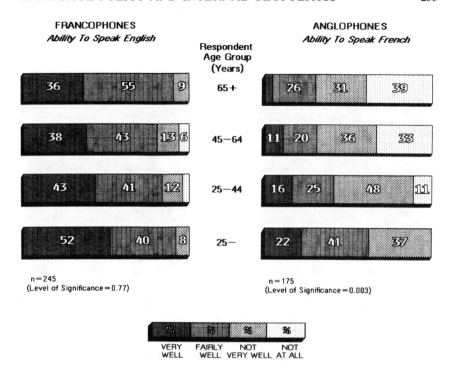

FIGURE 8.5   *Ability to speak the second official language by French and English mother-tongue populations, Eastern Ontario*

(Figure 8.7). Almost 50% of the youngest anglophones said that they "strongly favour" learning French. This shift in attitude among the younger anglophones emerges in the usage of the second language. In language usage with friends and at work (Figures 8.8 and 8.9) there is a statistical significance among the anglophone age groups. The youngest use French "occasionally" and "often", more so than the older cohorts. In social situations beyond the home the youngest francophones *and* anglophones interact at least "occasionally" in the language of the other.

Although it must be stressed that these data are preliminary and only a part of more extensive research, early results are encouraging in this portion of the zone of transition, for there is an apparent shift to acceptance and greater usage of the French language among the younger anglophones. We cannot tell whether this shift is transitory. Rather than wait to see if it begins to wane and then formulate a policy to re-establish the trend, it is reasonable to reinforce the shift by applying that policy now.

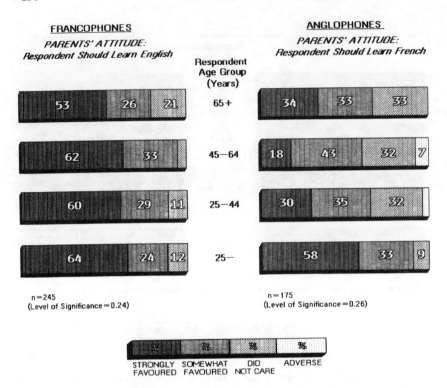

FIGURE 8.6   *Attitudes among French and English mother-tongue populations, eastern Ontario, toward learning the second official language*

The creation of an official languages zone in Ontario will not replace the "functional" policy that is now utilized in the province. Services in the minority language will continue to be provided in areas outside the zone of transition where demand has been recognized and where it is consistent. The relatively low percentages of language retention and measures on the index of language intensity (Table 8.1) indicate that Franco-Ontarians beyond the proposed zone are highly selective in the use of their mother tongue beyond the home. Some social scientists refer to this as the patterned evasion of language usage whereby the minority will use the language of the majority in certain situations in their community even though use of their mother tongue is sanctioned by law or by arrangement (Streib, 1974). This pattern of usage has developed over a long time during which the minority/majority have learned to accommodate each other. Research in central and western Ontario has

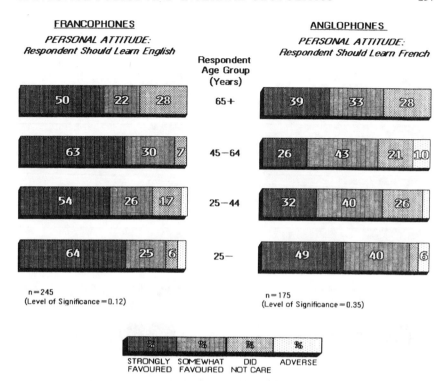

FRANCOPHONES

PERSONAL ATTITUDE:
Respondent Should Learn English

Respondent
Age Group
(Years)

50	22	28	65+
63	30	7	45–64
54	26	17	25–44
64	25	6	25–

n=245
(Level of Significance = 0.12)

ANGLOPHONES

PERSONAL ATTITUDE:
Respondent Should Learn French

39	33	28	
26	43	21	10
32	40	26	
49	40	6	

n=175
(Level of Significance = 0.35)

%	%	%	%
STRONGLY FAVOURED	SOMEWHAT FAVOURED	DID NOT CARE	ADVERSE

FIGURE 8.7 *Attitudes among French and English mother-tongue populations, eastern Ontario, toward learning the second official language*

confirmed this pattern of usage and also revealed that Franco-Ontarians were satisfied with the services that they received in French (Cartwright & Taylor, 1979; Bennett, 1980). The strength and pervasiveness of English in central and western Ontario (Table 8.1) is such that official-language status will neither create a bicultural environment nor is it likely to change the pattern of language usage that has evolved within these communities over several generations. Community harmony in this part of the province is more likely to be sustained if minority-language services continue to be provided through a functional organization of territory. This awareness of community harmony was expressed when bilingual districts were being considered as a means of formal territorial organization to provide federal services within minority enclaves. The concept of enclaves beyond the zone of transition was rejected by some members of the minority because, "They would be happy to have their services but they do not want to

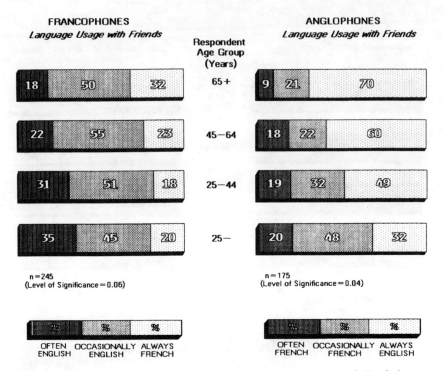

FIGURE 8.8 *Language usage beyond the home, French and English mother-tongue populations, eastern Ontario*

irritate fellow members of their community through a proclamation at this time" (B.D.A.B. Minutes, 1976, vol. 6: 46). During visits to these communities, by members of the Board that was responsible for recommending the location of districts, it was learned that the two services considered by isolated minorities to be most crucial were schools and high quality radio and television broadcasting (B.D.A.B. Report, 1975. See minority report by Eleanor Duckworth). For these reasons, one may conclude that official-language status for one part of the province would not be completely objectionable to Franco-Ontarians in central and western Ontario.

Within eastern and northern Ontario, the measures of language retention and the index of language intensity (Table 8.1) indicate greater range of French mother-tongue usage throughout the community. The indices for the English language, particularly when presented by age-cohort components, suggest that this language is not yet as pervasive as

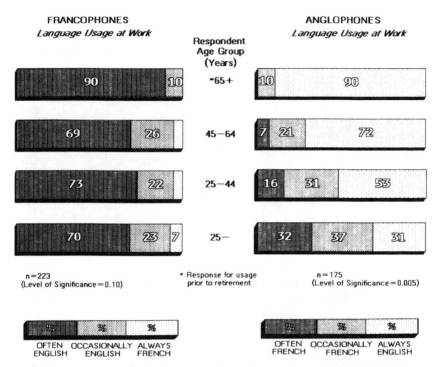

FIGURE 8.9 *Language usage beyond the home, French and English mother-tongue populations, eastern Ontario*

elsewhere in the province. If the assessment of trends among young anglophones, as revealed through census data and field work analyses, is correct, the pervasiveness of English may not reach the levels found in central and western Ontario as quickly as Lachapelle (1980) suggests. One way to help thwart the advance of English at the expense of French and, concurrently, reduce the process of territorialization, is through the addition of official status to the zone of transition.

From the research of others we know that in eastern and northern Ontario there are francophone institutions that are more extensive than those in central and western Ontario (Choquette, 1980; Coons, Taylor & Tremblay, 1977; Castonguay and Marion, 1974). This is a reflection of the size of the Franco-Ontarian population in the zone of transition, both in absolute numbers and in relation to total population (Table 8.1), their historical association with the area, and their geographical proximity to Quebec. The reasons for the extent of francophone institutions may also be taken as justification for assuming that anglophones in the zone would not object to the official-languages status. Furthermore, in several census subdivisions within the zone, anglophones are the minority.

A complementary development in this part of Ontario, that can promote minority-language usage beyond the home, falls into the domain of the private sector. If, with official territorial status, private corporations can be persuaded to extend their services in both languages, employment opportunities can develop beyond those that now exist mostly within the civil service for those with facility in both languages. The zone is more receptive to this type of private-sector development because patterns of language usage are not as entrenched as in the minority-language enclaves described above. This perception of the role and willingness of the private sector is not quixotic, for many have expressed a desire to extend services in this manner (Bilingual Districts Advisory Board, Minutes of Meetings, 1971 to 1973). Both the measures of language retention and the index of language intensity indicate that the French language is sufficiently strong and pervasive to justify this role for the private sector within the zone. Nor would such services appeal to only one age group within the francophone population and this is revealed in the profiles illustrated in Figures 8.1 and 8.2.

Lamy (1977) has stressed that structural remedies alone — French schools and universities, cultural centres, radio, television and newspapers — will not save Franco-Ontarians from assimilation. Developing a set of parallel institutions will not ensure that minority members will patronize them. But is it necessary to have all institutions parallel? Caldwell (1982) in his research among anglophones in Quebec revealed that bilingual anglophone professionals and businessmen are participating in predominantly French-speaking institutions at an increasing rate. If the younger anglophone cohorts are becoming more proficient in the second official language in eastern Ontario, is it quixotic to assume that co-operative membership within similar institutions is possible in the future? There is a parish in Prescott County in which the priest conducts the weekly service in both languages. "I think they count the number of words that I use in both languages," was the amused comment given to this writer by the priest. This example is anecdotal and hardly signifies a trend but one can be encouraged to discover that it does work and, in this instance, has for several years. It does not, at this time, seem to be a congregation that is in transition from one language group to another. It appears that Franco-Ontarians do need their own educational institutions (Mackey, 1981). Separate school systems within cultural transition zones can, however, increase social and cognitive distances between the young

(Buchanan, 1982; Douglas, 1983). But two school units can be accommodated within a single building and co-operative programmes in sporting and social events between two unilingual English/French sections can help to develop empathy among school-aged participants.[5] It requires imagination and resolve among educators to bring these young members of the two ethnic groups together to reduce social and cognitive distances and help to generate a spirit of accord. With such contact and interaction among the young it is possible that this spirit will continue into business and professional groups in the future. The zone is bicultural[6] and has as hallmark a history of accommodation between the two ethnic groups with urban service centres that are integral and not extrinsic as in most francophone settlements beyond the zone. But it is an accommodation that has yet to achieve balanced bilingualism and a true sense of biculturalism. It is the contention here that the zone has the greatest potential for a balanced and integrative bilingual/bicultural society in Ontario. Accord that is nurtured among the youths through imaginative application of programmes and the continued development of services in both languages in all sectors of society in the context of formal territorial organization can tip the "seesaw" toward social integration.

It is possible to argue that a precedent for the organization of territory described above now exists, whereby the functional organization provides the foundation upon which bilingualism is to be sustained and the formal organization is the framework within which biculturalism can develop. Under federal law services in both official languages are provided within the National Capital Region (N.C.R.) in both contexts. The rest of the country receives services from federal departments and agencies, but on a functional arrangement that relies upon local demand and the feasibility of providing these services (Commissioner of Official Languages, Official Report, 1982).

In a functional sense, the Region is organized so that communications with federal departments and agencies can be conducted in either language; planning for this permeates all federal activities in the Capital. In Ontario, the provincial and municipal governments have followed the federal example by providing similar language services within their portion of the Region. The N.C.R. has also been organized formally as an official-languages area through Articles 7,9(1) and 11(2) of The Official Languages Act. These sections of the Act specify the publication of information, provision of services, and court proceedings, and provide de jure status to the two languages in the area that is specified in the National Capital Act.

This arrangement for the Region has both symbolic and practical values. In his special study on the National Capital, Fullerton (1974) described the significance of the bilingual/bicultural development of the N.C.R. as, "... a unifying symbol for this country — a capital to which all Canadians can feel drawn with affection and respect" (p. 223). He recognized that formal, as well as functional, status was necessary for the area because of the sense of security that they provide for the parties within, and because of the opportunities for contact and interaction that can develop: "... it is only when a culture no longer feels threatened that it reaches out" (p. 156). The National Capital region is part of the area identified as the cultural zone of transition and it may now be propitious to extend these values beyond the region and involve the rest of the zone in Ontario.

The formal status recommended for this portion of Ontario accords, in part, with some recommendations that were made for the bilingual districts concept contained in the Official Languages Act of Canada. Although the federal government appears to have abandoned this concept, when it was being considered one member of the Advisory Board believed firmly that the cultural zone of transition, or "interface region" to use her term, was the only place in Canada suited to such formal organization of territory. "Outside the interface region, I do not believe that the declaration of bilingual districts is the best answer. In return for the costs involved, financially and in some cases politically, I think the benefits would be slight." (B.D.A.B. *Report*, 1975: 224). Beaujot (1979: 27) also acknowledged the value of districts for the same region but rejected the concept elsewhere in Canada. "In other areas there should be support for minority languages ... However, since these minorities are small and not very viable this support should not be entrenched in law." The official-languages zone, as recommended here for the province, is considered a more viable recommendation than the federal bilingual districts concept because it is not encumbered with the necessity of equal and simultaneous application on both sides of a provincial boundary (Cartwright, 1980; Castonguay, 1976).

If the territorialization process does proceed as Lachapelle has suggested, the opportunities for interaction between the two official-language groups will become circumscribed. The potential for the growth of intergroup understanding and empathy will be severely restricted. It is within the cultural zone of transition that the two ethnic communities can interact regularly. What a pity if an opportunity to enhance this cultural environment, with all positive fanfare, is allowed to pass.

Notes to Chapter 8

1. This chapter is a revised version of a publication that originally appeared in *Canadian Public Policy*, Vol. xi, n. 3, 1985 entitled "An Official-Languages Policy for Ontario".
2. A bilingual population for any area (those who responded "both" to the official-languages question) can be analysed to determine whether it consists mainly of anglophones or francophones and thereby provide a useful measure of who must switch languages to accommodate the other (Vallee & Dufour, 1974). There are, however, two weaknesses in using bilingual-population data to ascertain the level of ascendancy of one language within a community. The definition of ability to speak both official languages — "well enough to conduct a conversation" — makes it perhaps the vaguest and most subjective of the language-related census questions. Distance from the core area of French Canada may exacerbate the confusion in responding to this question; a resident of British Columbia or Newfoundland who responds "yes" may wish to give a different response after a four-week sojourn within the bilingual zone of Ontario or Quebec. Second, a respondent who answered "French" to mother tongue and "English" to language-of-the-home, or vice versa, was classified by Statistics Canada as bilingual *regardless* of the response to the official-languages question (Kralt, 1976). It is not fanciful to envisage someone who learned French as a child and may still have some small understanding but no longer feels competent to speak it, because of having married someone of English mother tongue or having lived in an English-dominant environment for decades. Nevertheless, that person is classified as bilingual.
3. This statement applies to the county-level of analysis. With variation in the scale of analysis and location within the zone some communities would have a higher profile on the index than those illustrated.
4. This research is being conducted in association with Professors H.W. Taylor and M.F. Goodchild, Department of Geography and Professor Rod Beaujot, Department of Sociology, U.W.O.
5. The suggestion here is that French and English-language schools be combined to produce teams that would compete against similar combinations elsewhere. The same type of arrangements can be made for other youth organizations but where feasible such groups — Cubs, Scouts, Girl Guides, etc. — should be operated jointly for the two linguistic groups.
6. Only 6.8% of the provincial population whose mother tongue is neither English nor French (allophones) live within the cultural transition zone. The policy recommended here should not conflict with a multicultural policy applied by either the federal or provincial governments.

References

BEAUJOT, R.P., 1979, A demographic view on Canadian language policy, *Canadian Public Policy*, 5: 16–29.

BENNETT, JOHN R., 1980, Cultural maintenance in a language island: Welland, Ontario. London, Ontario: The University of Western Ontario, Department of Geography. mimeographed.

BOAL, FREDERICK W. & DOUGLAS, J. NEVILLE H., 1982, *Integration and Division: Geographical Perspectives on the Northern Ireland Problem*. London: Academic Press.

BUCHANAN, RONALD 1982, The planter and the Gael: Cultural dimensions of the northern Ireland problem. In F.W. BOAL & J.N.H. DOUGLAS (eds), *Integration and Division: Geographical Perspectives on the Northern Ireland Problem*. London: Academic Press. pp. 49–74.

CALDWELL, GARY, 1982, Anglo-Quebec on the verge of its history, *Language and Society*, 8: 3–6.

CANADA, ROYAL COMMISSION ON BILINGUALISM AND BICULTURALISM, 1967, *Report, General Introduction*. Book I. Ottawa: Queen's Printer.

CANADA, COMMISSIONER OF OFFICIAL LANGUAGES, 1982, *Annual Report*. Ottawa: Ministry of Supply and Services Canada.

CANADA, BILINGUAL DISTRICTS ADVISORY BOARD, 1972/73, *Minutes of Meetings*. Ottawa: Public Archives of Canada.

—— 1975, *Report*. Ottawa: Ministry of Supply and Services.

CARTWRIGHT, DON, 1980, *Official Language Populations in Canada: Patterns and Contacts*. Montreal: The Institute for Research on Public Policy.

—— 1984, The impact of minority on language policy and the impact of language policy on minority in Quebec. In J. COBARRUBIAS & J-D. GENDRON (eds), *Language Policy in Canada: Current Issues*. Quebec: International Center for Research on Bilingualism, Laval University Publication B-150. pp. 37–59.

—— 1987, Accommodation among the anglophone minority in Quebec to official language policy: a shift in traditional patterns of language contact, *Journal of Multilingual of Multicultural Development*, 8, 1, 193–94.

CARTWRIGHT, DON & TAYLOR, HARRY W., 1979, Bilingual accommodation in language islands: Essex County and Penetang, Ontario, *Canadian Ethnic Studies*, 11: 99–114.

CARTWRIGHT, DON & WILLIAMS, COLIN H., 1982, Bilingual districts as an instrument in Canadian language policy, Institute of British Geographers, *Transitions*, N.S. 7: 474–93.

CASTONGUAY, C., 1976, An analysis of the Canadian bilingual districts policy. *American Review of Canadian Studies*, 6: 57–73.

CASTONGUAY, C. & MARION, J., 1974, Une realité l'anglicisation du Canada, *Le Droit*, February 8 and 9, p. 14.

CHOQUETTE, ROBERT, 1980, *Ontario français, historique*. Montreal/Paris: Editions Etudes vivant.

COMPTON, PAUL A., 1982, The demographic dimension of integration and division in Northern Ireland. In F.W. BOAL AND J.N.H. DOUGLAS (eds), *Integration and Division: Geographical Perspectives on the Northern Ireland Problem*. London: Academic Press. pp. 75–104.

COONS, W.H., TAYLOR, D.M. & TREMBLAY, M.A., 1977, *The Individual, Language and Society in Canada*. Ottawa: The Canada Council.

DOUGLAS, J. NEVILLE H., 1983, Political Integration and Division in Plural Societies — Problems of Recognition, Measurement and Salience. In N. KLIOT & S. WATERMAN (eds), *Pluralism and Political Geography: People Territory and State*. London: Croom Helm Ltd. pp. 47–68.

EDWARDS, VIVIAN, 1984, The quest for linguistic equality in New Brunswick, *Language and Society*, 4: 10–14.

FULLERTON, D.H., 1974, *The Capital of Canada: How it Should be Governed* (2 vols.). Ottawa: Information Canada.

GAFFIELD, C., 1982, Boom and bust: The demography and economy of the lower Ottawa valley in the nineteenth century. Paper presented to the Canadian Historical Association, Annual Meetings.

HOUSE, J.W., 1981, Frontier Studies: An Applied Approach. In A.D. BURNETT & P.J. TAYLOR (eds), *Political Studies from Spatial Perspectives*. New York: John Wiley and Son. pp. 291–304.

JOY, RICHARD J., 1972, *Languages in Conflict: The Canadian Experience*. Toronto: McClelland and Stewart.

KRALT, J. (1976), *Languages in Canada*. Profile Studies No. 99–707. Ottawa: Statistics Canada.

LACHAPELLE, RÉJEAN 1980, The Evaluation of Ethnic and Linguistic composition. In R. BRETON, J.G. REITZ & V.F. VALENTINE (eds), *Cultural Boundaries and the Cohesion of Canada*. Montreal: Institute For Research of Public Policy. pp. 15–39.

LACHAPELLE, RÉJEAN & HENRIPIN, JACQUES, 1982, *The Demolinguistic Situation in Canada: Past Trends and Future Prospects*. Montreal: The Institute for Research on Public Policy.

LAMBERT, WALLACE & TUCKER, RICHARD G., 1982, Graduates of early French immersion. In G. CALDWELL & E. WADDELL (eds), *The English of Quebec from Majority to Minority Status*. Quebec: Institute Quebecois de recherche sur la culture. pp. 261–77.

LAMY, PAUL, 1976, Language planning and language use: Canada's national capital area, *American Review of Canadian Studies*, 6: 74–87.

—— 1977, The French language in Ontario: Renaissance, stagnation or collapse? Paper presented at the annual meeting of the American Anthropology Association, Houston, Texas, mimeo.

LAPIERRE, ANDRE, 1977, Le français des milieux ruraux de Prescott-Russell, *Bulletin de centre de recherche en civilisation canadienne-*

française. Université d' Ottawa, 14: 5–14.

MACKEY, WILLIAM F., 1981, Safeguarding Language in Schools, *Language and Society*, 4: 10–14.

MACKEY, W.F. & CARTWRIGHT, D.G., 1979, Geocoding language loss from census data. In W.F. MACKEY & J. ORNSTEIN (eds), *Sociolinguistic Studies in Language Contact: Methods and Cases.* The Hague: Mouton Publishers. Pp. 69–96.

MAHEU, ROBERT, 1970, *Les francophones du Canada, 1941–1991.* Montreal: Editions Parti Pres.

SAVARD, PIERRE, 1978, De la difficulté d'être franco-ontarien, *Revue du Nouvel Ontario*, 1: 11–22.

STREIB, GORDON F., 1974, The Restoration of the Irish Language: Behavioral and Symbolic Aspects, *Ethnicity*, 1: 73–89.

UNITED STATES OF AMERICA, *Congressional Record – Senate* (March 7, 1984) 130:26:S2412–S2413.

VALLEE, FRANK G. & DUFOUR, ALBERT, 1974, The bilingual belt: A garotte for the French? *Laurentian University Review*, 6:2: 19–44.

VALLEE, FRANK G. & SHULMAN, NORMAN, 1969, The viability of French groupings outside Quebec. In MASON WADE (ed.), *Regionalism in the Canadian Community, 1867–1967.* Toronto: University of Toronto Press. Pp. 83–99.

VALLIERES, GAETAN, 1982, The Franco-Ontarian experience. In R. BRETON & P. SAVARD (eds), *The Quebec and Acadian Diaspora in North America.* Toronto: The Multicultural History Society of Ontario.

9 Language Planning and Regional Development: Lessons from the Irish Gaeltacht

COLIN H. WILLIAMS
Department of Geography and Recreation,
North Staffordshire Polytechnic, Stoke-on-Trent, U.K.

The central question I want to address is the relationship between ethnolinguistic maintenance and regional economic development. The literature on regional development is characterized by an almost total disregard for the multi-ethnic basis of the population in most West European states. As a consequence, linguistic and cultural considerations are hardly ever made explicit in regional or local planning proposals, even though they may on occasion entail drastic consequences for the maintenance of minority language communities. The theme of this chapter is that minority language communities are a special type of "consumer", for whom traditional planning priorities and practices are inadequate, and often totally inappropriate, both in terms of policy formulation and regional planning implementation.

It is generally accepted that modernization imposes severe structural strains upon minority cultural groups, especially when such modernization processes are spatially uneven and are accompanied by challenges to the social organization and ideology of peripheral collectivities (see Giles & Saint-Jacques, 1979; R. Williams, 1981). One assumption which characterized developmental theories of the late 1960s was that modernization almost inevitably meant cultural absorption for peripheral minorities. Within the marginal regions of West European states it was asserted that this transformation from "tradition" to "modernity", because it took place in a relatively short span, produced social and economic ruptures, which could only be ameliorated by the closer integration of the periphery into the national economic space, thereby facilitating the diffusion of state-wide benefits into the periphery.[1]

One outcome of these societal ruptures has been a consistent questioning of the power structure in West European states by dissident political movements (Hayward & Berki, 1979; Giner & Archer, 1978; Blacksell, 1981). Many of these movements base their appeal in part on the failure of the unitary state's planning programmes to improve the socio-economic condition of their constituents in the periphery. Regionalist, autonomist and ethnic separatist movements have flourished of late in the advanced industrial societies of Europe (C.H. Williams, 1982, 1980b). Many nationalist leaders cite their incorporation into an "alien" state as the essence of their multifarious problems and assert that until political independence is secured their future will inevitably be that of a dependent group in an under-developed territory.[2] The logic of this perspective is that economic marginality is a function of political subordination and can only be changed through increased political autonomy.[3]

I want to examine certain regional planning policies which seek to reduce the element of incvitability portrayed in the above scenario by concentrating on the Irish experience of language resuscitation. Conventionally the Gaeltacht is analysed alongside other European minority areas as a "classic" problem region of the periphery. A number of common elements characterize such problem regions; for example, they are in the main culturally unique; marginally located vis à vis the centres of trade and political authority within the European Economic Community; predominantly agrarian-based economies; often characterized by a regional autonomist movement, ranging in style from constitutional parties, as in Wales, to semi-constitutional movements, as in Catalonia and Flanders, to all of the above plus extra-constitutional movements as in Corsica and Euskadi. Most of these ethnic minorities pin their grievances squarely on the door of the government whom they claim represents the interests of the dominant class/ethnic group, and to whom they are often subordinated in a form of patron–client relationship within the multi-ethnic state. In the past lack of power, resources and influence, hindered the development of ethnolinguistic minorities, such as the Welsh, Basques, Catalans, Bretons and Galicians as language groups.

However, what happens when a minority group shares the spatial and economic marginality outlined above, but is incorporated within its *own* independent and sovereign state? Clearly other national minorities cite lack of political freedom as the main structural barrier to group development. In the Irish case the interesting question is, can independent states deal more effectively with the problem of regional culture maintenance in advanced industrial societies?

It is a truism in cultural affairs that political independence does not guarantee minority language survival, it merely allows the choice of development priorities to be determined primarily *within* rather than *outside* the value system of the host group. We acknowledge that many other factors impinge on the situation; for example, the international geo-political location of Ireland and its role in the conflict of faiths, trade and power which have characterized the North Atlantic triangle. Other, more pressing, factors would include the historic legacy of the former ruler (i.e. British influence in Ireland), the general Western processes of industrialization and urbanization, group self-esteem, the economic resources available to the newly independent polity, the "universality" of the former dominant language (in this case a world language, English), migration patterns, and the opportunity for upward social advancement within the speech community of the minority group.[4] In this context, the application of regional planning theory often threatens the cultural integrity of minority communities by creating patterns of social and spatial mobility that endanger further the linguistic balance. This appears to be the central dilemma. How can a sympathetic government achieve both economic advancement and linguistic preservation in a marginal and peripheral region?

Before answering that question we need to ascertain the precise nature of the linguistic situation, both in history and contemporaneously, for the geolinguistic context sets the limits of possibility for government policy and action.

The pre-census pattern of spoken Irish

Pre-census sources are notoriously difficult to interpret in order to establish the geographical extent of spoken Irish. Several commentators have pointed to the fact that census data in the late nineteenth century are likely to have underestimated the numbers reared as predominantly Irish-speaking. Garret Fitzgerald (1984: 117–55), the former Taoiseach of the Republic has recently examined the degree to which one can establish the minimum level of Irish-speaking from 1771–1871. Using the 1881 census as his primary data source, he calculated "the proportion in each barony of the survivors in Ireland of various decennial cohorts born from 1801 onwards who replied positively to the census question about Irish-speaking."[5] He also employed the less reliable data from the 1851 and 1861 census sources in order to extrapolate age-group cohorts back to 1771–1781. By mapping the resultant pattern for each decennial age cohort from 1771–1781 to 1861–1871 he has established a very detailed basis for the construction of the Irish geolinguistic landscape in the pre-census era.

The resultant evidence, summarized below in Figures 9.1 and 9.2, suggests a very sharp decline in the level of Irish-speaking amongst the young. The pattern reveals a spatially complex, but inexorable, process of language loss during the century. Fitzgerald suggests two critical conclusions from his study. First that there is a geographically contiguous consistency amongst age cohorts in neighbouring areas, what he terms "buffer zones of lower intensity of Irish-speaking interweaving between areas where there was a high level of Irish-speaking and areas where the language seems to have been disappearing or to have disappeared so far as a particular cohort is concerned" (p. 137). This neighbourhood effect is a consistent pattern in geolinguistic analysis and is worthy of more detailed study. Secondly, Fitzgerald suggests that the pattern is consistent over time. The major distinction is evident from Figures 9.1 and 9.2; the south and west, which contained some 45% of the total population in the earlier period, showed little overall erosion, whereas the rest of the country (with the exception of parts of Meath and Lenister) revealed a low level of Irish-speakers even in the late eighteenth century.

The work of Fitzgerald, earlier work by Adams on Ulster, and Ó Cuív are critical contextual studies of the pre-independence period and deserve closer scrutiny for their rich methodological and interpretative contributions to historical geolinguistics.

Language planning

The Gaelic basis to Irish nationhood, drawing on the revolt of Hugh O'Neil, and the long established separateness of Gaelic culture, was an important factor in national consciousness. Damid O'Neil has argued that the Irish language was important in the cultural revitalization of Ireland at about the turn of the century because "it reinforced the belief that there was an ancient Irish culture with a non-Anglo-Saxon base. It encouraged the belief that this culture was developed and significant. It contributed a camaraderie to those involved in the lingual effort, many of whom would move into the separatist cause" (O'Neil, 1983: 6). This is a common role for language to fulfil in nationalist movements and the Irish case replicates that of Hungary, Finland, Wales, Euskadi and Norway.

But the language issue *per se* was not as central in Ireland's struggle with Britain as one might have imagined. Ireland's quest for identity was based on a wider cultural platform of Catholic Irish identification, even though for long periods, paradoxically, it was the Protestant Ascendancy which animated the nationalist drive most forcibly. And yet, on achieving independence in 1921 the government committed itself to the legitimization of Gaelic and to a concern with language revival, primarily in the Gaeltacht, but also more generally throughout the young state. Initially, language reforms were confined to education and government agencies, but in recent years, as we shall see, successive governments have adopted more comprehensive language planning policies.

In order to understand the relation between interests, problems, linguistic work and development, Weinstein has suggested that there are ten stages in the *ideal* language-planning process which take into account both linguistic and non-linguistic factors. It is not suggested that each of these has been followed in the Irish context, although many have in the course of the years. They are:

1. Coalescence of language "ideology" or attitudes
2. Perception of communication inadequacy
3. Nongovernmental correction
4. Governmental decision-making
5. Creation of a bureaucracy to carry out policy choices
6. Implementation or "planning" in the narrow sense
7. Acceptance or rejection by the language users
8. Evaluation methods applied by the bureaucracy: determination of whether or not inadequacy has been corrected
9. Continuation of implementation or cessation: reports back to government
10. Government maintenance or change of policy (Weinstein, 1983: 42).

Weinstein argues in his book, *The Civic Tongue*, (Chapter Three) that the first stage in government participation in language decision making is that of altering the status of a language by its promotion as a language of state affairs. Thus the development of a bilingual school system, the specification that University entrants or government employees need to speak certain languages, or to demonstrate bilingual capabilities is evidence of "status planning". If, then, a government should decide

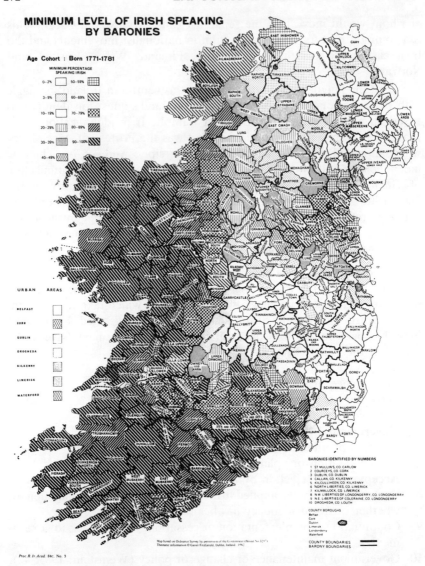

FIGURE 9.1   *Minimum level of Irish speaking by baronies: 1771–1781.*
Reproduced by kind permission of G. FitzGerald and the Royal Irish Academy from
FitzGerald (1984).

that in order to serve a specific function in the future, a language must
be developed by specialists, this is evidence of "corpus planning". Such
planning, argues Weinstein, usually concentrates on development, that is
reduction of a language to writing (graphization), modernization, or

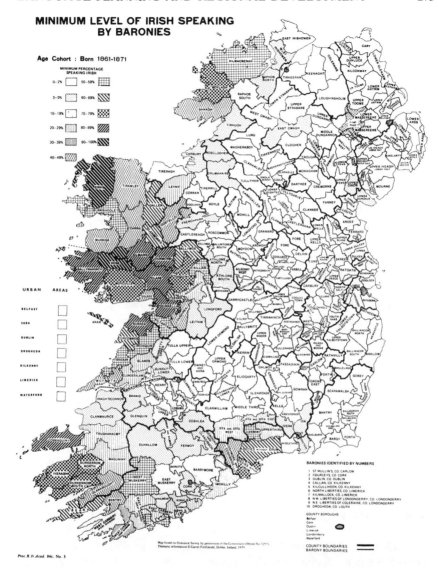

FIGURE 9.2   *Minimum level of Irish speaking by baronies: 1861–1871.*
Reproduced by kind permission of G. FitzGerald and the Royal Irish Academy from
FitzGerald (1984).

expanding the stock of words and styles; and standardization, or choosing
and maintaining a norm. Others have criticized this distinction between
"status" and "corpus" planning, arguing that as language is a seamless
web, such distinctions in its planned functions are artificial.

In its initial post-independence period the Irish state made great advances both in status and corpus planning for Gaelic. It institutionalized the language in the state bureaucracy and guaranteed the individual's right to exercise a language choice in his/her dealings with State agencies. The fact that in reality individual language behaviour did not always conform to the public rhetoric of government did not dissuade activists, but rather strengthened further official promptings to encourage Gaelic as a medium of communication throughout the land.[6]

Despite its concern with language planning *per se*, the government was faced with markedly different problems when it sought to switch attention from individual status planning to regional-community planning for the Gaeltacht. Language legislation alone would not prove effective in redressing the primarily socio-economic grievances of the "problem region." A more comprehensive set of planning agencies was needed, agencies which could address three basic but profoundly significant questions posed by O'Riagain (1978).

1. What is the current linguistic situation and how is it changing?
2. What social, economic and spatial variables are causing change?
3. Which of these variables can be influenced by regional planning policies?

Conscious that it could ameliorate the Gaeltacht's problems, the Irish state sought to achieve both language preservation and economic development through the regional planning process. Initially, its aims were applauded by other cultural minorities, especially by fellow Celts. Subsequently, severe doubts were raised as to the efficiency of government action, as we shall see below.

The Gaeltacht

Despite the foundation of the Irish state in 1921, the Gaeltacht areas have been declining both in terms of population and territory (Table 9.1). The demographic decline, only recently arrested, has caused particular concern for policy-formulation, as it threatens to undermine attempts at regional stability prior to development. The official Irish-speaking area is fragmented, peripheral and weak, constituting 1/42nd of the total population of the Irish Republic in 1971, comprising some 71,000 inhabitants (not all of whom are Irish-speakers) scattered in the hamlets and small market centres of the extreme west of Ireland. Since 1911 the number residing in these areas had dropped by 50%, while the population of the Irish State is generally showing a slight increase over its 1911 level. Nationally, within the Republic some 72.6% have indicated in 1981 that they are non-Irish-speakers, but as we shall see below, the definition of Irish-speaking and the distribution of self-defined Irish-speakers cause problems for both census enumerators and those planners who would seek to build a language criterion into their regional policies.

At the beginning of the present century (1901) some 641,000 were recorded as being able to speak Irish in the island of Ireland. The total population at this time was 4,459,000, of whom some 3,309,000 were identified as Catholic and 1,150,000 as Protestant. Thus from pre-Independence days the situation of the Irish-speakers could be described as tenuous. But of the 641,000 able to speak Irish, 619,710 were living in the territory of the present Republic, and of these only about 150,000 were living in communities where Irish was the normal language of everyday life.[7] Irish was confined, almost exclusively, to rural communities, and to craft occupations, small scale farmers and to fishermen of the western coastal districts. Its status in sociolinguistic terms was very low and as a consequence of its weakness in terms of individual social advancement within the British empire, it was not likely to be demanded as a prerequisite for employment within the larger Irish or British society. Its relevance in these times seemed determined more by political rather than by social considerations, for the independence movement used language as a key marker of group identity, and after the 1921 settlement Irish became the first official language. Consequently, it became an obligatory subject in primary schools and for entrance into one of the Republic's two universities.

It was also obligatory at secondary school level where one was required to pass in Irish in order to receive the Certificate of Education, otherwise if one failed in Irish one was deemed to have failed the whole diet of examinations. This condition has now been lifted, but one is still obliged to receive instruction in Irish, as might be expected, given the high public profile which the language has consistently held.

State-wide education policy, particularly at the primary level, has resulted in a gradual revival of the language, such that by 1971 some 789,429 claimed to be Irish-speaking. And yet there remained a remarkable paradox in Irish national life, the numbers claiming to possess a knowledge of the national language increasing at the same time that the functional usage of that language was decreasing.

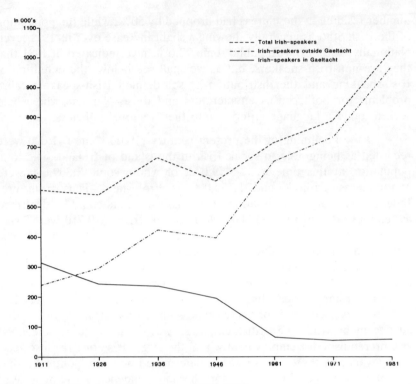

FIGURE 9.3   *Total Irish speakers: 1911–1981*

TABLE 9.1   *Knowledge of Irish as reported at censuses, 1851–1911*

Year	Population	Total able to speak Irish		Persons able to speak Irish only	
		Number	%	Number	%
1851	5,111,557	1,485,050	29.1	318,998	6.2
1861	4,402,111	1,077,087	24.5	162,764	3.7
1871	4,053,187	804,547	19.8	103,320	2.5
1881	3,870,020	924,781	23.9	64,075	1.7
1891	3,468,694	664,387	19.2	38,178	1.1
1901	3,221,823	619,710	19.2	20,945	0.7
1911	3,139,688	553,717	17.6	16,869	0.5

Source: Calculated from Census of Ireland, 1851 . . ., 1911 reproduced with permission from Coakley (1980)
Note: All figures refer to the present territory of the Republic of Ireland.

The reality, of course, is that the strong constitutional and legal position of the Irish language and its prominent place in the rhetoric of political parties gives a misleading picture of its strength. We may illustrate this by reference to the census statistics since 1911. Table 9.2 reports on the number of people with a knowledge of Irish 1926–1981 and gives an estimate of actual usage for 1911. Because the census of Ireland, like that of Scotland and Wales, has traditionally questioned ability rather than actual usage, the census results have to be interpreted with great caution and sensitivity as to what they actually demonstrate. Since 1961 the decennial census question on Irish-speaking has been phrased in the following manner: "Ability to Speak the Irish Language. This question should be answered for persons aged three years and over. Leave blank for children under three years of age. Write 'Irish only' for persons who can speak only Irish. Write 'Irish and English' for those who can speak Irish and English. For persons who can read but cannot speak Irish, write 'Read but cannot speak Irish'. Do not write anything opposite names of persons who can neither read nor speak Irish" (Census of Population, 1981: x).

As with all mass self-administered questionnaires there are problems as to what the derived data actually measure in linguistic terms. Further, when these data are mapped, the resultant distribution pattern of language ability rather than language usage conveys a distorted impression of the ubiquity of Irish speech in certain areas.[9] The data recorded in Table 9.1 appear to indicate a gradual decline from 29% in 1851 to a low of 18% in 1911, followed by an equally gradual revival. However, as Coakley observes, the 28% returned as Irish speakers in 1971 were a radically different group from the 29% returned 120 years earlier. This is a major problem of interpretation, for time-series data are often treated as if they related to identical, undifferentiated populations, when clearly they do not. Compare the 1971 population with that of 1851 for example:

"The former were mainly native English-speakers who had acquired some knowledge of Irish at school; the latter were predominantly native Irish-speakers who had learned English at school or as a consequence of life in an environment where most transactions took place through the medium of English. Furthermore, knowledge of Irish is subjectively assessed, and many people who return themselves as Irish-speaking on census forms may be expressing a strong emotional attachment to the language rather than claiming that they possess a reasonable degree of fluency in Irish". (Coakley, 1980[10]).

TABLE 9.2 Knowledge and estimated usage of the Irish language 1911–1981

Year	Total Population	Gaeltacht Population	Irish-speakers in Gaeltacht		Irish-speakers outside Gaeltacht		Total Irish-speakers	
			Number	%	Number	%	Number	%
1911	3,139,688	530,320	313,508	10.0	240,209	7.7	553,717	17.6
		(189,555)	(149,677)	(4.8)	(404,040)	(12.9)		
1926	2,971,992	476,186	246,811	8.8	296,700	10.6	540,802	19.3
		(168,279)	(130,074)	(4.6)	(413,437)	(14.8)		
1936	2,968,420	426,685	238,338	8.5	428,263	15.3	666,601	23.7
		(148,179)	(123,125)	(4.4)	(543,476)	(19.4)		
1946	2,955,107	398,202	192,963	7.0	395,762	14.3	588,725	21.2
		(137,193)	(104,941)	(3.8)	(483,784)	(17.5)		
1961	2,818,341	74,261	64,275	2.4	652,145	24.7	716,420	27.2
1971	2,978,248	66,840	55,440	2.0	733,989	26.3	789,429	28.3
1981	3,226,467	75,000	58,026	1.7	960,286	29.7	1,018,413	31.6

Sources: Derived from Census of Ireland, 1926 …, 1971. Reproduced with permission from Coakley (1980), Census of Ireland (1981: 12, table 7).

Note: The Gaeltacht refers to the territory so defined in 1925, as altered in 1956. The 1971 figures include the Meath Gaeltacht colonies (population 858). From 1925 to 1956 a second more rigorous and more realistic definition of the Fíor-Gaeltacht (truly Irish-speaking area) was also in existence, and the figures in brackets above refer to this territory.

All percentages refer to Irish-speakers aged three and over as a percentage of the total population aged three and over, apart from those for 1911 which refer to the whole population. The number of Irish-speakers in the Gaeltacht is a crude indicator of language usage.

Similarly, there is a discrepancy between the areas officially designated as Gaeltacht, and the actual or real Gaeltacht. Thus in 1971, the census declared the population aged 3 years and over of the official Gaeltacht to be 66,840, of whom some 55,940 were Irish speakers. In 1975–76 Desmond Fennel undertook a survey of this area and found the really Irish-speaking parts — the "real Gaeltacht" — had a population of only 29,000, while the other 42,000 people lived in districts where the everyday language was English (Fennell, 1980a,b, 1981). The 29,000 people just referred to were located in three main districts: *Gaothdobhair* – Western Donegal, *Iarchonnacht*, South Connemara, Aran Islands and Galway district, *Corca Dhuibhne* – Western Kerry.

Government planning policy

The Gaeltacht breeds paradoxes. A critical one facing any government charged with the responsibility of simultaneous economic development and cultural maintenance has been described by Edwards (1984: 486) in the following manner:

"the Gaeltacht is vital to the language since it provides the only sizeable groups of Irish speakers. At the same time, it is constantly being encroached upon by modern influences of all kinds ... If nothing is done, the Gaeltacht will continue to shrink, if things ARE done there is the very real danger of creating an enclave which is seen, by those inside as well as by those without, as essentially artificial — an area not allowed to follow larger social and economic currents".

Government economic policy has been consistently orientated towards a reduction of out-migration from the Gaeltacht, and has attempted a series of job-creation programmes to offset unemployment. Each of the Government agencies, as we shall see, has a specific brief to take into consideration the effects its policies might have on the preservation of Irish, but in general it is fair to say that the language policy has been mainly formulated in regional planning terms in accordance with the old maxim: "No jobs, no people; no people, no Gaeltacht".

The equating of employment and population stability with language and culture stability is not without its difficulties. For example, we need to know for whom are jobs created? Where are the jobs to be created? Are they to be concentrated in key growth centres or dispersed throughout the region? What changes will the development programme induce in

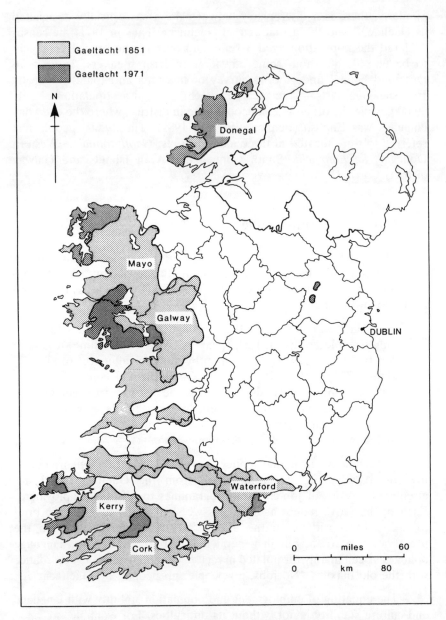

FIGURE 9.4 *The territorial shrinkage of the Gaeltacht, 1851–1971*

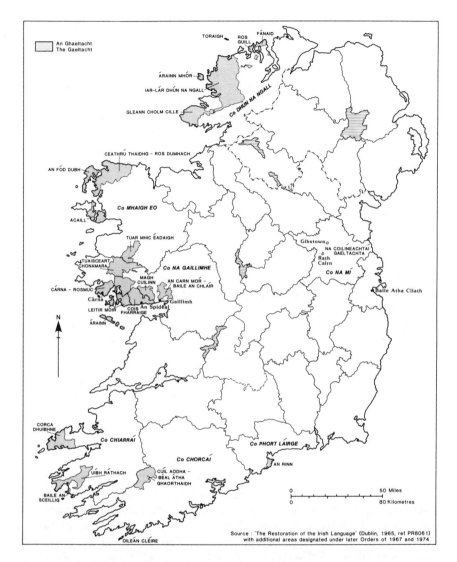

FIGURE 9.5   *The "Official" Gaeltacht*
Source: "The Restoration of the Irish Language" Dublin (1965), (ref PR8061) with
additional areas designed under later Orders of 1967 and 1974.

language patterns? What type of employment and industry will be attracted
to marginal industrial sites? Are they to be long-term, viable projects?
Above all we must ask whether the initial capital costs involved in
preparing industrial sites, in providing a modern infra-structure and

subsidized housing, an economic cost which cultural considerations can afford to sustain. P.N. O'Farrell has suggested two other questions which one might pose; namely, what is the opportunity cost in terms of the losses to national output of subsidizing Gaeltacht investment rather than an equivalent volume of investment at a more efficient location? Is it a cost that can be justified on cultural grounds? Certainly Gaeltarra Eireann seem not to have estimated it.[11] Clearly the Irish government was faced with making difficult economic and political decisions in order to honour its longstanding commitment to the national tongue. It sought to tackle the problem primarily through the development of rural industries.

Industrial development in the Gaeltacht

The principal instrument of government policy was Gaeltarra Eireann, a state sponsored body established under the Gaeltacht Industries Acts of 1957–1975. Formed in 1958, it was charged "to make further and better provision for the organization, conduct and development of the rural industries", which were then being administered by the Department of Gaeltacht. Gaeltarra was given the additional objective of actively encouraging the use of Irish within the Gaeltacht, as well as being the principal governmental instrument for economic development.

In the initial period, 1958–1966, a number of problems faced the Board of Gaeltarra, chief of which was that the Gaeltacht was an unattractive location for private enterprise industrial development. This was because fragmentation reduced any possibility of scale advantages and economic viability, and the isolated pockets of population reduced the potential for a varied and skilled labour force. Even with protected home markets, all the rural industries that were taken over by the Board since 1958 had lost money consistently; many of them had closed, leaving the Gaeltacht with some of the highest unemployment and emigration rates in the Irish Republic. Underlying all this was that in terms of natural resources it was amongst the poorest of West European regions, with little possibility of self-sustained growth.

In essence the Board was admitting its paralysis in the face of overwhelming odds stemming from the Gaeltacht's dependency situation. It was a situation shared by other West European peripheries, but intensified in the Gaeltacht because the rest of the Irish economy was not performing as well as most of its competitors. There emerged a form of associated-dependent development. Cooke (1982) has outlined the theoretical pre-conditions of dependent development. His analysis, when applied to Ireland, would suggest that capital movements to dependent economies, as envisaged by Gaeltarra, are stimulated by the abundant supply of cheap labour and the "capacity of international corporations for organising manufacturing to maximise profits by framing a new international division of labour"; the stresses that the domestic variations in the availability of associated supply factors, "such as financial and infra-structural incentives, guaranteed labour force quiescence, relaxation of business regulations, and local private and state financial participation in new ventures, condition the direction and intensity of foreign investment" (p. 213). In turn these variations are contingent on the vagaries of local and national class relations and on the conflict of interests which operate in all dependent economies.

Typically the industrialisation of dependent economies produces a new social stratification system.[12] In ideal terms this is comprised of a professional sector divided into a private "clientele" segment, and a large state bureaucracy geared to directing regional development policy and extending state agencies to the local populus. The non-professional labour-force, according to Cooke's analysis, is divided into a "relatively well-paid manufacturing segment, a less well-paid agrarian and mining segment, and a sub-employed or marginalised residual segment" (p. 213). The Gaeltacht was not initially characterized by the emergence of an ideal type form of development described by Cooke as a "components outpost" location; that is a region where "valuable skills and/or relatively sophisticated technology are cheaply available and where local consumption is negligible but products are exported for assembly within industrial platforms or larger markets".[13] The Gaeltacht experienced meagre levels of ephemeral indigenous and foreign capital investment which had, by the early 1960s, failed to usher in the required economic transformation. Consequently, the government initiated a range of radical policy measures to invigorate industrial life in the region.

Radical policies

Given the locational disadvantages of the Gaeltacht and the chronic underinvestment in the region's infra-structure, it was evident by 1966 that any policy of economic development and cultural maintenance had to deal with the central problem of continuous out-migration in search of employment. In assessing the predicament, MacGabhann (1978) argues that a number of factors influenced the government's thinking, chief of which were the need to invest heavily in the existing labour-intensive and loss-making spinning, weaving, knitting, plastics and toy-making operations. New plant and machinery, new management methods, new products and new techniques were all required, and these were to be provided within the constraints imposed by a democratic society on state-owned industry, by regional competition elsewhere in Ireland, and above all by the needs of the language.[14]

In response to these perceived needs the powers and role of Gaeltarra were considerably extended in 1966, such that it became a partner in a number of service industries; for example, a computer bureau, hotels and tourist developments, horticultural and agricultural activities and fish-farming projects.[15] The radical advocacy policy transformed Gaeltarra's role, such that its industrial concerns now were often in direct competition with private enterprise, whereas in the past national specialist public agencies had normally only had a promotional or consultative role.

By concentrating on employment creation through industrial development Gaeltarra was criticized for not guaranteeing that the very processes it sought to encourage would not prove detrimental to the linguistic vitality of the region. If modernization, critics argued, was the root cause of depopulation and cultural erosion in the marginal districts, then it was the utmost folly to hasten such decline through introducing new agents of modernization.

Gaeltarra's defence rested on eight criteria which sought to safeguard their cultural objectives. MacGabhann, a former chief executive of Gaeltarra, outlined their strategy to offset the deleterious effects of modernisation, as follows:[16] their efforts were 1) concentrated initially on areas where the language was strongest (i.e. not necessarily the most-favoured economic locations within the Gaeltacht); 2) they emphasized employment for Irish-speakers (thus arousing fears of cultural apartheid and reverse discrimination); 3) they worked for the most part through the medium of Irish (e.g. Board meetings, office work and documentation); 4) they endeavoured, where possible, to work with other state agencies in Irish; 5) they developed a management development programme for Irish speakers; 6) they gave maximum assistance to projects being established by Irish speakers; 7) they gave preferential treatment to Gaeltacht co-operatives; 8) they re-located their Head Office in the Gaeltacht rather than in Dublin. These were important psychological as well as practical boosts to the regular use of Irish in the affairs of the local state, but how effective were they in serving the needs of the Gaeltacht's population?

The initial period of the new policy, 1967–70, was devoted to a rationalisation of existing industrial commitments (plastics, toy making, spinning, weaving and knitting) by putting them on a proper footing before proceeding with a job-creation programme. From 1970 onwards, MacGabhann argues that policy was orientated towards job creation and the restructuring of the regional economy through direct investment of the Board's capital in its associated companies. The results of direct investment and advocacy planning may be demonstrated through the sharp increase in the turnover of the Board's enterprises. In 1967 Gaeltarra had five trading divisions with an annual turnover of £8,000,000. By 1978 Gaeltarra was involved with 50 companies with a turnover of £24,000,000. Similarly, employment in Gaeltarra assisted projects rose from 680 in 1967 to about 4,211 in 1978.[17] Many of the associated companies are American or European in origin, often drawing on their own company personnel and industrial patterns of behaviour. Other things being equal (which they never are) the Board recommends that positions should be filled by Irish speakers, and an attempt has been made to train local managers. To date, it is a moot point as to whether most activities financed by Gaeltarra capital actually use Irish as the working language of daily industrial life.

In a review of its progress up to 1978 the Board recognized that a piecemeal approach to regional development was unlikely to bring about economic recovery, thus permitting population stability. With a view to wresting more independent decision-making authority, it pressed on the government the complexity of the task it faced. MacGabhann lists the several problems as follows:
1) The Board recognized that there was a need to offer higher incentives to attract industry to unprofitable locations, and to restructure the incentive scheme[18]; 2) the economic recession and increased unemployment levels had resulted in the Industrial Development Authority being empowered to invest capital in joint ventures anywhere in Ireland. This led, in MacGabhann's view, to the elimination of the only specific policy advantage enjoyed by Gaeltarra, and severely weakened its original strategy of offsetting locational disadvantages by financial compensation; 3) the infrastructure remained chronically inadequate; 4) there was little tradition of local enterprise or initiative in the region; 5) the poor public image of the whole scheme.[19] These problems were compounded by the various conflicts of interest identified by MacGabhann as a three-way split between a business strategy which dictated profits and expansion, a government need for increased employment, and the original goal of language preservation and cultural group development.

Language activists, unimpressed by government promises for the region, claimed that increased commercial activity and industrial penetration would result in increased exposure to outside influences, and would accelerate the effect of deleterious anglicizing processes. Regional planners could claim, with much justification, that compared with the situation some thirty years ago, the Gaeltacht was now prospering.[20] But in the last remaining Gaeltacht districts the language is changing inexorably to English, leading Fennell (1980a,b, 1981) to ask whether the Gaeltacht can be saved. For the successful economic development — in the sense of raising living standards and halting overseas emigration — has not stemmed the process of language shift. To cultural activists the picture is bad enough, but the problem of marginality is now compounded by evidence which suggests that the economic base of the recent prosperity is fragmented and incapable of self-sustained development.[21]

A survey commissioned for the Irish Business Journal concluded that the Údarás na Gaeltachta attracted weak and short-term companies, and that the vast majority of the 68 companies in which it held an equity stake at the year ending December 1979, were weak even at the drawing board stage.[22] Why does the Údarás seem to attract loss-making ventures? The survey points to the original laws governing Údarás involvement in new industries. In 1967, if the Údarás grant exceeded £10,000 it was compelled to take a share-holding of not less than 26% in the company.[23] The survey argues that for those companies unable to secure outside finance this equity involvement became in effect a non-repayable loan. When a company faced difficulties, as many of the 68 did, the Údarás, rather than close them, injected more capital which bought more of the company until eventually it owned 100% of a bad loss-making concern. The Údarás's own rulings, it concludes, made it into an organization providing venture capital to projects which were totally unsuited to remote Gaeltacht areas.[24]

A more sympathetic analysis of the work of Údarás argues that though the Údarás strategy of employment creation is often expensive it does nevertheless produce "worthwhile investments both from an exchequer and economic viewpoint" (Keane, Cawley & O'Cinnéide, 1983[25]). A detailed analysis of the Donegal Gaeltacht revealed that the new employment opportunities had contributed to population stability and a reversal of the historical pattern of population loss. But an additional feature of note was the conclusion that the Údarás projects were "socially profitable", in that communities were strengthened by the injection of new employment and its consequent spill-over effect in wage expenditure and local resources and skill development. However, we should not ignore the fact that some of the problems raised above in relation to Gaeltacht firm closures were common to all firms in Ireland. The last decade was dominated by a recession, by rising labour costs, and as O'Farrell & Crouchley (1983) have demonstrated many of the traditional company activities, such as knitting, spinning, weaving and clothing, were vulnerable to labour cost competition elsewhere in the international system. Prospects for future industrial growth in Ireland generally, according to O'Farrell & Crouchley (1984), lie either in import substitution by supplying components for multinational enterprises, or by "firms currently serving only a regional or the national market exporting to the U.K., the rest of the E.E.C. or beyond". Small scale industrial activity represents a fairly buoyant pattern, but its effect in employment creation must remain limited. The chief problem facing Údarás now seems to be to consolidate its earlier work and to nurture the relatively small number of profitable concerns in which it holds a substantial interest. Profitability in economic concerns is difficult enough in this marginal periphery of Europe, and yet there remains the nagging language dimension, the initiator of regional planning proposals for the Gaeltacht.

Language considerations

Clearly government policy has met with only limited success in the economic sphere. In linguistic terms, some language experts have predicted the imminent collapse of the Gaeltacht. Why, despite government commitment, wasn't the Gaeltacht saved? Given the complexity of the situation, our attention will focus only on the most salient aspects of the decline. Fennell emphatically argues that the reason the State's effort failed was that successive governments assumed that the State bureaucracy, the semi-state companies, and particularly Gaeltarra Eireann,[26] *could* stop the Gaeltacht shrinking (Fennell, 1981: 36). Echoing the self-confidence of positive regional and social planning at that time, the Government gave the task to these planning agencies. But, Fennell argues, this assumption was misplaced, as is clearly seen if we return to political basics and ask a simple question, whose profundity has implications for all other minority ethnolinguistic communities. "If there is a territory in which a particular language is usually spoken, and it is contracting continually through language change on the fringes, who can stop this contraction?" (1984: 36). Fennell answers that only the people of the territory — by deciding to do so and taking the appropriate measures. He argues that the government failed to perceive this fundamental premise and made no serious attempt to persuade the people

of the Gaeltacht to decide to end the erosion.[27] For example, it did not
establish a regional assembly, or a regional institution until 1979, by
which time the problem was too deeply ingrained to be amenable to
remedial action. Furthermore, argues Fennell, the Gaeltacht was not
adequately defined for more than 30 years. When it was defined in 1956,
it included considerable English-speaking areas. By the early 1980s the
greater part of this Official Gaeltacht was English-speaking, still part of
what had to be saved.

Bord na Gaeilge, amongst other agencies, recognize the problems
posed by creeping anglicization. In a major policy review document it
cites the principle anglicizing influences operating in the Gaeltacht:

"1. The daily impact of a television service transmitting perhaps
     95% of its programme content in English;
 2. the extent to which central and local government agencies
     still conduct their business in the Gaeltacht through English
     (thereby diminishing the standing of Irish and conveying
     the impression of a lack of policy at central government
     level for its enhancement);
 3. the undermining of Irish as the community language of the
     Gaeltacht by the gradual influx of English speaking
     residents;
 4. certain inadequacies in the present educational arrange-
     ments;
 5. the extent to which young people in the Gaeltacht have
     had to rely on commercial entertainment in English." (Bord
     na Gaeilge, 1983: 7)

Industrialization and anglicization need not necessarily induce a total
language shift from Irish to English. Despite the overall trend to the
opposite, some areas which were predominantly English speaking ten
years ago are now Irish speaking.[28] The recent census data (1981) indicate
a marked increase in the total number of reported Irish speakers over
the past decade, from 789,429 (1971) to 1,018,413 (1981), constituting
some 31.6% of the Irish population of 3,226,467 aged three and over.
Within the Gaeltacht the numbers of Irish speakers rose from 55,440
(1971) to 58,026 (1981) (see Table 9.2). But the numbers of non-Irish
speakers also rose from 11,400 (1971) to 16,974 (1981), a figure neglected
by many analysts of the language situation.

Table 9.3 indicates the age distribution of the Gaeltacht population.
It is evident that the younger age groups show a preponderance of Irish
over non-Irish speakers that must bode well for the future. But we should

look beyond the aggregate data, and consider both the overall Irish situation and the structural preconditions of Irish maintenance in the Gaeltacht, especially as there is recent evidence that emigration has recommenced.

Figures 9.6 and 9.7 show the number and percentage of Irish speakers by county, 1961–1981. It is evident that the Dublin hinterland dominates the numerical distribution of Irish speakers, although there remain substantial thresholds of Irish speakers within the Gaeltacht. This pattern is confirmed if we scan the percentage of Irish speakers by county (Figure 9.7), where small but significant elements of growth are identified in most counties, but particularly in Waterford, Meath, Cork and Kerry. However, within the traditional core areas of the west, i.e. Donegal, Galway and Mayo, the pattern is not so encouraging. I have discussed the details of the 1961–1981 census results elsewhere and do not wish to elaborate upon the data here.[29] Of more critical interest than mere aggregate totals of potential Irish speakers for our present concern is the actual practice of speaking Irish in the several employment contexts of the Gaeltacht. A recent survey by Irish geographers indicated that many native Irish speakers within Gaeltacht industries were employing English as their prime language of communication, and they suggested that without a positive language strategy, economic development alone would not restore the language as a natural medium for discourse in these areas (O'Cinnéide, Keane & Cawley, 1985). Clearly industrialization *per se*, they argue, does not necessarily conduce to language decline, but without positive discrimination to redress such forces it is likely so to do. A key practical question as to the appropriate spatial dimension for language policy remains an acute concern.

A fundamental problem concerned the efficacy of a formal or a functional organization of state territory, a traditional problem of regional planning (see, for example, Cartwright, 1980). Each of the state agencies, charged with the responsibility of regenerating the Gaeltacht, operated in any given area largely independently of other bodies, such that the Gaeltacht areas were fragmented by multifarious administrative boundaries which attached different parts of them to adjacent English speaking districts. This spatial fragmentation led to administrative inefficiency and the subordination of the minority Gaeltacht problem to the wider departmental concerns of Government agencies. The ability of Údarás na Gaeltachta to initiate, co-ordinate and monitor activities in the areas must prove a major improvement in the execution of policy for the Gaeltacht.

TABLE 9.3   Number and percentage of Irish-speakers, 3 years of age and over in the Gaeltacht areas (as then defined), 1971 and 1981

Gaeltacht Areas	Irish speakers 1971	Irish speakers 1981	Non-Irish speakers 1971	Non-Irish speakers 1981	Irish speakers as percentage of total 1971	Irish speakers as percentage of total 1981	Percentage change 1971–81 in population 3+
					%	%	%
Total Gaeltacht Areas	55,440	58,026	11,400	16,974	82.9	77.4	*
Cork	2,703	2,681	383	560	87.6	82.7	+5.0
Donegal	18,321	19,209	3,636	5,113	83.4	79.0	+10.8
Galway	17,698	19,819	2,328	4,945	88.4	80.0	+23.7
Kerry†	6,214	6,264	1,174	1,584	84.1	79.8	*
Mayo	9,270	8,457	3,449	4,162	72.9	67.0	−0.8
Meath	500	493	358	407	58.3	54.8	+4.9
Waterford[1]	734	1,103	72	203	91.1	84.5	*

* Not available

Source: Census of Population of Ireland, 1981, Volume 6, Table D, p. xviii.
Note: 1. The Gaeltacht areas of Counties Kerry and Waterford were extended under the Gaeltacht Areas Order, 1974 (S.I. No. 1921, 1974). In Table 9.3 above, the 1971 figures for Irish speakers and non-Irish speakers for both these Counties relate to pre-1974 areas whereas the 1981 figures relate to the new (extended) areas. The total populations in 1971 of the areas added were as follows:-
Co. Kerry: 755 persons Co. Waterford: 198 persons.
It has not been possible to disaggregate these figures by age group or ability to speak the Irish Language.

State education policies also contributed to the general sociolinguistic decline. Despite recognizing the special features of Gaeltacht social geography, school catchment areas continue to combine Gaeltacht and non-Gaeltacht districts. We have a situation where children attending Irish-medium schools in the Gaeltacht, from non-Irish speaking homes, results in the under-emphasis of Irish as the primary medium of instruction. Conversely, Irish speaking children attend English-medium schools outside the Gaeltacht. In such a geolinguistic milieu English tends to predominate and the official primacy of Irish gives way to the unofficial, but instrumental, primacy of English. Edwards (1984: 271) reports that "now, most parents in the Gaeltacht have decided to bring up their children in English, a process reminiscent of the nation-wide shift a century or more ago. It goes without saying that this poses the gravest possible risk for the maintenance of Irish in its naturally-spoken forms".

TABLE 9.4 *Total population, by language and age, in designated Gaeltacht areas*

	Total 3+	3–4	5–9	10–14	15–19	20–24	25–34	35–44	45–54	55–64	65+
Total Gaeltacht areas	75,000	2,966	7,699	7,777	6,632	5,081	9,819	7,600	6,719	7,736	12,971
Irish speakers	58,026	1,566	5,642	6,485	5,531	3,960	7,259	5,717	5,365	6,284	10,217
Non-Irish Speakers	16,974	1,400	2,057	1,292	1,101	1,121	2,560	1,883	1,354	1,452	2,754
Irish Speakers as a percentage of total %	77.4	52.8	73.3	83.4	83.4	77.9	73.9	75.2	79.8	81.2	78.8

Source: Census of Population of Ireland, 1981, Volume 6, Table 8A, page 36.

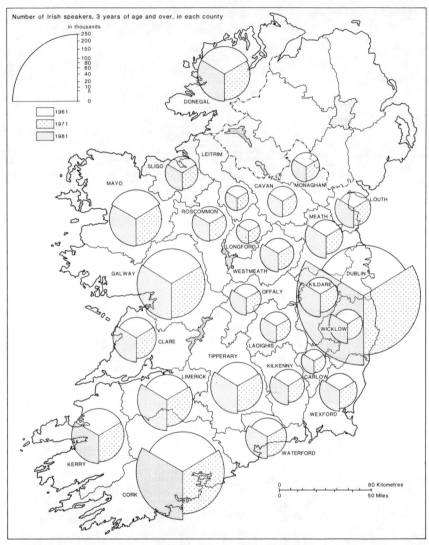

FIGURE 9.6   *Numbers of Irish speakers aged 3 years of age and over in*
each county
Source: Calculated from the Irish census of population for 1961, 1971 and 1981

Critics claim that the content of Irish-medium teaching also has
impoverishing effects on the quality of Irish in the Gaeltacht, because
the curriculum reflected the national standardization of education. In the
teaching of Irish language and literature, for example, it was common
for Gaeltacht pupils to study a course in Irish designed for second-

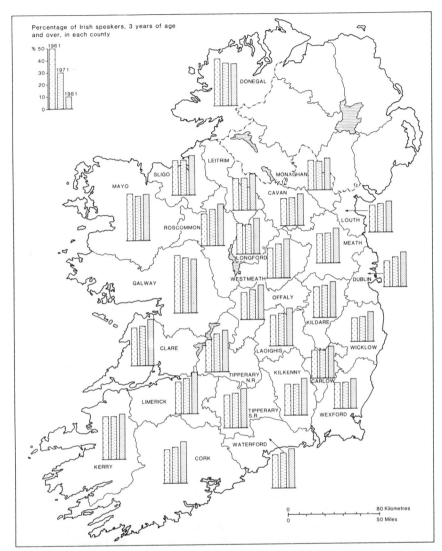

FIGURE 9.7   *Percentage of Irish speakers, 3 years of age and over in each county*
Source: Calculated from the Irish census of population for 1961, 1971 and 1981

language learners. A lack of a firm educational foundation in Irish not only militates against the general survival of the language, but also limits the instrumental motivation for learning the language. It reduces the practical necessity of insisting on fluency in Irish as a prerequisite to employment in most Údarás financed companies. A vicious circle of redundancy and irrelevancy for the language ensues, accelerating the general pattern of sociocultural erosion.

However, not all is gloom and doom on the language front. Ever since the publication of the Committee on Irish Language Attitudes Research Report in 1975, researchers have sought to analyse the various reasons why Irish has not "taken off" as a revised language. Attitudes to English *vis à vis* those to Irish are, of course, paramount, reflecting both the attraction (power) and ubiquity of English in modern Irish history. The education system itself, though, is fraught with difficulties if one compares it with the spectacular success of the Welsh revival (see Edwards, 1984; Welsh Office, 1983; Bellin, 1984). The reasons for the inability of the education system to institute Irish as a high status popular medium of communication are complex and need not be discussed in detail here,[30] except to highlight Edwards' point that given the very special nature of Irish as an official language of the state, it is acutely disappointing to have to admit the relative failure of the language revival, especially when one can no longer blame the "occupying forces" but accept that the "mass of the Irish people were more or less active contributors to the spread of English for pragmatic reasons brought into being by longstanding historical forces".[31]

Concluding remarks

Substantial improvements in the economic future of the Gaeltacht must be tempered by modest expectations of language survival in the region. Several of the weaknesses identified herein are being addressed by both government agencies and other organizations, and it should be evident that both sources of encouragement have often complementary effects upon language choice. However, let me end on a note of caution. Several commentators from within the language minorities of Western Europe have expressed severe reservations about the nature of formal language planning, especially as such planning is often deemed to be on behalf of the "improvement and development" of the minority. There may be a strong case for arguing that geolinguistic research should shift its attention away from the examination of census data and employment patterns, in isolation, so to speak, from government and multinational corporation activity. It might rather seek to supplement such valuable empirical information as has already been gleaned with a wider discussion of the role of the state, the community and the individual in terms of their respective legitimate expectations and rights. For without specifying this complex relationship our spatial patterns remain void of human dynamism and social conflict.

Acknowledgements

I wish to thank the following for their comments on the chapter, which proved very helpful: Desmond Fennell, P. O'Farrell, John Edwards, Michael Keane, I also wish to thank Mrs P. Thornberry of the Census of Population Division, Central Statistics Office, Dublin and Officers of the Údarás na Gaeltachta and the Bord na Gaeilge for providing me with data, Mrs Jane Williams, Cartographer at North Staffordshire Polytechnic for drawing the maps and diagrams, Dr G. FitzGerald and the Royal Irish Academy for permission to reproduce Figures 9.1 and 9.2.

Notes to Chapter 9

1. For discussion of the "diffusion" perspective in state-formation see Hechter (1975), Smith (1981) and a somewhat looser treatment in Allardt (1979). John Edwards has pointed out that a combination of the diffusion and internal-colonial models seems appropriate because the diffusion model explains language decline more adequately than the internal-colonial version. Also he points to the neglect of the important process of language shift in theories couched in internal-colonial terms. J. Edwards, private correspondence, 9.9.84.
2. This is the major economic/political grievance of a number of minority separatist movements, e.g. *Plaid Cymru* in Wales, the *Volksunie* in Belgium, *Süd Tiroler Volks Partei* in Italy's Alto Adige region, *Action pour la renaissance de la Corse* in Corsica, *Esquerra Democratica* and *Llige* in Catalonia and *Euzkadi ta Askatasuna* in the Basque country of the Spanish state. See Krejci & Velimsky (1981), Rokkan & Urwin (1982), and also Shiels (1984).
3. I recognize that I am oversimplifying the issues here. For a conceptual critique of what autonomy implies see Wood (1981). For a discussion of the historic development of these claims to autonomy see Orridge & Williams (1982).
4. Mitchinson (1980). For details of Irish history see Hepburn (1980); and Porter (1975); Boyce (1982). See the government sponsored studies on the influence of modernization on the preservation of the Irish language i.e. *Report of Commission of Inquiry into the Preservation of the Gaeltacht (1976); Report of Commission on the Restoration of the Irish language (1964); Report of Committee on Irish language attitudes research (1976).*
5. FitzGerald (1984). I am grateful to Jim MacGlaughlin, University College Cork, for bringing this work to my attention.
6. For a good discussion of the relationship between the Irish and English languages see Edwards (1984); for a complementary historical account of the

Irish language see Price (1984).
7. The data, derived from official census reports, are discussed in Coakley (1980) and in a more provocative manner by Fennell (1981).
8. For the comparative situation in Scotland and Wales see MacKinnon (1977); and G. Williams (1978); C.H. Williams (1980a). Durkacz (1983) Trudgill (1984) and Price (1984).
9. There is an additional reason for interpreting census results cautiously. Michael Keane has pointed out to me that there may be good economic reasons for being "officially able" to speak Irish, for thereby one qualifies for additional government grants and subsidies.
10. Coakley (1980); here again Keane would add an economic incentive to the emotional attachment to the language cited by Coakley. The details are given by Fennell (1981: 33), "for every child of a Gaeltacht family who was certified by the school inspector to be Irish-speaking, a grant, first of £2, later of £10, was to be paid to the parents and qualification for these grants by the children of a family was made the qualifying criterion for various other benefits: for example, special house-building grants, scholarships to third-level education reserved for Gaeltacht children, and recognition of the family in question as a suitable family to lodge students attending summer language colleges in the Gaeltacht."
11. P.N. O'Farrell, private correspondence, 26/11/86. For details of the operation of Gaeltarra Eireann see the special series of Gaeltarra Information Leaflets, e.g. No. 1, *The Gaeltacht Areas*, No. 2, *Selected Investment from Overseas*, No. 6, *Transport Services and Communications* and No. 7, *Incentives Towards Establishing Industry in the Gaeltacht* (Gaillimh: Na Forbacha, 1976).
12. Cooke's description is amplified in a remarkable discussion of social relations and development in his *Theories of Planning and Spatial Development* (1983).
13. The other forms of dependent development he describes are a) former colonial enclaves, where international concerns, often operating through local affiliates, control natural resource exploitation; b) industrial platforms, regions of low labour cost located close to large export markets and c) new consumer markets susceptible to foreign penetration (Cooke, 1982: 212–13). An additional perspective applied to Ireland is that she faces severe constraints precisely because of the late timing of industrialization. O'Malley for example, suggests that in view of the competitive advantages of established industrial producers, indigenous industries would tend to be limited to sectors using simple, or standardized technologies, and having characteristics such as labour intensity, local craft intensity, low value added to local primary resources, low value/bulk ratio and clear advantages arising from sustained close contact with a local market. The fact that Irish enterprises have been successful in these sectors led to the particular choice of industry in the Gaeltacht, but Irish private industry is severely limited to these sectors and has little potential for diversification. See O'Malley (1980). Given this analysis of Ireland as a dependent periphery within the modern world-system, there seems little logic in expecting industry to perform better in the Gaeltacht, the periphery within the periphery.
14. MacGabhann reminds us that these constraints were imperative, especially in view of the impending implementation of the Anglo-Irish free trade agreement.
15. For details of these activities and the range of incentives introduced to attract

new industry and upgrade the infrastructure (telex, telephones, roads, sewage pipes, electricity etc) see MacGabhann (1978).

16. MacGabhann (1978) is the authoritative source on the activities of Gaeltarra in this period. The data reported in this section comes from his 1978 paper.

17. Gaeltarra's company operations are of two types, according to MacGabhann. First, 25 subsidiary companies, covering such activities as horticulture, hotels, textiles and fish-farming. These are scattered geographically and the Board's chief activity is one of supervision, seeking to ensure the survival of flagging industries. A second type involves some 25 associated companies in electronics, food processing and an American data processing company.

18. MacGabhann (1978). The existing incentive scheme's chief disadvantage was the government's obligation to take shares in assisted companies. It was argued that as healthy companies do not need state subventures, the policy was attracting weaker companies with only marginal profits.

19. Critics claimed the scheme was perceived as a "state give-away organization", increasing the dependency mentality amongst the local populus and deterring the more commercially-minded entrepreneurs from accepting Gaeltarra as a partner.

20. Recent work has highlighted the efficacy of Irish attempts to offset regional unemployment by attracting multinational enterprises. Indeed, the evidence presented by O'Farrell suggests that foreign enterprises — far from exacerbating regional disequilibria — have been marginally more likely than Irish ones to locate in Development Areas. For elaboration see O'Farrell (1980).

21. Recent doubts have been expressed as to the Irish economy's ability to diversify sufficiently to allow surplus capital and government subsidy to develop the Gaeltacht. Some, such as D.C. Perrons, argue that the fragmented units of production established largely in a sporadic manner by the Industrial Development Authority have succeeded in attracting a large number of overseas investors. Indeed, it is the very 'peripherality' of the country in the world division of labour which has proved to be attractive to the foreign branch plants. Labour surplus is a definite advantage, labour costs are more problematical, as Stanton and Paine make clear. However, Perrons insists that in comparison with other European countries, Ireland offers significant advantages to these branch plant opeators. They include a free access to the E.E.C., government incentives with a fair degree of freedom of location for the prospective operator, a widely developed industrial and social infrastructure, in particular good educational levels, a young fecund population and a stable political system. See Perrons (1981); for a discussion on labour costs see Stanton (1979), see also Paine (1979).

22. "Údarás na Gaeltachta – Attracting Lame Ducks", *Irish Business*, March 1981, pp. 2–9. In the two-year period 1979–1981 15 companies with a combined investment of £9.3 million were closed down with a loss of 461 jobs. I am grateful to Desmond Fennell for bringing this critique to my attention.

23. Clearly many entrepreneurs with potentially profit-making projects sought finance elsewhere rather than sell part of their company, *Irish Business*, pp. 2–9.

24. Though the £10,000 grant rule was relaxed on a number of occasions, it took the government thirteen years and over 26 disasters to change the ruling

completely. The Údarás is no longer compelled to take an equity stake and now judges projects solely on their ability to survive in a competitive environment. This could be the death knell for many of the Údarás's subsidiary and associated companies.

25. Keane, Cawley & O'Cinnéide (1983: 57). The authors do note that in the Donegal Gaeltacht eight failures occurred, 1979–1981, with a total investment of £9m written off on these ventures, representing 58% of the total investment for the period of £15.5m (p. 50). For a review of the "cost per job" argument see Keane (1984).

26. Since the 1979 Act, the Board of Údarás na Gaeltachta (The Gaeltacht Authority) replaced the old Gaeltarra Eireann. Mr Joe Maquire of Údarás has supplied me with the following key developments in the activities of the Board. Údarás was established on the 1st of January 1980, unlike the Gaeltarra Eireann; the majority of its members are elected by the Gaeltacht population using the proportional representation system.
It may acquire additional powers to those set out in the Act. The Údarás is a non-management Board, having 13 part-time members. Six members, including the Chairman, are appointed by the Minister for the Gaeltacht, and seven are elected, two for the Donegal area, one for Mayo, two for Galway and Meath, and two for Kerry/Cork/Waterford. All but one of these seven were, in the event, party nominees of the main political parties.

27. It must also be noted that, unlike the Welsh situation, the people of the Gaeltacht did not mobilize themselves in this period. To blame the Irish state alone for this impasse is a little harsh in my view. See C.H. Williams (1977).

28. This is the claim made by Frank Flynn, Chief Executive of Údarás na Gaeltachta in an address to the German–Ireland Chamber of Commerce, 27th January 1983.

29. Consideration of the geography of the Irish language is made in a text on geolinguistics which I am preparing for publication. Interested readers might like to write to me for details.

30. A variety of factors contributes to the low actual usage of Irish, including i) the overburdening of the school system as the main agency of language reproduction; 2) the insufficient training of teachers in all subjects, many of whom resented being the "whipping boys" for the failure of the revival; 3) lack of continuity and consistency in teaching methods from primary to secondary school; 4) the failure to prepare adequate Irish-medium materials both for school use and for use in the wider community, e.g. popular magazines, television and radio provision. For a very good discussion of the often emotive and politicized role of education see Edwards (1984a).

31. Edwards (1984a: 494); who quotes Brook's view that the Irish committed suicide rather than having been murdered.

References

ALLARDT, ERIK, 1979, *Implications of the Ethnic Revival in Modern Industrialised Society*. Helsinki: Commentationes Scientiarium Socialium.

BELLIN, W., 1984, Welsh and English in Wales. In P. TRUDGILL (ed.),

Language in the British Isles. Cambridge: CUP. 449–79.

BLACKSELL, MARK, 1981, *Post-War Europe: A Political Geography*. London: Hutchinson.

BORD NA GAEILGE, 1983, *Action Plan for Irish* 1983–1986. Dublin: Bord na Gaeilge.

BOYCE, D., 1982, Separatism and the Irish national tradition. In C.H. WILLIAMS (ed.), *National Separatism*. Cardiff: University of Wales Press, and Vancouver: University of British Columbia. 75–103.

CARTWRIGHT, DON, 1980, Bilingual Districts: The elusive territorial component in Canada's Official Language Act. *Discussion Papers in Geolinguistics* No. 1.

COAKLEY, J., 1980, Self-Government for Gaelic Ireland: The development of State Language Policy, *Europa Ethnica*, Vol. 37, no. 3. 114–24.

COOKE, P., 1982, Dependency, supply factors and uneven development in Wales and other problem regions, *Regional Studies*, Vol. 16 no. 3, 211–27.

—— 1983, *Theories of Planning and Spatial Development*. London: Hutchinson.

COMMITTEE ON IRISH LANGUAGE ATTITUDES RESEARCH. 1975, Dublin: Government Stationery Office.

DURKACZ, V.E., 1983, *The Decline of the Celtic Languages*. Edinburgh: John Donald.

EDWARDS, D.G., 1984, Welsh-medium education, *Journal of Multilingual and Multicultural Development*, Vol. 5, nos 3 and 4. 249–57.

EDWARDS, J., 1984a, Irish and English in Ireland. In P. TRUDGILL (ed.), *Language in the British Isles*. Cambridge: CUP. 480–99.

—— 1984b, Irish: Planning and preservation, *Journal of Multilingual and Multicultural Development*, Vol. 5, nos 3 and 4.

FENNELL, D., 1980a, The last days of the Gaeltacht, *The Irish Times*, 3/6/1980.

—— 1980b, Why the Gaeltacht wasn't saved? *The Irish Times*, 4/6/1980.

—— 1981, Can a shrinking linguistic minority be saved? Lessons from the Irish experience. In E. HAUGEN *et al.* (eds), *Minority Languages Today*. Edinburgh: Edinburgh University Press. 32–39.

FITZGERALD, G., 1984, Estimates for baronies of minimum level of Irish-speaking amongst decenniel cohorts: 1771–1781 to 1861–1871, *Proceedings of the Royal Irish Academy*, Vol. 84c.

GILES, H. & SAINT-JACQUES, BERNARD (eds) 1979, *Language and Ethnic Relations*. Oxford: Pergamon.

GINER, SALVADOR & ARCHER, SCOTFORD (eds) 1978, *Contemporary Europe: Social Structures and Cultural Patterns*. London: Routledge and Kegan Paul.

HAYWARD, J.E.S. & BERKI, R.N. (eds) 1979, *State and Society in Contemporary Europe*. Oxford: Martin Robertson.

HECHTER, MICHAEL, 1975, *Internal Colonialism: The Celtic Fringe in British National Development, 1536–1966*. London: Routledge and Kegan Paul.

HEPBURN, A.C., 1980, *The Conflict of Nationality in Modern Ireland*. London: Arnold.

KEANE, M.J., 1984, Can we afford the Gaeltacht? An analysis of job creation costs. mimeo. Department of Economics, University College Galway. April.

KEANE, M.J., CAWLEY, M. & O'CINNÉIDE, M., 1983, Industrial development in Gaeltacht areas: The work of Údarás na Gaeltachta, *Cambria*, Vol. 10, no. 1. 47–60.

KREJCI, J. & VELIMSKY, V., 1981, *Ethnic and Political Nations in Europe*. London: Croom Helm.

MACGABHANN, C., 1978, Industrial development in the Gaeltacht. Paper given at the *Conference on Regional Development and Language Planning*, Galway, March.

MACKINNON, KENNETH, 1977, *Language, Education and Social Processes in a Gaelic Community*. London: Routledge and Kegan Paul.

MITCHINSON, R. (ed.) 1980, *The Roots of Nationalism*. Edinburgh: John Donald.

O'CINNÉIDE, M.S., KEANE, M. & CAWLEY, M., 1985, Industrialization and linguistic change among Gaelic-speaking communities in the west of Ireland, *Language Planning and Language Problems*, Vol. 9, I, Spring. 3–16.

O'FARRELL, P.N., 1980, Multinational enterprises and regional development: Irish evidence, *Regional Studies*, Vol. 14. 141–50.

O'FARRELL, P.N. & CROUCHLEY, R., 1983, Industrial closure in Ireland 1973–81: Analysis and implications, *Regional Studies*, Vol. 17, no. 6, 411–27.

—— 1984, An industrial and spatial analysis of new firm formation in Ireland, *Regional Studies*, Vol. 18, no. 6, 221–36.

O'MALLEY, EOIN, 1980, Dependency and the experience of industry in the Republic of Ireland, *Bulletin of the Institute of Development Studies*, Vol. 12, no. 1, 42–47.

O'NEIL, D., 1983, Irish cultural revitalization, *Plural Societies*, Vol. 14, no. 1/2. Spring/Summer.

O'RIAGAIN, PADRAIG, 1978, Regional planning in Irish bilingual areas, *Cambria*, Vol. 5, no. 2, 182–87.

ORRIDGE, ANDREW & WILLIAMS, COLIN H., 1982, Autonomist nationalism:

A theoretical framework for spatial variations in its genesis and development, *Political Geography Quarterly*, Vol. 1, no. 1, 19–39.

PAINE, S., 1979, Replacement of the West European migrant labour system by investment in the European periphery. In D. SEERS, B. SCHAFFER & M-L. KILJUNEN (eds), *Underdeveloped Europe*. Brighton: Harvester. 65–96.

PERRONS, D.C., 1981, The role of Ireland in the new international division of labour. *Regional Studies*, Vol. 15, no. 2. 81–100.

PORTER, BERNARD, 1975, *The Lion's Share*. London: Longman.

PRICE, G., 1984, *The Languages of Britain*. London: Arnold.

Report of Commision of Inquiry into the Preservation of the Gaeltacht 1976, Dublin: Stationery Office.

Report of Commission on the Restoration of the Irish Language 1964, Dublin: Stationery Office.

Report of Committee on Irish Language Attitudes Research 1976, Dublin: Stationery Office.

ROKKAN, S. & URWIN, D.W. (eds) 1982, *The Politics of Territorial Identity*. London: Sage.

SHIELS, F.L. (ed) 1984, *Ethnic Separatism and World Politics*. Lanham, MD: The University Press of America.

SMITH, A.D., 1981, *The Ethnic Revival*. Cambridge: CUP.

STANTON, R., 1979, Investment and host-country politics: The Irish case. In D. SEERS, B. SCHAFFER & M-L. KILJUNEN (eds), *Underdeveloped Europe*. Brighton: Harvester. 103–24.

TRUDGILL, P. (ed.) 1984, *Language in the British Isles*. Cambridge: CUP.

WEINSTEIN, B., 1983, *The Civic Tongue*. New York: Longman.

WELSH OFFICE, 1983, *Welsh in the Secondary Schools of Wales*. Cardiff: H.M.S.O.

WILLIAMS, C.H., 1977, Non-violence and the development of the Welsh language society, *Welsh History Review*, Vol. 8, no. 4, 426–55.

—— 1980a, Language contact and language change in Wales, *Welsh History Review*, Vol. 10, no. 2, 207–38.

—— 1980b, Ethnic separatism in western Europe, *Tijdschrift voor Economische en Sociale Geografie*, vol. 71, no. 3, 142–58.

—— (ed.) 1982, *National Separatism*. Cardiff University of Wales Press, and Vancouver: University of British Columbia Press.

WILLIAMS, GLYN (ed.), 1978, *Social and Cultural Change in Contemporary Wales*. London: Routlege and Kegan Paul.

WILLIAMS, RAYMOND, 1981, *Culture*. London: Fontana.

WOOD, JOHN R., 1981, Secession: A comparative analytical framework, *Canadian Journal of Political Science*, Vol. 14, no. 1. March. 107–34.

10   Conclusion

*Department of Geography and Recreation,
North Staffordshire Polytechnic, Stoke-on-Trent, U.K.*

We trust that the contents of this volume have been reflective of the growing interest and awareness of the geographic aspects of language in society. We are conscious that the focus on four areas elaborated upon in the introduction, *viz.* geolinguistic origins and principles, the macro-social context of language in social space, the methodological problems of data collection and interpretation, and applied language planning, are but partial statements of interest within the research community. We recognize that we have not dealt with the myriad aspects of, for example, dialect geography (Trudgill, 1984; Chambers & Trudgill, 1980), or computer-aided geolinguistic analysis (Thomas, 1973, 1980). We trust that a projected companion volume will incorporate many of the interesting developments in these cognate areas.

In signalling neglected aspects I am reminded that one of the pressing concerns is for more work on the epistemological foundations of human geography, and in particular upon the language employed in analysing linguistic geography. Recent work in sociolinguistics on discourse analysis (Williams, 1986) has pointed to the ideological nature of much presumed "value-free" social science research and the manner in which consensus theories are dominant in the field of language planning. It is time that geographers also re-examined several key theories and concepts employed in the examination of sociocultural patterns and processes (Williams, 1984). Several of the chapters herein have attempted to move away from the perspectives which were dominant within geography in the 1960s and 1970s, but it is debatable as to whether or not one can as yet talk of a truly theoretically informed practice of geolinguistic research.

A more positive note may, however, be sounded in terms of applied geolinguistic planning. The recent work of McRae (1983, 1986) and

Laponce (1984) illustrates how structural factors of language change are influenced by political conflict and inter-group tension. They have examined the extent to which linguistic tensions have been accentuated or diminished by changes in disparities of income and wealth, by upward social mobility, by the rise of ethno-regionalism. Central to such conflicts in multilingual societies has been the formal organization of government services and the corresponding elaboration of group rights and state obligations.

Illustration of the centrality of political factors was provided in this volume by Don Cartwright, who reminded us that language groups were increasingly dependent upon the institutional support of the central and local state. However, the provision of institutional support, such as separate educational facilities for minority groups, need not necessarily encourage sectionalism and division within society. Given imagination and resolve, an accord can be built between language groups in contact, despite the fact that they are often in direct competition for the same resources. This obviously depends in part upon the formal organization of territorial services in multilingual societies, but ultimately it depends also on the attitude of the dominant cultural group towards its constituent minorities within the polity. Part of the State's response to the demands of its minorities has been the elaboration of group rights and language planning and in Canada and Ireland, as elsewhere, geolinguistic principles have already been incorporated into public policy. The cogency of Cartwright's argument for an official language zone in Ontario is testimony to the fact that such principles are likely to be even more relevant in the future. However, let me add a note of caution. Territorial language planning could be a two-edged sword, because, although language planning is an essentially technical field, it is also an expression of a political relationship between constituent power groups.

The power wielded by such groups is not merely a function of their relative demographic size and distribution (economically and spatially), it is also an expression of their decision-making ability as to how, when and where particular languages, or forms of language are restricted to specific domains. Such rules of language legitimization are often determined by the dominant group in society, and attempts to defy the rules are characterized as deviant behaviour or anti-state activity. Recent events in Quebec, Euskadi and Catalonia demonstrate that in order to break out of restrictive domains, language can be used as an instrument of resistance and of group mobilization. They also demonstrate that "intrusive" languages have to be institutionalized within new domains in order to maintain patterns of language behaviour as normal and worthwhile. This requires power and economic inducement, often supplied by the local state, to offset the challenge of the once dominant, high status language of the wider majority.

In modern technological societies, it is the local state which sets the conditions and possibility for cultural reproduction, through the formal agencies of the law, education, public administration and the like. There is a real danger that, if language planning in these spheres is adopted uncritically by the constituent group, it could lead to an even greater dependency on the state. The irony is that the local state is often the only institution which can afford to mount the expensive services now deemed essential to minority cultural reproduction, so that for the foreseeable future language considerations will be ultimately related to the formal power exercised by the state.

Up until the twentieth century most minority groups engaged in the struggle for liberty and equality, if not fraternity, demanded freedom from state and government control and influence. The current demands of minorities within advanced industrial societies are for freedom to have their culture and aspirations institutionalized within the bureaucratic structure of the plural state. This new, interventionist freedom, suggests a new basis for the relationship between the state and its constituent groups, a relationship which is likely to be not only of interest to geolinguistic research, but of vital concern to minority groups themselves in their struggle for representation and survival.

Part of this struggle will be related to the need for more information on the actual position of the language groups themselves, information which can be of vital import in the formulation and execution of policy. It is a truism that most of the information which informs public policy in advanced western states is that derived from official government surveys and reports. Hardly any of the vast data banks currently collected by government agencies are appropriate for a comprehensive analysis of language groups. To compound the problem, much of the available data is collected and published at high levels of aggregation, the province, region or county level. We know that formal language policy formulation is often a highly pragmatic process, making use of mapped information at whatever unit scale happens to be available (Ambrose & Williams, 1987).

In consequence many of the key geographic concepts employed in formal policy reports, let alone the geographic literature, tend to be inadequate, "culture regions", "zones of collapse", "bilingual belts", "heartlands" or "core areas" — the definition of all these tends to have its origins in scale selection. Within and between such units, sub-sets of the population may become net beneficiaries or losers, depending on chance factors of location (Ambrose & Williams, 1987).

On occasion the mapped distributions of language-related activities or needs may thus hide as much as they reveal, and this is a common predicament in the linguistic sciences where there often tends to be a "trade-off" between the quantity and quality of linguistic data. In cases where we have to compromise on detail we may still produce interesting linguistic mapping exercises, by adopting, for example, time-series data sets for the same places. Many of the most pressing needs for the application of geolinguistic research, as argued by my colleague, John Ambrose, and myself, is in situations of code-shifting and code-conflict, to understand patterns in the dynamics of language use. We know, and have demonstrated in Chapter 5, that decisive patterns of change can take place in short time periods. The evidence from many borderland situations suggests that ameliorative language policies can become outdated even before they have time to be implemented. In urban areas the processes are probably even more rapid, and the need for understanding correspondingly more pressing, yet little work has been undertaken by geographers on the dynamics of language at the urban and intra-urban scale.

In short, there is much to be gained from applying fundamental geographic principles to language-related problems and our hope is that this volume will serve as a reminder that the geographic context is a prime requisite for understanding the nature of languages in contact.

References

AMBROSE, J.E. & WILLIAMS, C.H., 1987, The geographical processing of linguistic data. Paper presented to the International Seminar on Geolinguistics, North Staffordshire Polytechnic, May.

CHAMBERS, J.K. & TRUDGILL, P., 1980, *Dialectology*. Cambrdge: Cambridge University Press.

LAPONCE, J., 1984, The French language in Canada: Tensions between geography and politics, *Political Geography Quarterly*, Vol. 3, pp. 91–104.

MCRAE, K.D., 1983, *Conflict and Compromise in Multilingual Societies: Switzerland*. Waterloo: Wilfred Laurier University Press.

—— 1986, *Conflict and Compromise in Multilingual Societies: Belgium*. Waterloo: Wilfred Laurier University Press.

THOMAS, A.R., 1973, *The Linguistic Geography of Wales: A Contribution to Welsh Dialectology*. Cardiff: The University of Wales Press.
—— 1980, *Areal Analysis of Dialect Data by Computer: A Welsh Example*. Cardiff: The University of Wales Press.
TRUDGILL, P., 1984, *On Dialect*. Oxford: Blackwell.
WILLIAMS, C.H., 1984, Ideology and the interpretation of minority cultures, *Political Geography Quarterly*, Vol. 3, No. 2, pp. 127–47.
WILLIAMS, G., 1986, Language planning or language expropriations, *Journal of Multilingual and Multicultural Development*, Vol. 7, No. 6, pp. 309–18.

Index